PowerPoint® 2000
fast&easy™

Send Us Your Comments

To comment on this book or any other PRIMA TECH title, visit our reader response page on the Web at **www.prima-tech.com/comments**.

How to Order

For information on quantity discounts, contact the publisher: Prima Publishing, P.O. Box 1260BK, Rocklin, CA 95677-1260; (916) 632-4400. On your letterhead, include information concerning the intended use of the books and the number of books you wish to purchase. For individual orders, visit PRIMA TECH's Web site at **www.prima-tech.com**.

PowerPoint® 2000

fast&easy™

Coletta Witherspoon

A DIVISION OF PRIMA PUBLISHING

A Division of Prima Publishing

Prima Publishing and colophon are registered trademarks of Prima Communications, Inc. PRIMA TECH and Fast & Easy are trademarks of Prima Communications, Inc., Rocklin, California 95765.

Publisher: Stacy L. Hiquet

Associate Publisher: Nancy Stevenson

Managing Editor: Dan J. Foster

Senior Acquisitions Editor: Deborah F. Abshier

Project Editor: Kim V. Benbow

Technical Reviewer: Jacqueline Harris

Copy Editor: Susan Christophersen

Interior Layout: Shawn Morningstar

Editorial Assistant: Brian Thomasson

Cover Design: Prima Design Team

Indexer: Emily Glossbrenner

ISBN: 0-7615-1763-4

Library of Congress Catalog Card Number: 98-68148

Printed in the United States of America

02 03 DD 10 9 8 7 6 5 4 3 2

In memory of E. S. Witherspoon

Acknowledgments

Many thanks to everyone at Prima Tech for taking such good care of my manuscript and turning it into this awesome book. I'd especially like to thank Debbie Abshier, Kim Benbow, Susan Christophersen, and Jacqueline Harris. Thanks for all your help and dedication. And, none of this would be possible if it weren't for the love and support of my family and friends.

About the Author

Coletta Witherspoon is the author of several *Fast & Easy* series books from Prima Tech. Coletta and her husband, Craig, have been writing about computers, software, and networks since the 70s. In addition to writing and editing computer books, they produce training programs for their corporate clients.

Contents at a Glance

Contents

CONTENTS

PART IV
COLLABORATING WITH POWERPOINT 233

Chapter 14 Working on a Presentation with a Group 235

Chapter 15 Sharing Files with Office Applications 251

PART V
COMPLETING YOUR PRESENTATION 271

Introduction

This *Fast & Easy* guide from Prima Publishing will help you master Microsoft PowerPoint 2000 so that you can create stunning and informative presentations. PowerPoint is a popular presentation design program that provides a complete and easy way to create presentations to fit any need. PowerPoint has been popular with users for many years, and with each new version of the software, new features and abilities have been added to make PowerPoint more user friendly and compatible with other Microsoft Office programs. PowerPoint 2000 also has been upgraded to add new and improved Web features that allow you to use your presentation on the Internet or as a standalone kiosk.

PowerPoint 2000 is a versatile and creative presentation design and management program. PowerPoint makes it easy to add the extra bells and whistles to your presentation with the help of wizards, and it contains many other tools to help you create sophisticated presentations. Whether you have an existing presentation that you want to improve or you are creating your first presentation, you'll find the information you need in this book.

Who Should Read this Book?

This book is directed toward the novice computer user who needs a hands-on approach. The generous use of illustrations makes this an ideal tool for those who have never used a presentation design program before. This book is also for those who are familiar with previous versions of the PowerPoint software and want to quickly apply their skills to PowerPoint 2000.

This book is organized so that you can quickly look up tasks to help you complete a job or learn a new trick. You may need to read an entire chapter to master a subject, or you may need only to read a certain section of a chapter to refresh your memory.

Added Advice to Make You a Presentation Wizard

You'll notice that this book keeps explanations to a minimum to help you learn faster. You will find other features in this book that provide more information on how to work with PowerPoint 2000.

- **Tips** offer help hints about PowerPoint 2000 that make your job a little easier and help you create presentations efficiently.

- **Notes** offer additional information about PowerPoint 2000 to enhance your learning experience with the software.

Also, the appendix shows how to install PowerPoint 2000 on your computer.

Knock 'em speechless at your next presentation!

PART I

Creating Your First PowerPoint Presentation

1

Getting Started with PowerPoint 2000

You've just been told that you need to give a presentation in front of an audience. Are you shaking in your boots yet? No need to fear; PowerPoint is here! PowerPoint can help you get past your fear of public speaking by providing audio/visual tools that will take your audience's eyes away from you and direct them toward an organized, colorful, and animated presentation. Before you dive into creating a presentation with PowerPoint, take some time to get familiar with the program's basic interface. In this chapter, you'll learn how to:

- Start PowerPoint
- Explore the elements found on the PowerPoint screen
- Use menus, shortcuts, and toolbars
- Exit PowerPoint

Starting PowerPoint 2000

Before you can begin your exploration of PowerPoint, you must first open the program. This section shows you three different methods for getting started, but feel free to use the method that works best for you.

Beginning at the Start Menu

No matter which version of the Windows operating system you use, you can access every software program or utility installed on your computer by clicking on the Start button.

1. **Click** on the **Start button** on the Windows Taskbar. The Start menu will appear.

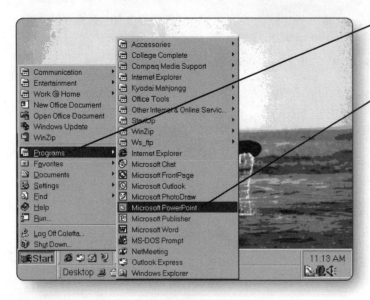

2. **Move** the **mouse pointer** to Programs. The Programs menu will appear.

3. **Click** on **Microsoft PowerPoint**. PowerPoint will open, and the PowerPoint getting started dialog box will appear.

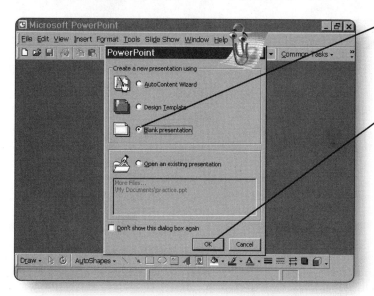

4. **Click** on the **Blank Presentation option button**, if it isn't already selected. The option will be selected.

5. **Click** on **OK**. The New Slide dialog box will appear, and the Title slide will be selected.

NOTE

You'll be using this blank presentation to get familiar with the PowerPoint interface. You'll learn how to get a quick start on a presentation in Chapter 3, "Creating a Quick and Easy Presentation."

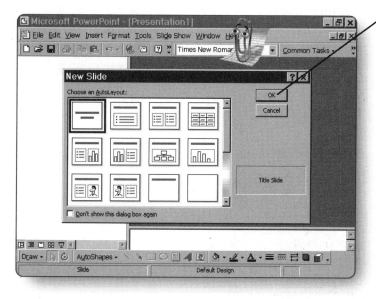

6. **Click** on **OK**. The PowerPoint screen will appear, showing the blank presentation.

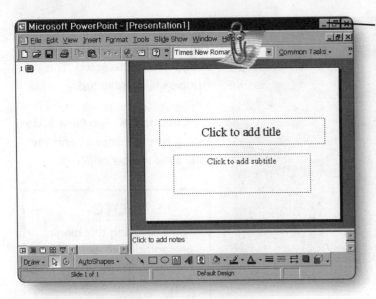

7. Click on the **Minimize button** (▬). The program window will be reduced to an icon on the Windows Taskbar.

TIP

When you are ready to work with PowerPoint, click on the PowerPoint icon on the Windows Taskbar to display the program on your monitor.

Displaying the Office Shortcut Bar

The Office Shortcut Bar provides a quick way to access all the programs installed on your computer. The Office Shortcut Bar displays on your screen and is always visible when you are working with an open program. When the Office Shortcut Bar is displayed, you can open a program by clicking on the associated icon.

1. Click on **Start** on the Windows Taskbar. The Start menu will appear.

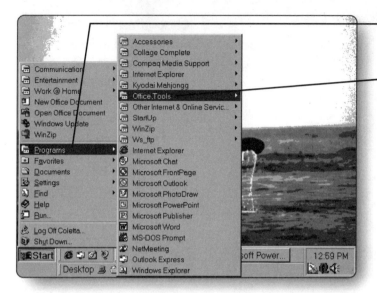

2. Click on **Programs**. The Programs menu will appear.

3. Click on **Office Tools**. The Office Tools menu will appear.

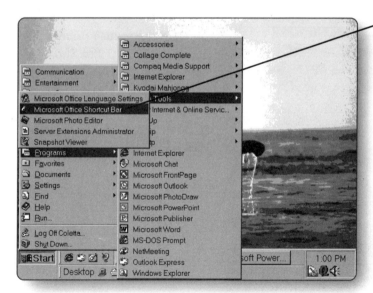

4. Click on **Microsoft Office Shortcut Bar**. The Microsoft Office Shortcut Bar dialog box will appear.

5. **Click** on **Yes**. The Office Shortcut Bar will appear on your screen, and from then on, every time you start your computer, the Office Shortcut Bar will be displayed on your screen— ready to give you quick access to your favorite programs.

6. **Hold** the **mouse pointer** over one of the Office Shortcut Bar icons. A ToolTip will appear that indicates the program that will open if you click on the icon. To open one of these programs, click on its icon.

Putting PowerPoint on Your Desktop

Another way to save a few mouse clicks when you want to open PowerPoint is to put a shortcut to the program on your Desktop.

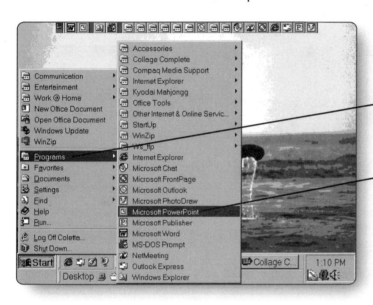

1. **Click** on the **Start button** on the Windows Taskbar. The Start menu will appear.

2. **Move** the **mouse pointer** to Programs. The Programs menu will appear.

3. **Right-click** on **Microsoft PowerPoint**. A shortcut menu will appear.

TIP

You can select any software program and add a shortcut for that program to your Desktop.

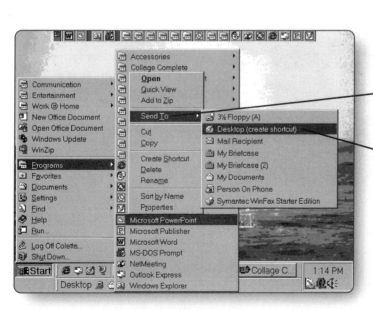

4. **Click** on **Send To**. The Send To submenu will appear.

5. **Click** on **Desktop (create shortcut)**.

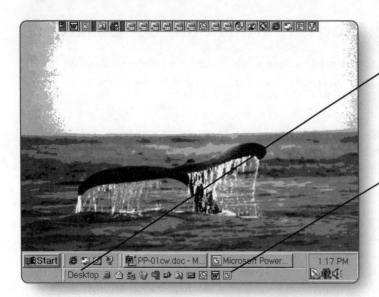

NOTE

If you have added the Desktop toolbar to the Windows Taskbar, you'll see an icon for PowerPoint on this toolbar.

A shortcut to PowerPoint will appear on your Desktop. If you click on this shortcut, the program will open.

6. Click on the **PowerPoint icon** that was created on the Windows Taskbar when you minimized the program. The PowerPoint window will appear on your screen. You are now ready to follow along with the next section and learn more about the elements that make PowerPoint tick.

Exploring the PowerPoint Screen

You'll notice that PowerPoint contains some of the same elements, such as toolbars and menus, that are found in Microsoft Office and other Windows programs. You'll also notice a few other elements that are unique to PowerPoint. In this section, you'll be introduced to the different elements found in PowerPoint and what these elements can do for you.

Learning About Toolbars

The various toolbars found in PowerPoint contain buttons that are shortcuts for many menu commands. To find out which command will be executed when you click on a toolbar button, place the mouse pointer over the button to display a ToolTip. Each of these toolbars has a different function, and this section describes the different types of tasks you can perform with each toolbar.

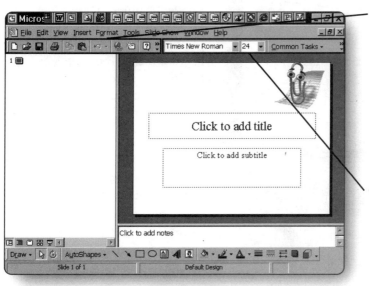

- The **Standard toolbar** contains buttons that are shortcuts to frequently used menu commands. From this toolbar, you can create a new presentation, save a presentation, print a presentation, and cut and paste text or graphics.

- The **Formatting toolbar** allows you to apply formatting to text such as font styles, bolding and italics, and paragraph alignment.

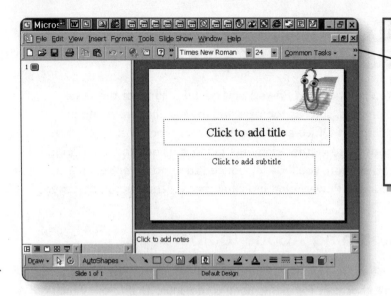

TIP

A double right-pointing arrow at the right side of a toolbar means that there are more buttons to be found. Click on the arrow to display the rest of the toolbar buttons.

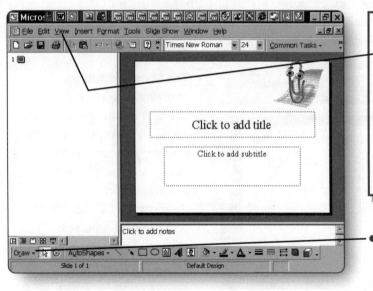

NOTE

PowerPoint also contains several other toolbars that you can find under the Toolbars command in the View menu. These toolbars perform specialized tasks and are discussed in later parts of this book.

• The **Drawing toolbar** makes it easy for you to draw shapes, create original artwork, add artistic effects to text, and insert clip art on your presentation slides.

Understanding Your Viewing Options

When you first open PowerPoint, you'll notice that the window is divided into three panes. This is PowerPoint's Normal View and it contains the most frequently-used viewing elements needed to create a presentation.

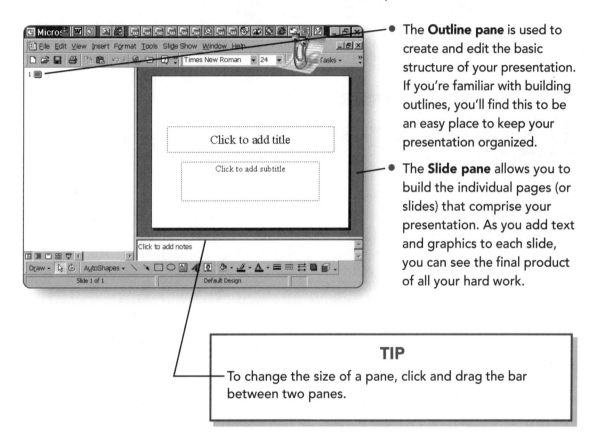

- The **Outline pane** is used to create and edit the basic structure of your presentation. If you're familiar with building outlines, you'll find this to be an easy place to keep your presentation organized.

- The **Slide pane** allows you to build the individual pages (or slides) that comprise your presentation. As you add text and graphics to each slide, you can see the final product of all your hard work.

TIP
To change the size of a pane, click and drag the bar between two panes.

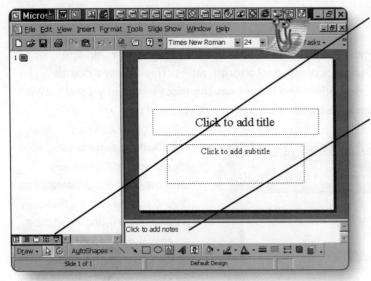

- The **View buttons** make it easy for you to switch to the other views that you can use to see different parts of your presentation.

- The **Notes pane** is where you make notes that you can use to help or remind yourself while you're making the presentation. You can also use this pane to add notes that you want to share with your audience in printed handouts.

NOTE

You'll learn more about working with the various views in Chapter 4, "Viewing Your Presentation."

Working with PowerPoint

When you look at the PowerPoint window, you'll notice an assortment of buttons, icons, menus, and scroll bars. These screen elements help you perform every task and function available in PowerPoint. If you've used other Office or Windows programs, you'll see similarities between PowerPoint and these programs. This section shows you the basics of working with the various PowerPoint elements.

Using Menus

You can find PowerPoint's menus, which are a collection of commands grouped into related categories, at the top of the program window. These menus can execute any function in PowerPoint. You'll find a new feature in the Office 2000 programs called *adaptive menus*. This feature shows only your most frequently used commands in the menu. But if you wait for a second, all the menu commands will magically appear.

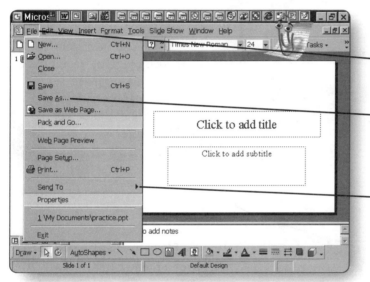

1. Click on a **menu item**. A drop-down menu will appear.

- When an ellipsis (...) follows a menu command, a dialog box will appear if that command is selected.

- When a right-pointing arrow follows a menu command, a submenu will appear when you move the mouse pointer over the arrow.

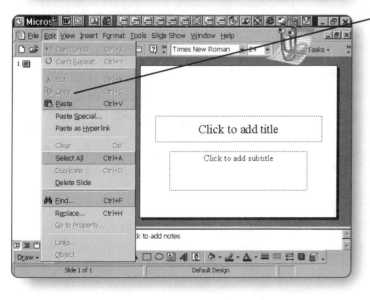

- When a menu command is grayed out, the command is not available during the particular task you are performing.

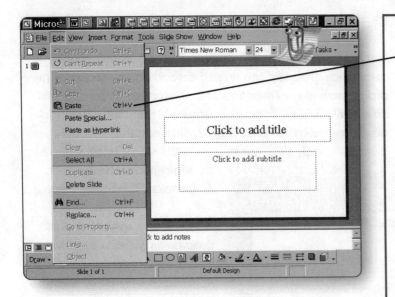

TIP

Some menu commands have keyboard shortcuts listed next to them. Type the keyboard shortcut listed next to a menu item to execute that command. That is, you hold down the Ctrl key while pressing the indicated letter. If you like, you can cut down your mouse usage by remembering these keyboard shortcuts (see the Table at the end of this chapter).

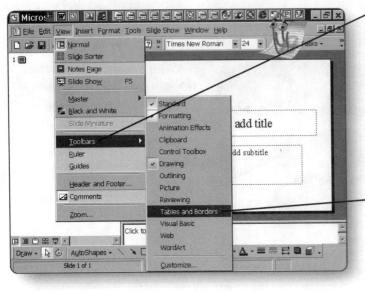

2. **Place** the **mouse pointer** over a menu command with a right-pointing arrowhead. A submenu will appear.

3. **Move** the **mouse pointer** over a command on the submenu. The command will be highlighted.

4. **Click** on a **command**. The command will be executed.

Finding Shortcut Menus

If you're looking for an alternate means of executing commands, try using the right-click method. When you right-click on any element inside a component window, a shortcut menu will appear. This menu contains all the commands that can be executed for the element you selected.

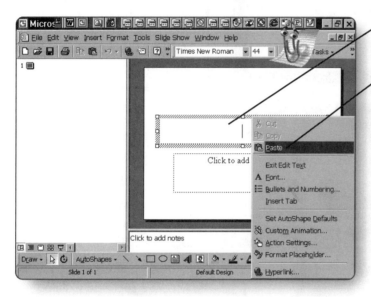

1. Right-click on the **object**. A shortcut menu will appear.

2. Click on a **command**. The command will be executed.

Working with Dialog Boxes

Dialog boxes group several related functions in one place. They allow you to perform a number of tasks regarding the menu command to which they pertain. This section shows you the Options dialog box. This dialog box controls how you and PowerPoint work together. Take some time to familiarize yourself with the options in this dialog box.

1. Click on **Tools**. The Tools menu will appear.

2. Click on **Options**. The Options dialog box will open.

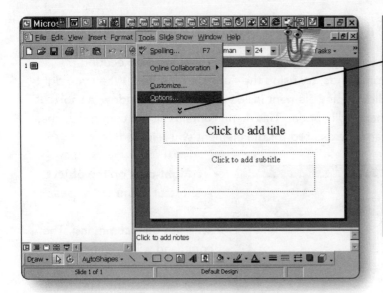

TIP

If you don't want to wait for the menu to automatically expand, click on the double down-pointing arrow. Or, you could double-click on the menu item so that the full list of menu commands displays when the menu opens.

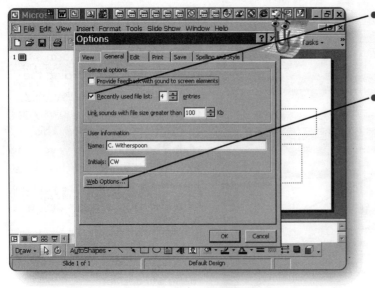

● Turn features on and off by clicking on the check box located at the left of the feature name.

● Access a secondary dialog box by clicking on a button.

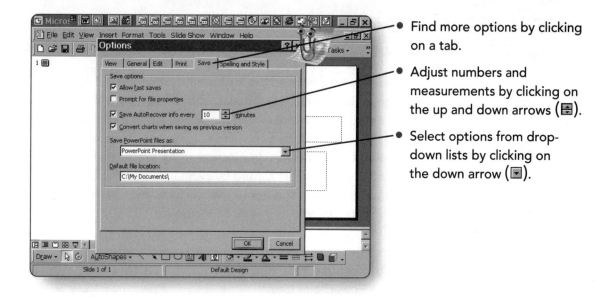

- Find more options by clicking on a tab.

- Adjust numbers and measurements by clicking on the up and down arrows (⬍).

- Select options from drop-down lists by clicking on the down arrow (▾).

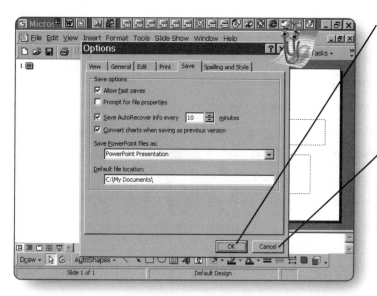

3. Click on **OK**. The dialog box will close, and the options will be applied to the presentation.

NOTE

If you want to close a dialog box without accepting any of the changes you have made, click on the Cancel button.

Bypassing the Mouse with Keyboard Shortcuts

You may have noticed the keyboard shortcuts listed on the right side of each of the menus. You can use these shortcuts to execute commands without opening a menu and clicking on the command. By becoming familiar with these keyboard shortcuts, you will not only increase your productivity but also decrease wrist strain caused by excessive mouse usage. The following table lists a few of the more common keyboard shortcuts that you may want to memorize.

To execute this command	Do this
Use PowerPoint Help	Press the F1 key
Create a new presentation	Press the Ctrl and N keys simultaneously (Ctrl+N)
Open a different presentation	Press Ctrl+O
Save a presentation	Press Ctrl+S
Print a presentation	Press Ctrl+P
Delete selected text	Press Ctrl+X
Make a copy of the selected text	Press Ctrl+C
Paste the copied text	Press Ctrl+V
Spell check a presentation	Press the F7 key
Insert a new slide into a presentation	Press Ctrl+M

Exiting PowerPoint 2000

As is the case with all Windows programs, you have several options for closing PowerPoint components. You could go shuffling through the menus, but there is a faster way.

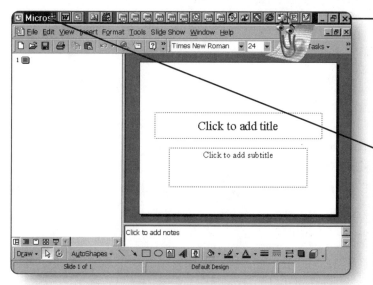

1. **Click** on the **Close button** (⊠) located in the upper-right corner of the PowerPoint window. The program will close.

TIP

If you want to close the Office Shortcut Bar, click on the shortcut bar icon (located at the far left of the bar) and select Exit from the menu that appears. You'll then see a dialog box that asks whether you want the Office Shortcut Bar to start automatically when you start Windows. The decision is up to you.

2

Getting Help

As the song goes, we all need a little help from our friends once in a while. Whether you're new to PowerPoint or using a feature for the first time, you'll want to use all your available resources so that you can work with the program efficiently. You'll find several ways to get the help you need from the PowerPoint Help system. You can also have some fun while you're at it. As with all Microsoft Office programs, the Office Assistant is at your beck and call, and you can enjoy the Office Assistant's antics at the same time. In this chapter, you'll learn how to:

- Use ToolTips to your advantage
- Ask the Office Assistant for help

Taking Advantage of ToolTips

ToolTips are the little boxes containing text that appear on your screen when you either hold the mouse pointer over an item or use the What's This? button. If you're uncertain about what function a command, option, button, or other screen element performs, using ToolTips is a quick way to answer your question. Before you begin this section, you'll need to reopen PowerPoint if you closed it in the last chapter.

Displaying ToolTips for Toolbar Buttons

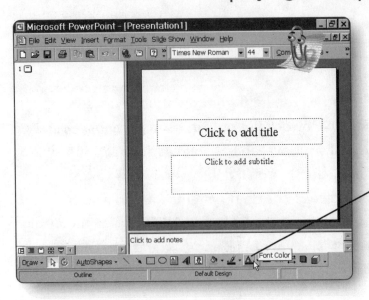

ToolTips are easy to find and use. All you do is hold the mouse pointer over a screen element. Some ToolTips just tell you the command that an element executes; others give directions for using the element. Try out the following example.

1. Place the **mouse pointer** over the Font Color button. A ToolTip will appear that tells you what function this button performs.

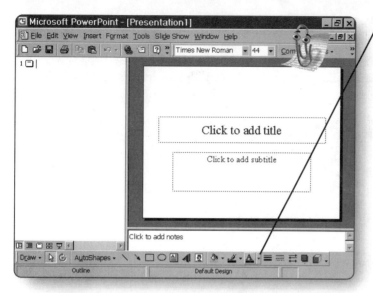

2. Click on the **down arrow** (▣) to the right of the Font Color button. A menu of available colors will appear.

NOTE

Toolbar buttons that have a down arrow on the right present further options. By clicking on the button, the default command is executed. By clicking on the down arrow, you can select from a list of choices.

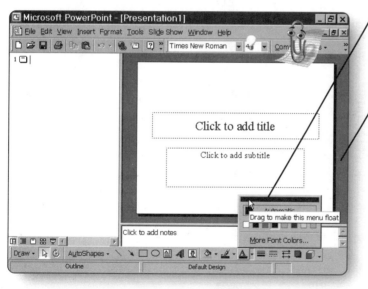

3. Place the **mouse pointer** over the menu bar. A ToolTip that gives you additional directions will appear.

4. Click anywhere **outside** the color menu. The menu will disappear.

Using the What's This? Button

If you need more help than what the basic ToolTips offer, you can display more detailed ToolTips by using the What's This? button.

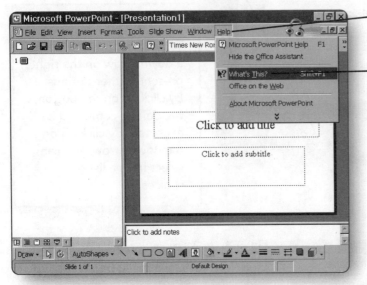

1. Click on **Help**. The Help menu will appear.

2. Click on **What's This?**. The mouse pointer will change to a pointer with a question mark attached to it.

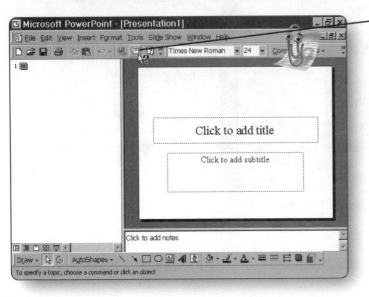

3. Click on the **screen element** that you want to learn more about.

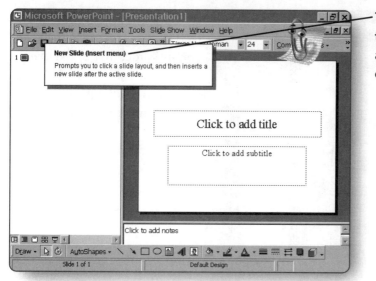

The ToolTip will appear. To make the ToolTip disappear, click anywhere outside the ToolTip, or press the Escape key.

Finding Help When Using Dialog Boxes

As you begin working with the various dialog boxes in PowerPoint, you'll notice a question mark in the upper-right corner of many of them. This question mark provides information about the options contained in the dialog box. Follow this example to see how to get help so that you can make the right choices.

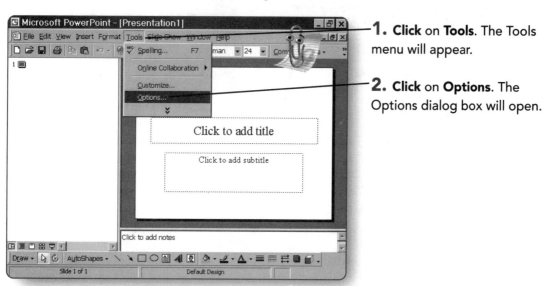

1. Click on **Tools**. The Tools menu will appear.

2. Click on **Options**. The Options dialog box will open.

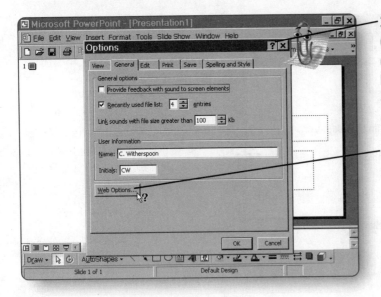

3. Click on the **question mark** (**?**) **button** located in the upper-right corner of the dialog box. The mouse pointer will change to a pointer with a question mark attached to it.

4. Click on any **element** in the dialog box.

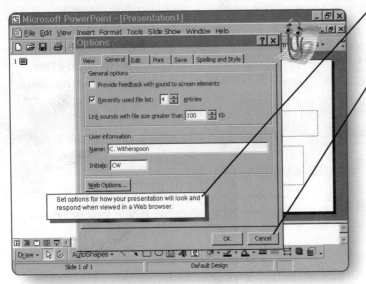

A ToolTip will appear that describes what function the dialog box element will perform.

5. Click on **Cancel**. The Options dialog box will close and any changes made in the dialog box will not be applied.

Asking the Office Assistant for Help

As you've been following along in this book, you may have noticed the paperclip cartoon character (called Clippit) in the upper-right corner of the screen. This is the Office Assistant.

The Office Assistant stands ready to answer any questions you may have while you're working with PowerPoint.

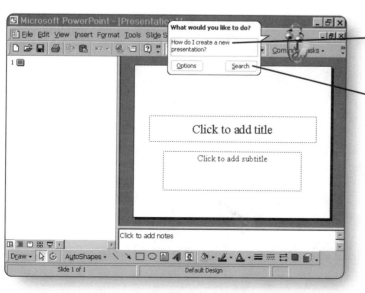

1. Click on the **Office Assistant**. The What would you like to do? message box will appear.

NOTE

If you don't see the Office Assistant on your screen, click on the Microsoft PowerPoint Help button on the Standard toolbar.

2. Type a **question or keywords** in the text box.

3. Click on **Search**. A list of possible help topics that may answer your question or matches to the keyword you typed will appear.

TIP

Are you getting tired of looking at Clippit? Right-click on the Office Assistant and select Choose Assistant from the menu that appears. You have a choice of eight different assistants.

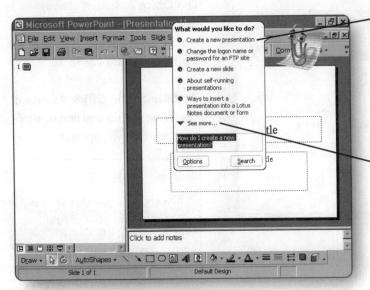

4. Click on the **topic** that you feel is the closest match to your question. The Microsoft PowerPoint Help dialog box will open.

NOTE

Click on the See more option to view other possible help topics.

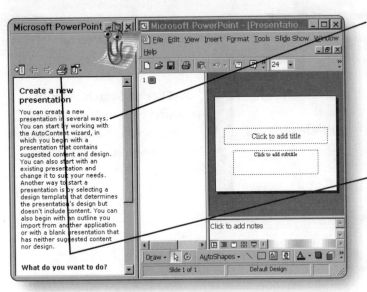

5. Read the **introduction** to the help topic and use the scroll bar to see a list of options that will further answer your question.

NOTE

Click on the Print button if you want to make a paper copy of the help topic that is displayed.

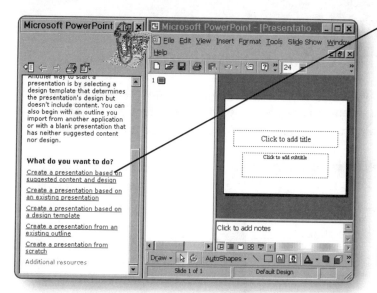

6. Click on the **topic** that you'd like to read more about. The help topic will appear in the dialog box.

TIP

Want to watch the Office Assistant perform a cool trick? Right-click on the Office Assistant and select Animate! from the menu that appears.

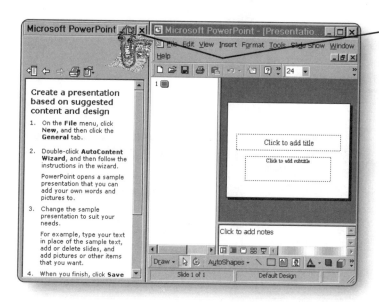

7. Click on the **Close button** (⊠) located at the upper-right corner of the dialog box when you are finished with the help topics. The Microsoft PowerPoint Help dialog box will close.

Working Around the Office Assistant

You may decide that you don't want to work with the Office Assistant. You can turn the Office Assistant off and access help from the Help menu when you need it.

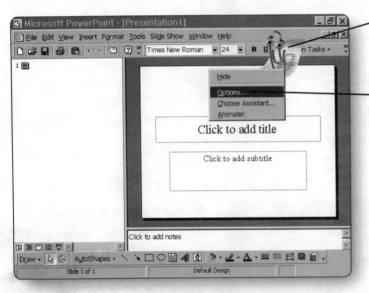

1. Right-click on the **Office Assistant**. A shortcut menu will appear.

2. Click on **Options**. The Office Assistant dialog box will open with the Options tab displayed.

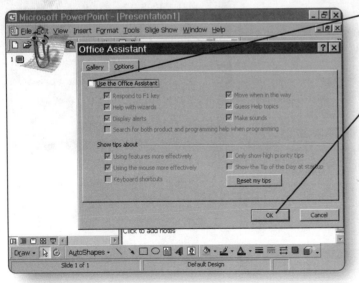

3. Click in the **Use the Office Assistant check box**. The check mark will be cleared and all the options will be grayed out.

4. Click on **OK**. The Office Assistant will disappear from your screen.

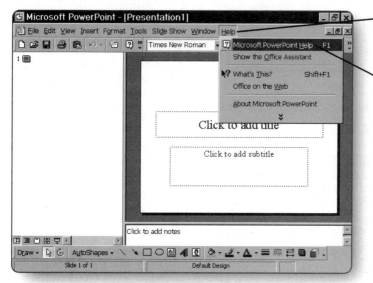

5. Click on **Help**. The Help menu will appear.

6. Click on **Microsoft PowerPoint Help**. The Microsoft PowerPoint Help window will appear.

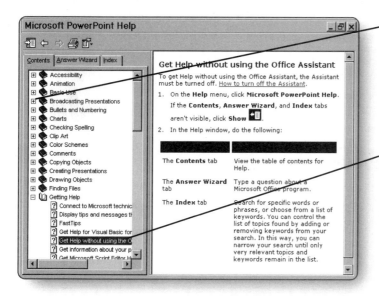

7. Click on the **plus sign** (⊞) next to the topic you want to know more about. The topic will expand to show the contents, and the plus sign will change to a minus sign.

8. Click on the **item** about which you need more information. The associated help file will appear in the right side of the window.

9. **Click** on the **Index tab**. The Help Topics index will appear.

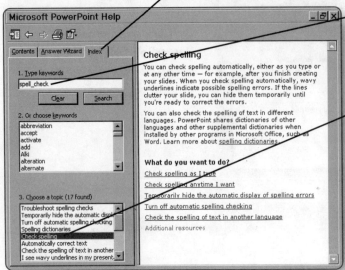

10. **Type** a **keyword** in the Type keywords text box. The closest match will appear in the Choose a topic list box.

11. **Click** on the **topic** in the Choose a topic list box that you want to view. The help topic will appear in the right side of the window.

12. When you are finished using help, **click** on the **Close** (☒) **button**. The Microsoft PowerPoint Help dialog box will close, and you can continue working with the program.

3

Creating a Quick and Easy Presentation

Now that you've been introduced to the basic workings of PowerPoint, it's time to start building your presentation. The hardest part of any project is getting started. To make this task easier, PowerPoint provides you with a helper, called the AutoContent Wizard. This wizard gets you started with a basic outline and design for your presentation. After the wizard finishes its job, you can then modify the presentation to fit your needs and taste. In this chapter, you'll learn how to:

- Get started on a presentation using the AutoContent Wizard
- Change the design of your presentation
- Save a presentation file
- Close the presentation file

Starting with the AutoContent Wizard

If you're looking for some professional advice on how to design and lay out a presentation, the AutoContent Wizard is at your command. The AutoContent Wizard will create a sample presentation based on how you answer the wizard's questions. When the wizard is finished, you'll have a sample outline that you can modify to fit the information you need to impart with the presentation. The wizard will also suggest a look (that is, a background for your presentation slides and color combinations for the text that appears on the slides) that you can change if you desire.

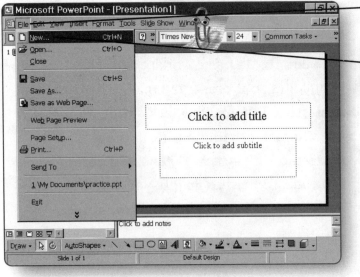

1. Click on **File**. The File menu will appear.

2. Click on **New**. The New Presentation dialog box will open, and the General tab should be on top.

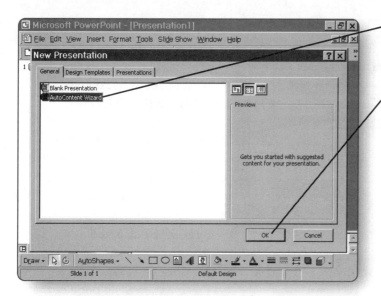

3. **Click** on **AutoContent Wizard**. The wizard will be selected.

4. **Click** on **OK**. The AutoContent Wizard will start.

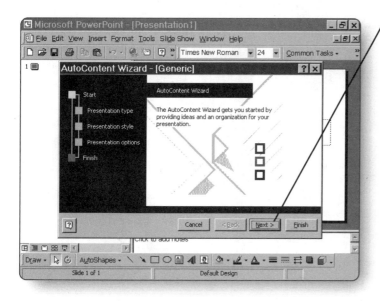

5. **Click** on **Next**. The Presentation Type page of the wizard will appear.

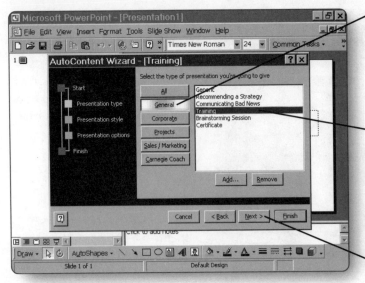

6. Click on the **button** that represents the type of presentation you'd like to give. A list of presentation types will appear in the dialog box.

7. Click on a **presentation type** that comes closest to the type of information that you want to discuss in your presentation. The presentation type will be selected.

8. Click on **Next**. The Presentation Style page of the wizard will appear.

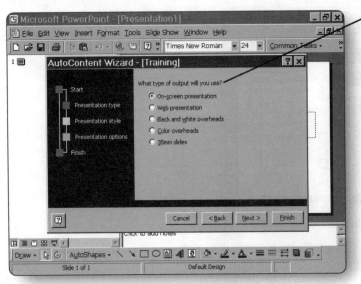

9. Click on the **option button** that corresponds to the method you will be using to give your presentation. The option will be selected. The following describes the presentation methods that are available to you:

- **On-screen presentation** allows you to run your presentation on a computer monitor or on a projector that is connected to a computer. The computer from which the presentation is being displayed will need to have PowerPoint installed on it, or else you will need to set up the file so that it can be viewed in the PowerPoint Viewer.

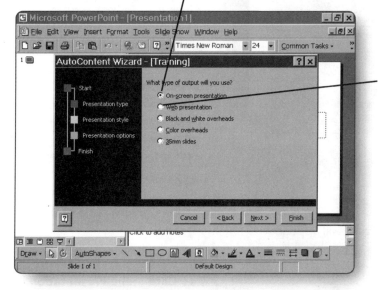

- **Web presentation** allows you to create a presentation in the appropriate format so that it can be viewed easily over the Internet or on your company's intranet. The presentation is viewed in a Web browser and can contain hyperlinks to take your audience to information contained outside the presentation. The presentation's outline serves as the navigation element, or you can add navigation buttons to take your audience from slide to slide.

- **Black and white overheads** creates a presentation that will be printed either on 8-1/2-by-11-inch paper or transparency sheets from a black-and-white printer. You can then either pass out paper hard copies to your audience or display the transparencies on an overhead projector.

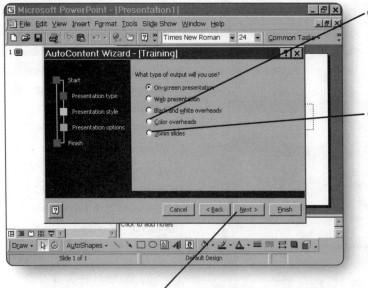

- **Color overheads** creates a presentation that will be printed on 8-1/2-by-11-inch paper or transparency sheets from a color printer.

- **35mm slides** allows you to use a slide projector to give a presentation. This option requires you to have a slide maker that accepts output from a computer. If you don't, you will need to take advantage of the services provided by a service bureau.

10. **Click** on **Next**. The Presentation Options page of the wizard will appear.

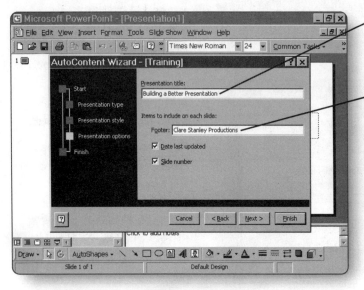

11. **Click** in the **Presentation title: text box** and type a title for your presentation.

12. **Click** in the **Footer: text box** and type the text that you want to appear in the footer of each slide.

NOTE

The footer will appear at the bottom of each slide and can contain any information you wish. You could use your name or your company name, copyright information, or the name of the group to which you are presenting.

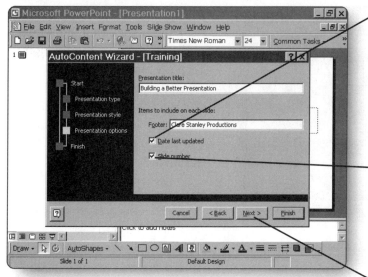

13. **Click** in the **Date last updated check box** if you do not want to display the last date on which you made updates to the presentation in the footer area of each slide. The check box will be cleared.

14. **Click** in the **Slide number check box** if you do not want to show the number order of each slide in the footer area. The check box will be cleared.

15. **Click** on **Next**. The Finish page of the wizard will appear.

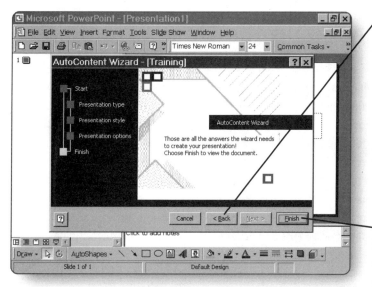

16. **Click** on the **Back button**, if you need to make any changes to the information you put into the wizard, until you reach the page in the wizard to which you want to make changes. When you've made your change, **click** on the **Next button** until you get to the Finish page of the wizard.

17. **Click** on **Finish**. The beginning of your presentation will appear in the PowerPoint window.

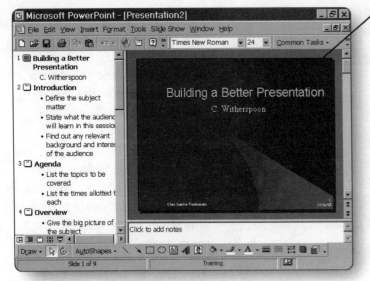

You'll notice a basic outline in the left pane and the title screen of the presentation on the right. Each presentation has a suggested design that best displays the method you will be using to give your presentation. You'll learn how to change this design in the next section.

Changing the Design Template

You now have a basic structure on which to build your presentation, and a predesigned look to go with it. The basic design elements (such as background, text style, and text color) that you see on the title slide are used on all the other slides in the presentation. This look is only a suggestion. PowerPoint provides you with other designs that you may like better and may be more pleasing to your particular audience. Take some time to look at the other designs that come with PowerPoint. When you change the design template, all the slides in your presentation will be changed automatically.

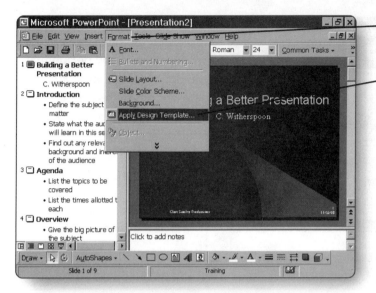

1. **Click** on **Format**. The Format menu will appear.

2. **Click** on **Apply Design Template**. The Apply Design Template dialog box will open.

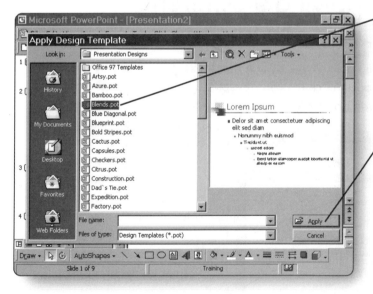

3. **Click** on the **template** that you want to apply to your presentation. The template will be selected and a preview of the design will appear in the preview window.

4. **Click** on **Apply**. The new design will be applied to all the slides in your presentation.

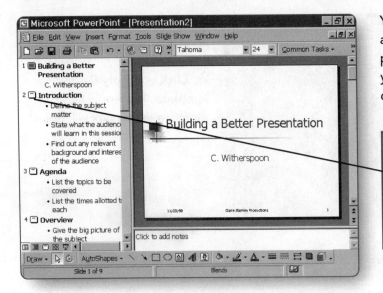

You'll see the new design applied to the title slide of your presentation. If you decide that you don't like this look, apply a different design template.

TIP

Click on the slide icons in the Outline pane to see how other slides look with the new design you chose.

Applying a Different Color Scheme

You now have a design that looks good and that you feel is a good match for your presentation. But what if the colors just aren't right? Maybe you'd like to change the color of the background or make certain text elements a different color. You can change the color scheme for the entire presentation, or just change the color of certain elements.

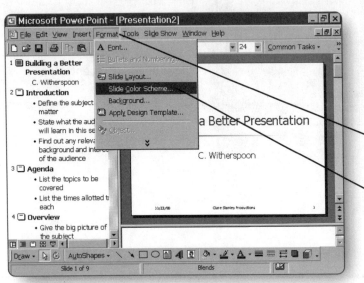

1. Click on **Format**. The Format menu will appear.

2. Click on **Slide Color Scheme**. The Color Scheme dialog box will open, and the Standard tab will be on top.

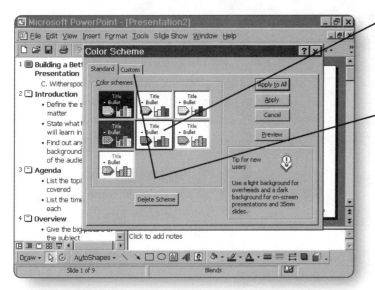

3. Click on the **color scheme** that you want to apply to the entire presentation. The color scheme will be selected.

4. Click on the **Custom tab** if you want to change the color of individual slide elements (such as text, bullets, background, or lines). The Custom tab will move to the front.

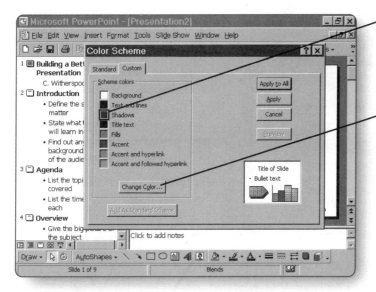

5. Click on the **Scheme color box** for the element that you want to change color. The color box will be selected.

6. Click on the **Change Color button**. The Color dialog box for the element will open.

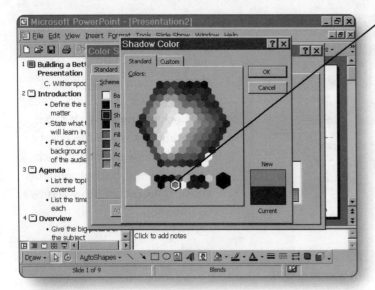

7. Click on the **color** that you want to apply to the element. The color will be selected. The preview pane at the bottom right of the dialog box will show you the selected color and the current color of the element.

8. Click on **OK**. You will return to the Color Scheme dialog box, and the color box for the element will be changed to the new color.

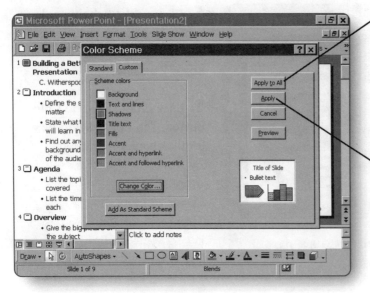

9. Click on the **Apply to All button**. The dialog box will close, and the new color scheme will be applied to every slide in the presentation.

TIP

To change the color of the current slide only, click on the Apply button.

Saving Your Presentation

That was a lot of fun! Now, it's time to make sure you don't lose all your hard work. The importance of saving your work can't be stressed enough. Computers are subject to a number of factors that can cause them to crash. Crashes may be caused by something as simple as an electrical surge or outage, or by something more complex, such as a hardware problem. To protect yourself from lost work, press that Save button every few minutes.

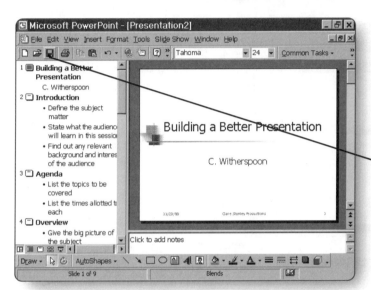

1. **Click** on the **Save button**. The Save As dialog box will open.

NOTE

The Save As dialog box only opens the first time you save your presentation.

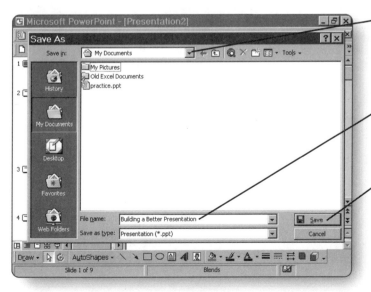

2. **Select** the **directory and folder** in which you want to store the file. The folder will be selected.

3. **Click** in the **File name: text box** and type a name for the presentation.

4. **Click** on **Save**. The file will be stored in the designated directory and folder on your computer, and the file name will appear in the title bar of the PowerPoint window.

Closing the Presentation File

It's time to take a short break, grab a cup of coffee, and stretch your legs. If you don't want others to see what you're working on, you can close your presentation file. You can easily reopen the file when you return.

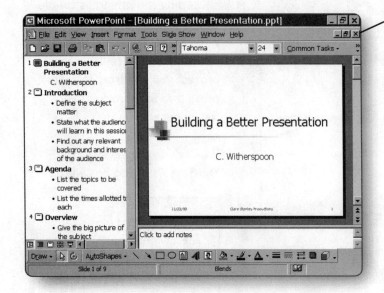

1. Click on the **Close button** (❌). The presentation file will close and the PowerPoint program will stay running.

4

Viewing Your Presentation

Before you get too involved in creating your presentation, you'll want to take some time to get familiar with the various ways in which you can look at your presentation. PowerPoint gives you a choice of several different views, and each view is best suited for performing particular tasks. In this chapter, you'll learn how to:

- Open an existing presentation
- View your presentation in different ways
- Use the Zoom feature for an up-close look at your presentation slides

Opening an Existing Presentation

Break time's over, and now you need to get back to work. You'll need to open the presentation file on which you were working. PowerPoint displays the last four presentation files with which you've worked in the recently-used files list, found at the bottom of the File menu. If you opened PowerPoint fresh to start this chapter, a dialog box will open that allows you to access the most recent PowerPoint presentations without going to the File menu. If you don't find your file in one of these two places, you'll need to search through your computer's file system.

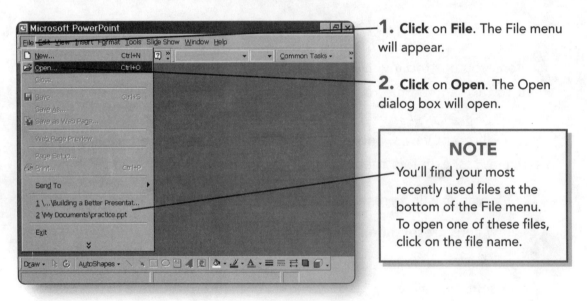

1. Click on **File**. The File menu will appear.

2. Click on **Open**. The Open dialog box will open.

NOTE

You'll find your most recently used files at the bottom of the File menu. To open one of these files, click on the file name.

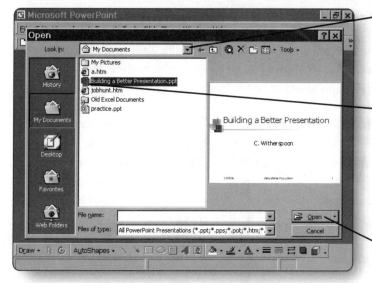

3. Select the **directory** in which the file is stored. The directory will appear in the Look in: list box.

4. Click on the presentation **file** that you want to open. The file will be selected, and a preview of the presentation title slide will appear in the preview window.

5. Click on **Open**. The presentation will appear in the PowerPoint Normal view.

Understanding the PowerPoint Views

As you work on your presentation, you'll be performing a variety of tasks such as creating the outline, rearranging slides, and adding text and graphics to a slide. To perform these various tasks more easily, you'll want to switch to the best view to use for each one.

Using the All Purpose Normal View

The Normal view is the most versatile view available to you. Normal view allows you to work on the outline, individual slides, and speaker notes from one convenient place.

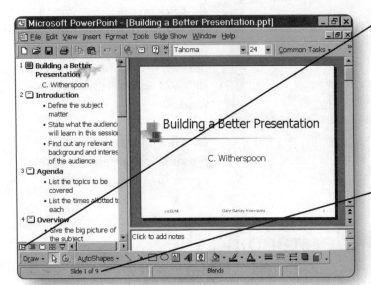

1. **Click** on the **Normal View button** if the Normal view is not displayed in the PowerPoint window. The PowerPoint window will be divided into three panes.

NOTE

The status bar indicates which slide number is displayed in the Slide pane.

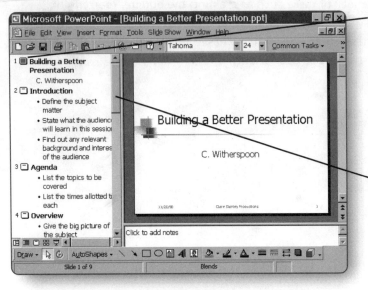

2. **Click** on a **slide icon** in the Outline pane. The outline text associated with the slide will be highlighted, and the selected slide will appear in the Slide pane.

TIP

Click on the scroll bar in the Outline pane to see more of your outline.

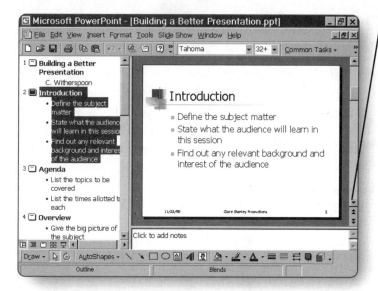

3. Click on the **down arrow** (□) at the bottom of the Slide pane scroll bar. The next slide in your presentation will appear in the Slide pane. You'll also notice that the slide icon for the associated slide will be highlighted in the Outline pane.

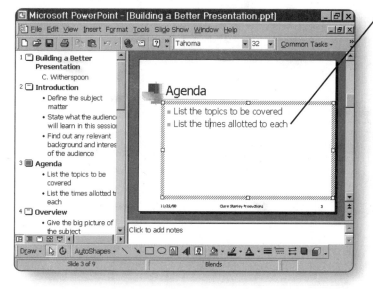

4. Click on the **text** contained in a slide. A text box will appear around the text. These text boxes are placeholders. When inserting text into a textbox, PowerPoint will automatically format the text so that it fits inside the placeholder.

Checking the Flow of Your Outline

The Outline view is the best place to work out the flow and organization of your presentation. From this view, you can rearrange headings and supporting text, add additional information, and see how well your presentation is organized.

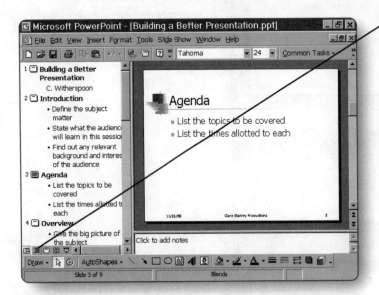

1. Click on the **Outline View button**. The Outline view will appear.

> **NOTE**
>
> You'll learn how to create an outline in Chapter 5, "Working with the Outline View."

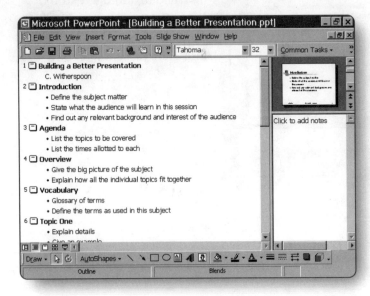

You'll notice the same three panes as you did in the Normal view except that the Outline and Notes panes are larger and the Slide pane shows only a thumbnail of the selected slide. To make it easier to build an outline, you'll want to display the Outlining toolbar.

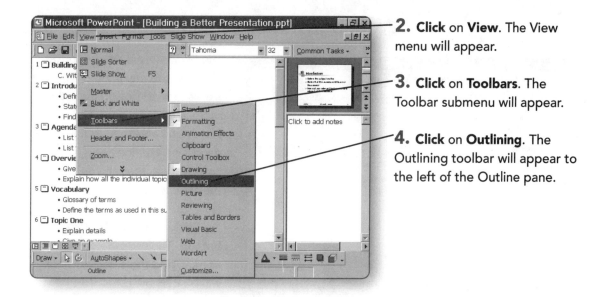

2. Click on **View**. The View menu will appear.

3. Click on **Toolbars**. The Toolbar submenu will appear.

4. Click on **Outlining**. The Outlining toolbar will appear to the left of the Outline pane.

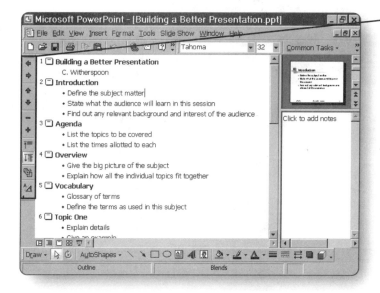

The Outlining toolbar contains buttons to promote and demote text within the outline, to move slides within the outline, to collapse and expand the outline to display only slide headings or the entire text found on a slide, and to show how text is formatted on the slide.

Working with Individual Slides

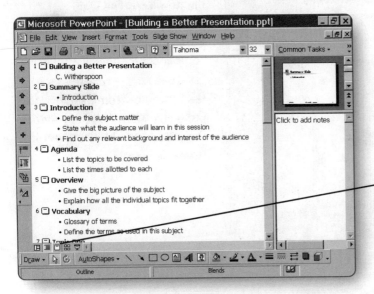

The Slide view is designed to give you the maximum workspace to design individual slides. This view contains the Slide pane and the Outline pane. The Outline pane is collapsed so that all you see is the slide icons.

1. **Click** on the **Slide View button**. The slide view will appear, and the selected slide will be displayed.

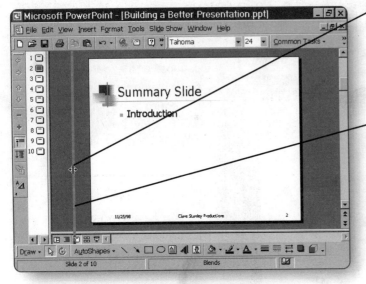

2. **Click and hold** the **mouse button** on the bar between the Outline and Slide panes. The mouse pointer will change to a double-pointed arrow.

3. **Drag** the mouse to the **right**. As the Outline pane becomes wider, you'll see the outline expand from displaying just title headings to the entire outline.

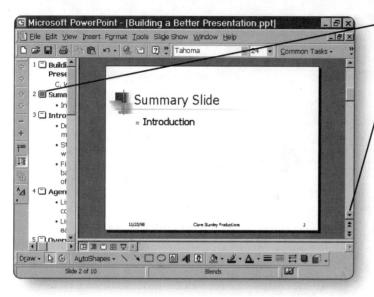

4. **Click** on a **slide icon** in the Outline view. The slide you selected will appear in the Slide pane.

5. **Click** on the **down arrow** (⬇) at the bottom of the Slide pane scroll bar. The next slide in the presentation will appear in the Slide pane.

Sorting through Your Slides

The Slide Sorter view allows you to see thumbnail versions of all the slides in your presentation in one convenient place. In addition to viewing your slides, you can also rearrange slides and view slide transitions.

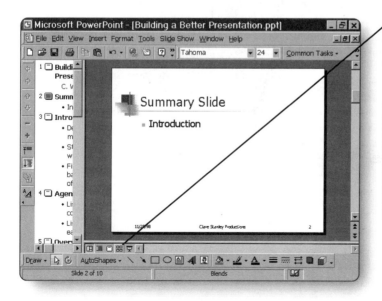

1. **Click** on the **Slide Sorter View button**. The Slide Sorter view will appear.

NOTE

You'll learn more about using the Slide Sorter view in Chapter 6, "Organizing Your Presentation."

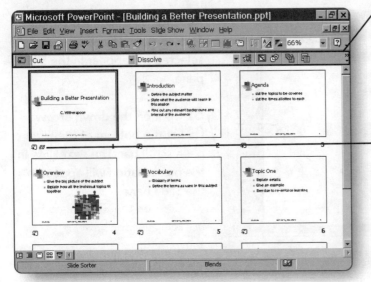

You'll notice that a new toolbar has been added to the PowerPoint window. This is the Slide Sorter toolbar, and it allows you to add transition effects to your slides.

2. Click on an **Animation Preview icon**. Any animation effects that have been applied to the slide or any of its elements will appear.

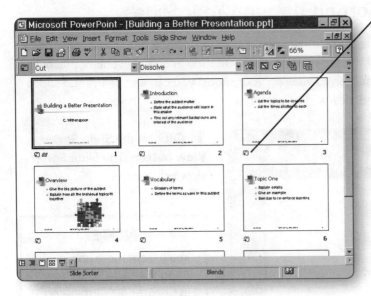

3. Click on a **Slide Transition icon**. Any slide transitions, such as fades or wipes, will appear.

NOTE

You'll learn how to add animations and transition effects in Chapter 10, "Displaying Special Effects."

Running a Slide Show

When you want to view your presentation onscreen, use the Slide Show view. This view allows you to see your presentation in full-screen mode, that is, without the PowerPoint interface.

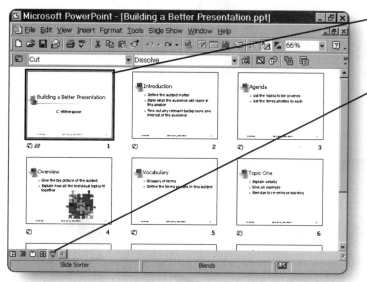

1. Click on the **slide** that you want to display first in the slide show. The slide will be selected.

2. Click on the **Slide Show button**. A slide show presentation will start and will show how your presentation will look onscreen.

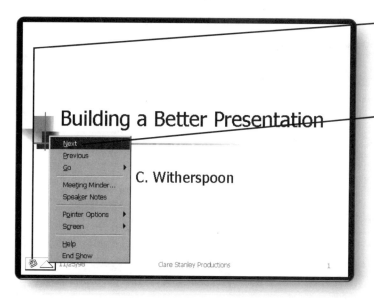

3. Click on the **control button** at the bottom left of the slide show. A shortcut menu will appear.

4. Click on **Next**. The next slide in your presentation will appear.

TIP

You can also use the right and left arrow keys on your keyboard to move forward and backward in your presentation.

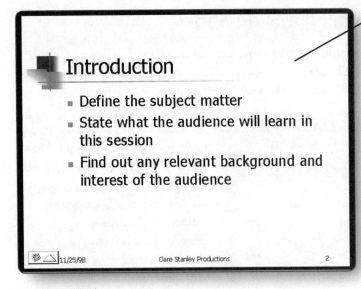

5. Continue previewing your presentation until you have reached the last slide.

TIP

To exit the slide show presentation and return to the PowerPoint window, just press the Escape key.

Zooming In on Your Work

If you have a slide that contains artwork, you may want to take a closer look at the picture so that you can make changes. Or, maybe the text is too small for you to see without your glasses.

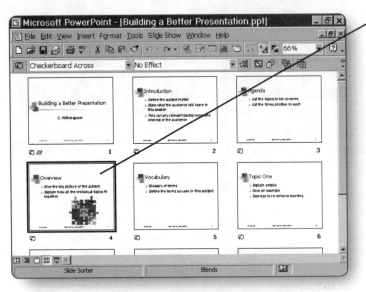

1. Double-click on the **slide** with which you want to work. The slide will appear in the Slide view.

NOTE

You'll learn about using graphics in Chapter 9, "Adding Graphics to a Presentation."

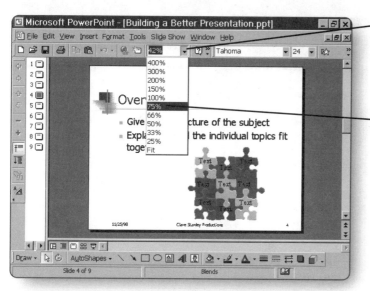

2. **Click** on the **Zoom down arrow** (⬛) on the Standard toolbar. A list of percentages will appear.

3. **Click** on a **percentage** of the original size of the slide in which you want to view the slide. The display size of the slide as it appears in the Slide pane will change. A thumbnail of the slide will appear in a separate window if you enlarge the slide more than 75%.

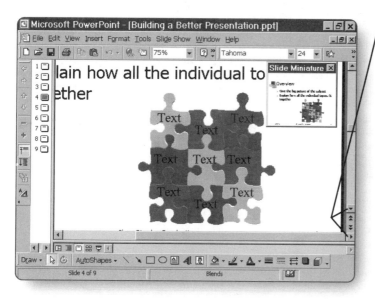

4. **Click** on the **arrows** at either end of the two scroll bars until the portion of the slide that you want to view appears in the Slide pane.

TIP

To hide the thumbnail of the slide, click on the Close (⬛) button.

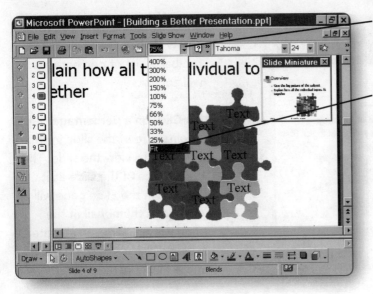

5. Click on the **Zoom down arrow** (▾). The list of zoom percentages will appear.

6. Click on **Fit**. The entire slide will be visible inside the Slide pane.

Part I Review Questions

1. *What are the two shortcut methods you can use to start PowerPoint? See "Starting PowerPoint 2000" in Chapter 1*

2. *What is the purpose of the three panes that display in the PowerPoint Normal view? See "Exploring the PowerPoint Screen" in Chapter 1*

3. *How can you quickly find out what command a toolbar button executes? See "Taking Advantage of ToolTips" in Chapter 2*

4. *Is it possible to use a different Office Assistant character? See "Asking the Office Assistant for Help" in Chapter 2*

5. *How do you turn off the Office Assistant? See "Working Around the Office Assistant" in Chapter 2*

6. *What is the easiest way to start a presentation? See "Starting with the AutoContent Wizard" in Chapter 3*

7. *How do you change the look of a presentation? See "Changing the Design Template" in Chapter 3*

8. *Why is it important to save your presentation often? See "Saving Your Presentation" in Chapter 3*

9. *Name the five different views that you can use to work with your presentation. See "Understanding the PowerPoint Views" in Chapter 4*

10. *How can you get a close-up look at elements in your presentation slides? See "Zooming In on Your Work" in Chapter 4*

PART II

Expanding Your Presentation

5

Working with the Outline View

So far, you've let PowerPoint do most of the work creating a basis for a presentation and customizing a design. Now it's your turn to add the real content that will make your presentation an attention grabber. The easiest place to create and organize your presentation is in the Outline view. You were introduced to the Outline view in Chapter 4, "Viewing Your Presentation." It's time to use this view to get creative and plot a course for your presentation. In this chapter, you'll learn how to:

- Work with text in an outline
- Organize items in the outline
- Use outlines created in other applications
- Send the outline to the printer

Editing the Presentation Outline

If you used one of PowerPoint's presentation templates, you'll find that a structure for designing a solid and informative presentation has been created for you. You can take this suggested outline and add or delete outline items to create a well-organized and smooth-flowing presentation.

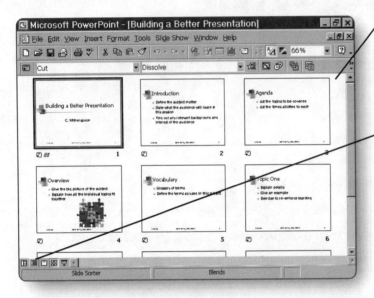

1. **Open** the **presentation** with which you want to work. The presentation will appear in the view in which it was last displayed.

2. **Click** on the **Outline View button**. The presentation will appear in the Outline view.

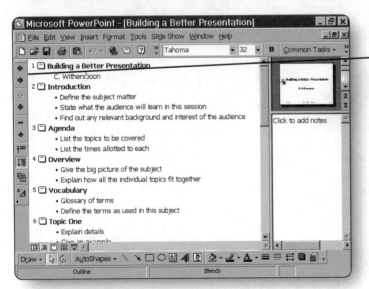

NOTE

Even though some of the outlining commands are available on the Standard and Formatting toolbars, you may want to display the Outlining toolbar. See Chapter 4, "Viewing Your Presentation."

Selecting Text

Before you can edit or format text, you'll need to select the text. Selected text appears inside a boxed background. The text you select can be a single letter or an entire document, but you can only select a single, continuous block of text.

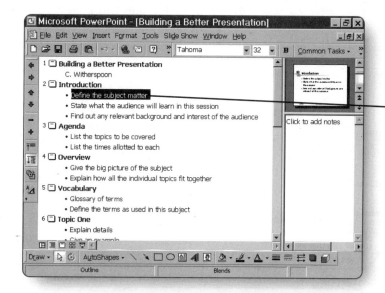

Here are a few tips for selecting text:

- To select a word, click twice on the word.

- To select a sentence, click three times on the sentence.

- To select a paragraph, click four times on the paragraph.

- To select the entire document, press Ctrl+A.

- To select a block of text, click at the beginning of the text and drag the mouse pointer to the end of the text you want to select. Release the mouse button.

Replacing Outline Text

When you want to change the text contained in a paragraph while retaining the position and formatting of the text, just replace the words with a few of your own.

1. Select the **text** that you want to replace. The text will be highlighted.

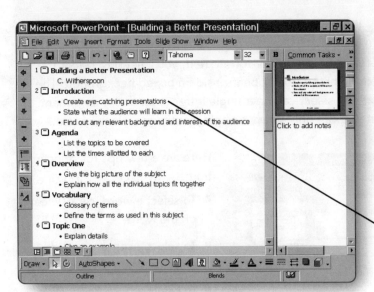

NOTE

Give your mouse a rest! Use the four arrow keys on the keyboard to move around in the outline. To select text, press and hold the Shift key while using the arrow keys.

2. Type the **new text**. The selected text will be deleted and replaced by the new text.

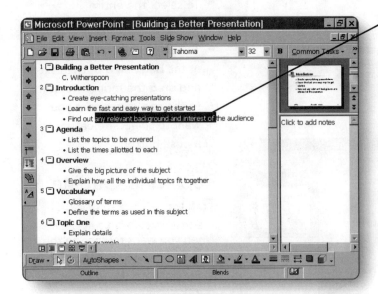

3. Replace text in the outline as needed.

TIP

Try out this obscure Microsoft Web site: **www. microsoft.com/education /curric/**. You'll find some online courses for several Microsoft applications.

Adding Items to an Outline

The outline structure that came with your presentation template isn't very specific when it comes to the topic you'll want to cover. Try your hand at adding items to the outline. You'll learn how to move items around in Outline view in the next section.

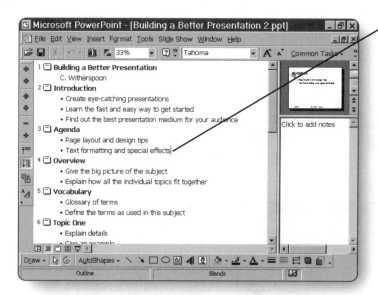

1. **Click** at the **end** of the line that is above the space where you want to add a new item in the outline. The cursor will appear at the end of the line.

2. **Press** the **Enter key**. A blank line will appear and the cursor will be in that blank line.

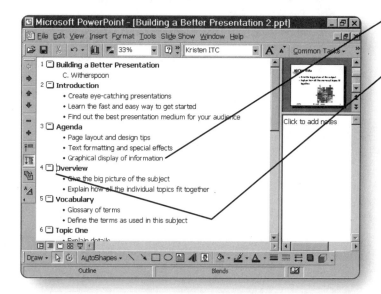

3. **Type** the **text** that you want to appear in the new line.

4. **Click** at the **beginning** of a line that you want to appear below the new text. The cursor will appear at the beginning of the line.

5. **Press** the **Enter key**. A blank line will appear, and the cursor will be in the line below the blank line.

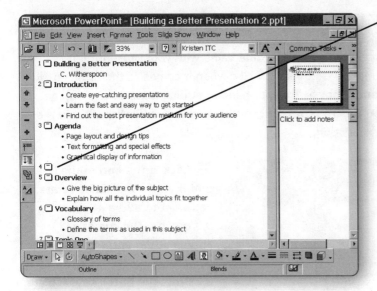

6. Click in the **blank line**. The cursor will appear in the blank line.

7. Type the **text** that you want to appear in the line.

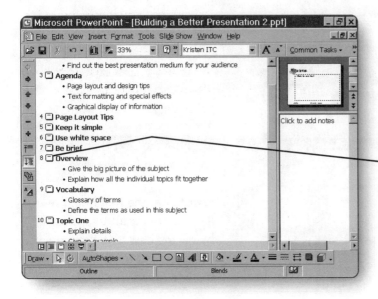

Deleting Items from an Outline

It's easy to get rid of those slides and outline items that you don't want to use.

1. Click on the **slide icon** next to the slide that you want to delete. The icon and its associated text will be selected.

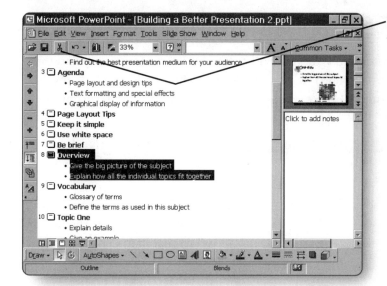

2. Click on the **Cut button**.
The outline item will be deleted.

TIP
You can move text to another location instead of deleting it. Select the text that you want to move, and click on the Cut button. Then, click on the new location where you want to put the cut text, and click on the Paste button.

Rearranging Items in an Outline

After you've added and deleted some text, you may find that outline items do not appear at the correct level within the outline. Here's where the Outlining toolbar comes in handy.

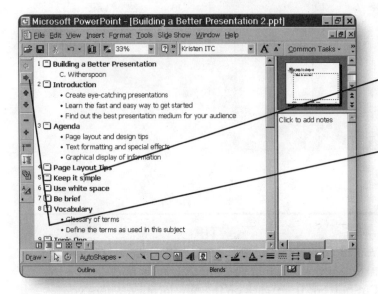

Demoting Outline Items

1. Click in the **line** of text that you want to demote. The cursor will appear in the selected line.

2. Click on the **Demote button**. The text will be demoted.

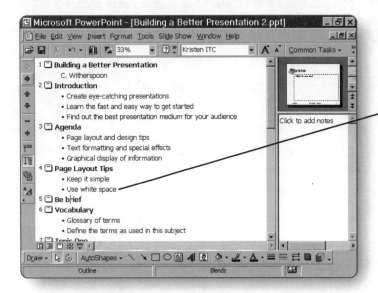

If the line you selected was originally a first-level heading, it will be demoted to a bullet point within the slide.

3. Demote other **lines** of text as needed.

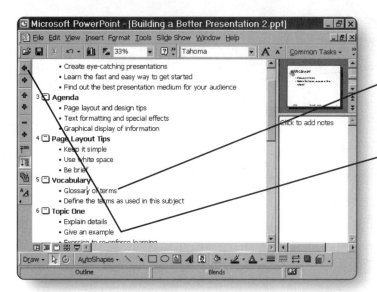

Promoting Outline Items

1. Click in the **line** of text that you want to promote. The cursor will appear in the selected line.

2. Click on the **Promote button**. The text will be promoted.

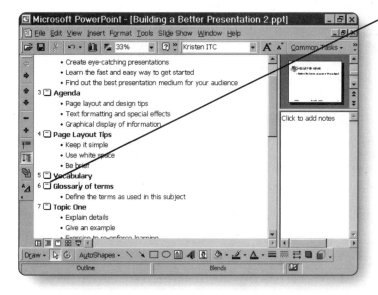

If the line you selected was originally a bullet point, it will be promoted to a first-level heading.

3. Promote other **lines** of text as needed.

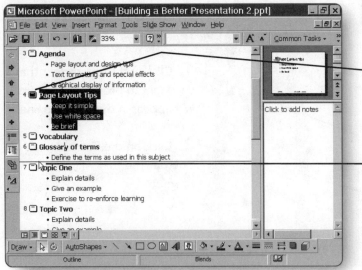

Moving Items Around

1. **Click and hold** the **slide icon** next to the text that you want to move. The slide and the text will be highlighted.

2. **Move** the **mouse pointer** to the location where you want to place the text.

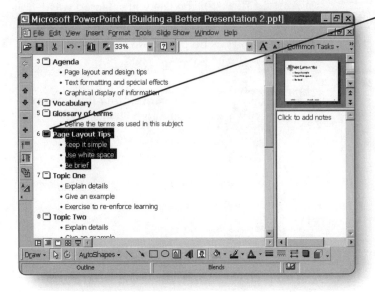

3. **Release** the **mouse button**. The text will be moved to the new location.

NOTE

You can also move outline items using the Move Up and Move Down buttons on the Outlining toolbar.

Using Keyboard Shortcuts

As you've seen, you can move any part of an outline by clicking the mouse pointer and a few assorted buttons. You can also use keyboard shortcuts to make the job of editing your outline easier. The following table shows these keyboard shortcuts.

To execute this command	Do this
Demote an item	Press the Alt, Shift, and right arrow keys simultaneously (Alt+Shift+Right arrow)
Promote an item	Atl+Shift+Left arrow
Move an item down in the outline	Alt+Shift+Down arrow
Move an item up in the outline	Alt+Shift+Up arrow
Show top level heading	Alt+Shift+1
Expand outline to show text	Alt+Shift+plus sign
Collapse outline to hide text	Alt+Shift+minus sign
Show all headings and text	Alt+Shift+A
Turn character formatting on and off	Slash (on the numeric keypad)

TIP
These keyboard shortcuts also work in the Slide Sorter view. Try them out when you want to move slides around to reorganize your presentation.

Sharing Outlines between Applications

If you created an outline in another application, you can easily use that information in a PowerPoint presentation. You can add outlines created in Microsoft Word or FrontPage to your presentation. Other file formats that PowerPoint can use include Rich Text Format (.rtf), plain text format (.txt), or HTML format (.htm). PowerPoint reads the heading styles and paragraph indentations in which the text is formatted to build an outline structure. PowerPoint can also export an outline so that other programs can use it as well.

Using an Outline Created in Another Application

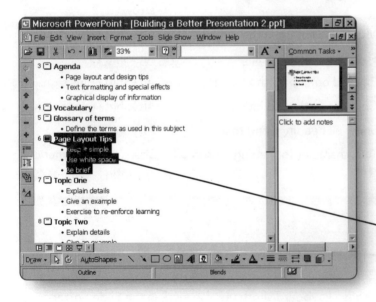

When importing an outline created in another application, PowerPoint does its best work when the imported outline uses Heading styles. If you don't use these styles, indent your outline items using tabs. Items without a tab character in front become the slide title (or first-level heading).

1. Click on the **slide icon** after which you want the outline to appear. The icon and slide text will be highlighted.

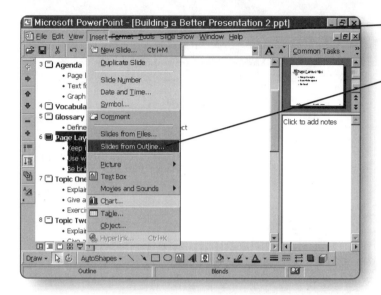

2. Click on **Insert**. The Insert menu will appear.

3. Click on **Slides from Outline**. The Insert Outline dialog box will open.

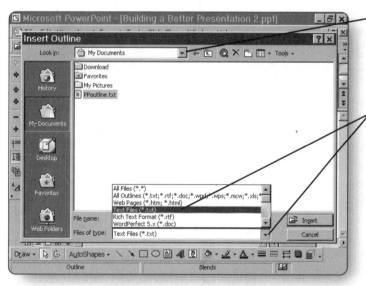

4. Display the **folder** in which you've stored the outline file. The folder will appear in the Look in: list box.

5. Click on the **down arrow** (🔽) next to the Files of type: list box, and select the file type in which you saved the outline that you want to add. The file type will appear in the list box.

TIP

If you're unsure of the file type, select All Outlines from the Files of type: list box.

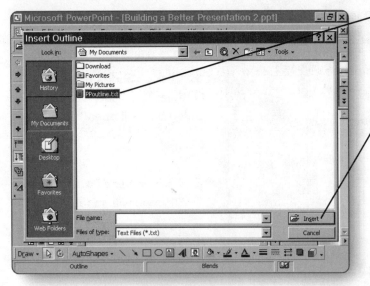

6. Click on the **file** that contains the outline information that you want to add to your presentation. The file will be selected.

7. Click on **Insert**. The outline will be inserted in the existing outline.

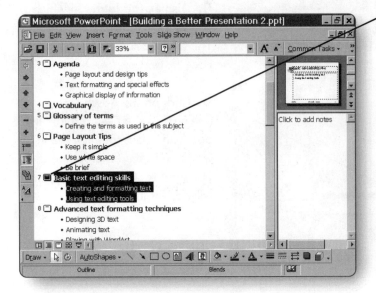

The new outline items will appear after the selected slide. The first outline item from the imported file will now be highlighted. If your outline didn't import properly, you may need to demote and promote items.

TIP

Create a new presentation from an outline created in Word. Display the outline in Word, then open the File menu and select Send To, Microsoft PowerPoint.

Sending the Outline to Microsoft Word

If you want to work on your outline in Word, or if you want someone else to look over your outline, PowerPoint can easily convert the presentation outline to a Word document.

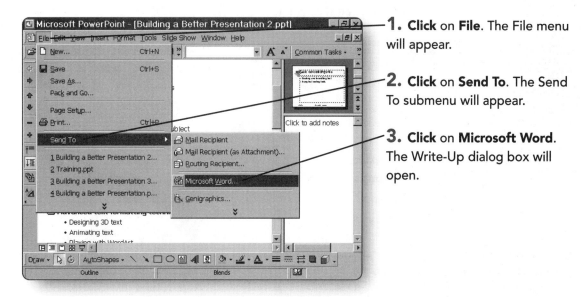

1. Click on **File**. The File menu will appear.

2. Click on **Send To**. The Send To submenu will appear.

3. Click on **Microsoft Word**. The Write-Up dialog box will open.

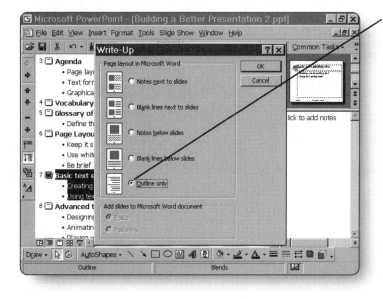

4. Click on the **Outline only option button**. The option will be selected.

5. Click on **OK**.

Printing the Outline

You may want to keep a paper copy of your presentation outline. Just click a few buttons, and you'll have it! But before you do this, you'll have to display the outline the same way you want it to print.

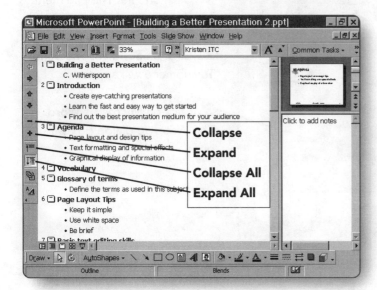

1. Display all **the items** in the outline that you want to print. The outline items will appear in the Outline pane.

TIP

If you want to print only the slide titles, collapse the outline. Use the Expand, Collapse, Expand All, and Collapse All buttons to display only the outline information that you want.

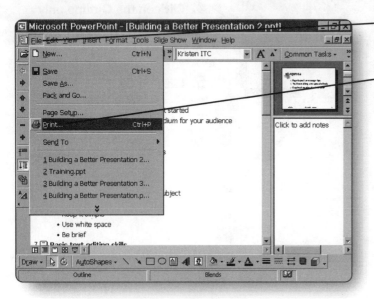

2. Click on **File**. The File menu will appear.

3. Click on **Print**. The Print dialog box will open.

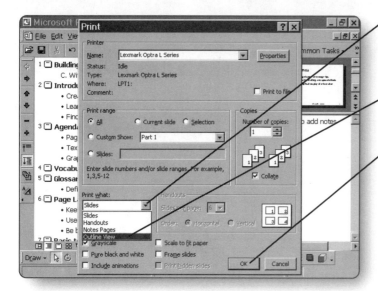

4. Click on the **down arrow** (▼) next to the Print what: list box. A list of print options will appear.

5. Click on **Outline View**. The option will appear in the list box.

6. Click on **OK**. The outline will be sent to your printer.

6

Organizing Your Presentation

When you're looking for a visual approach to organizing your presentation, try the Slide Sorter view. This view displays miniature representations of all the slides in your presentation, in the order in which they will appear in the presentation. You can perform those add, delete, and move tricks that you did in the Outline view, plus a few added goodies. In this chapter, you'll learn how to:

- Add, delete, and move slides in a presentation
- Change the format of individual slides
- Use Summary slides to better organize information

Working with Slide Miniatures

The Slide Sorter view displays all the slides in miniature version in neat rows across your screen. This is a great view of the "big picture." You can quickly see how your presentation is progressing and how the various slides fit together.

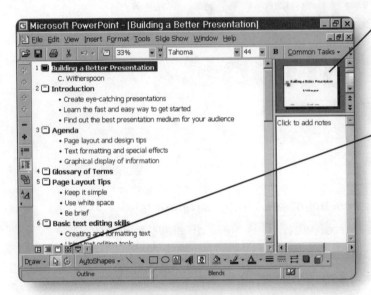

1. Open the **presentation** with which you want to work. The presentation will open in the view in which it was last displayed.

2. Click on the **Slide Sorter View button**. The presentation will appear in the Slide Sorter view.

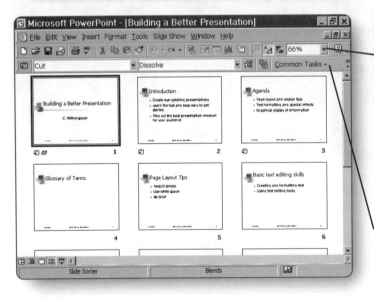

NOTE

Change the size of the slides in the Slide Sorter view. Click on the down arrow next to the Zoom button and select a zoom percentage. A lower zoom percentage displays more slides in each row.

The Slide Sorter view has an added toolbar, the Slide Sorter toolbar. You'll use this toolbar to work with slides and add animated effects.

Selecting Slides

Before you can perform some functions with slides, you'll need to select the slides with which you want to work. Selected slides have a border around them. You can select a single slide, a continuous group of slides, or random slides.

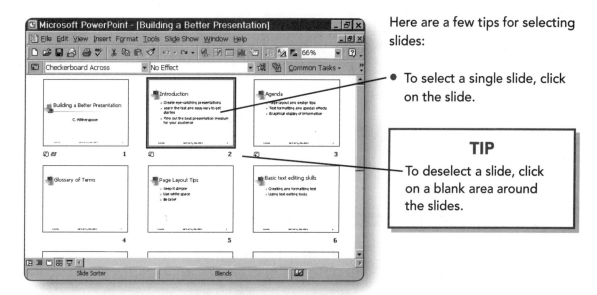

Here are a few tips for selecting slides:

- To select a single slide, click on the slide.

TIP

To deselect a slide, click on a blank area around the slides.

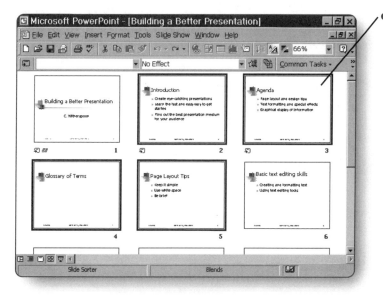

- To select a contiguous group of slides, click on the first slide, then press and hold the Shift key while clicking on the last slide in the group.

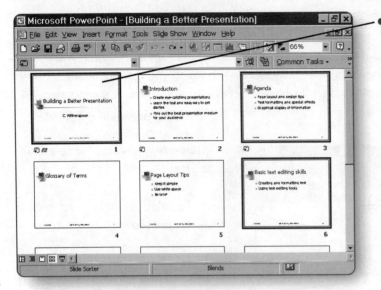

● To select random slides, click on the first slide, then press and hold the Ctrl key while clicking on the other slides you want selected.

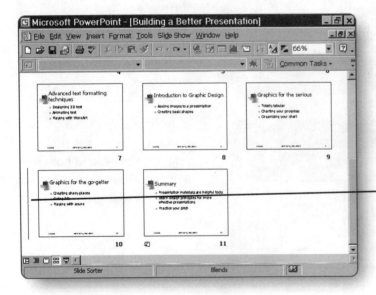

Adding Slides to a Presentation

As you're looking through the slide miniatures, you may see a place where an extra slide could be useful. Here's how to add a new slide to your presentation.

1. Click in the **space** between the two slides where you want the new slide to appear. The cursor will appear between the two slides.

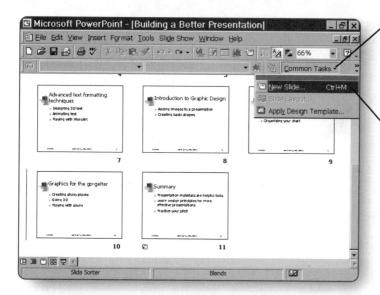

2. Click on the **Common Tasks button** on the Slide Sorter toolbar. The Common Tasks menu will appear.

3. Click on the **New Slide button**. The New Slide dialog box will open.

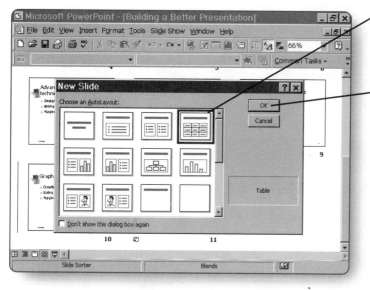

4. Click on the slide **layout** that you want to use for the new slide. The layout will be selected.

5. Click on **OK**. The new slide will appear in the Slide Sorter.

The new slide does not contain any text, but it does contain the template graphics and text formatting of the other slides in your presentation.

NOTE

To work with the slide, click on the Slide View button. You'll learn more about adding text to a slide in Chapter 7, "Editing Text."

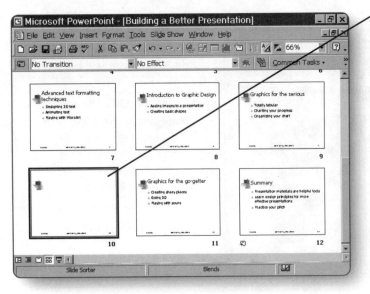

6. Double-click on the **slide** you just added. The Outline view will appear, and the icon for the new slide will be selected.

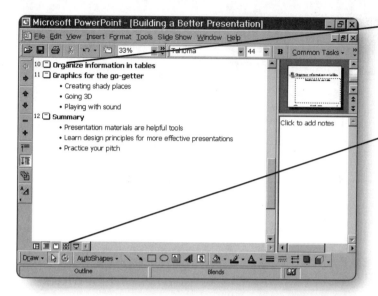

7. **Click** in the **text area** to the right of the slide icon, and type a title for the slide and any additional outline text that you want to add.

8. **Click** on the **Slide Sorter View button**. The Slide Sorter will appear, and the title will be displayed on the slide miniature.

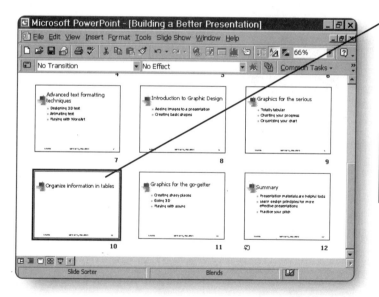

The new slide will be the selected slide in the Slide Sorter view.

NOTE

You'll learn how to use text and graphics in a table to help organize information in Chapter 11, "Adding Tables."

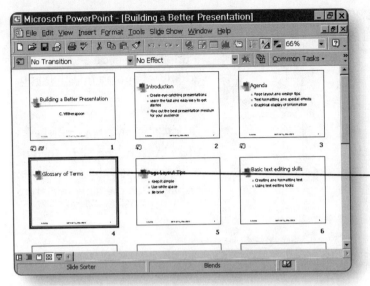

Duplicating Slides within a Presentation

When you want to make an exact copy of a slide, use the Duplicate function.

1. Click on the **slide** of which you want to make a duplicate copy. The slide will be selected.

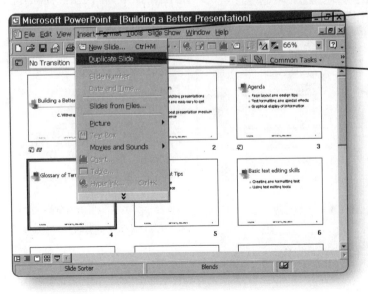

2. Click on **Insert**. The Insert menu will appear.

3. Click on **Duplicate Slide**. An identical slide will be created.

NOTE

The menu commands that you see in this book may not match what you see on your screen. This is due to the adaptive menus used in Office. If you don't see a command, either wait a second or two or click on the down arrow at the bottom of the menu.

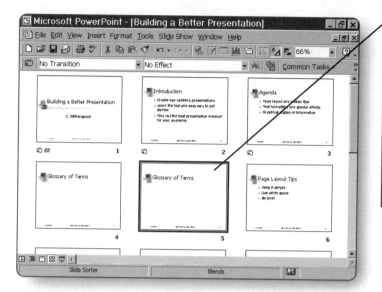

The duplicate slide will appear to the right of the slide you selected.

TIP

Move it anywhere! Click on the duplicate slide and drag it to a different place in the presentation.

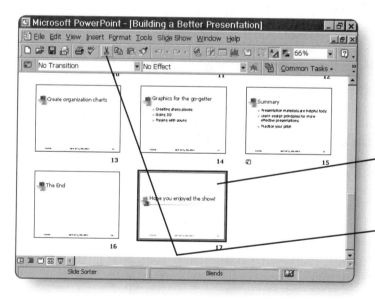

Deleting Slides from a Presentation

When you have a slide that just doesn't fit into your presentation, delete it.

1. **Select** the **slide or slides** that you want to delete. The slides will be selected.

2. **Click** on the **Cut button**. The slides will be removed from the presentation.

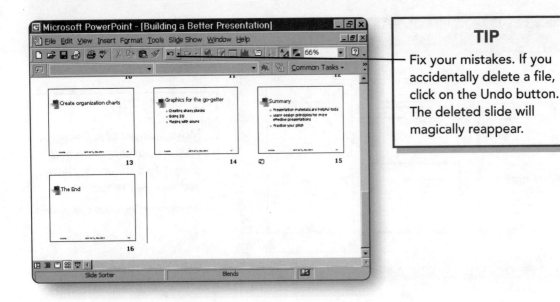

TIP

Fix your mistakes. If you accidentally delete a file, click on the Undo button. The deleted slide will magically reappear.

Moving Slides to Reorganize Information

The Outline view isn't the only place where you can move slides around to better present your information. It's a simple process of drag-and-drop when using the Slide Sorter view.

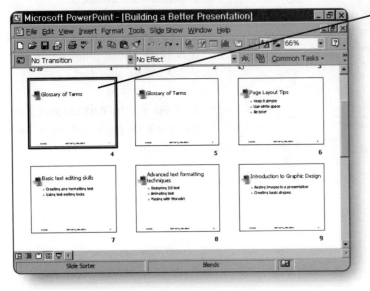

1. Select the **slides** that you want to move. The slides will be selected.

2. Click and hold a selected **slide**. The mouse pointer will turn into a vertical insertion bar.

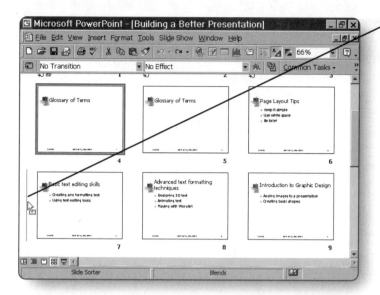

3. Drag the **insertion bar** until it appears in the place where you want to move the selected slides. The insertion bar will appear between two slides.

4. Release the **mouse button**. The slides will appear in their new position.

Changing the Slide Format

When you added new slides in the Outline view, you used the default slide format. This default format contains space for a slide title and several bullet points of text. There are several slide formats from which to choose. Take some time to look at the list.

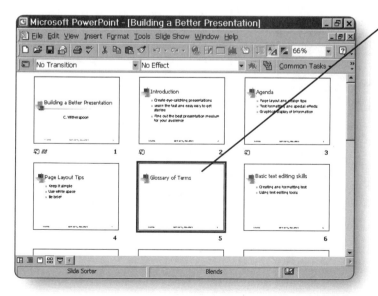

1. Click on the **slide** of which you want to change the layout. The slide will be selected.

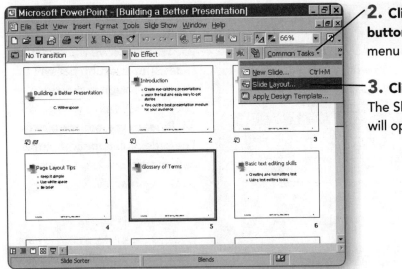

2. Click on the **Common Tasks button**. The Common Tasks menu will appear.

3. Click on **Slide Layout**. The Slide Layout dialog box will open.

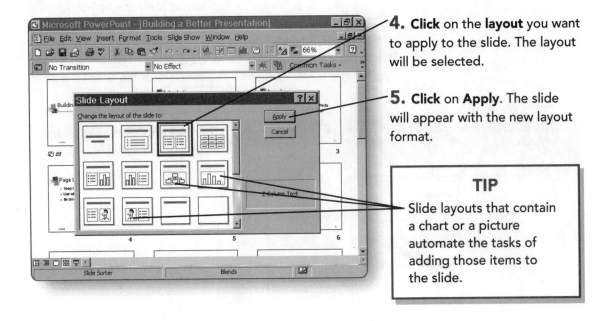

4. Click on the **layout** you want to apply to the slide. The layout will be selected.

5. Click on **Apply**. The slide will appear with the new layout format.

TIP

Slide layouts that contain a chart or a picture automate the tasks of adding those items to the slide.

Creating a Summary Slide

As you're working on your presentation, you may find places where it would be nice to have a slide that summarizes all the points of a group of slides. You could create this slide yourself, but who wants to do all that typing a second time? PowerPoint can automate this task for you using the Slide Summary feature.

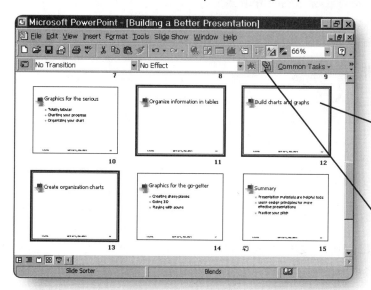

1. Select the **slides** whose titles you want to use to create the summary slide. The slides will be selected.

2. Click on the **Summary Slide button**. The Summary slide will appear in the Slide Sorter view.

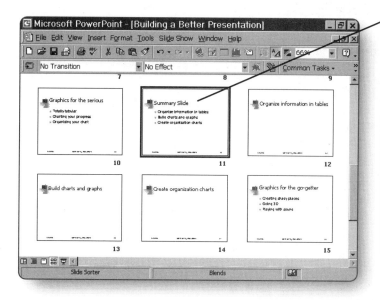

The Summary slide contains a bulleted list of the titles of the selected slides and appears in front of the first selected slide.

TIP

You can make changes to the text contained on the Summary slide. Double-click on the slide or click on the Slide View button.

Inserting Slides from Another Presentation

You may have created another presentation, or been given a presentation by another person, that you want to use in the presentation on which you are currently working. You can easily add all the slides from the other presentation, or only a few slides. If these inserted slides use a different design template, they will take on the look of the presentation into which they are added.

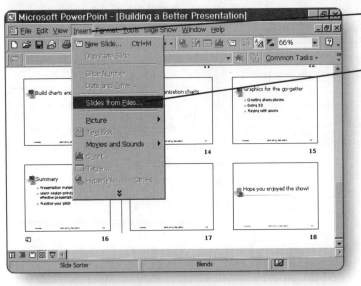

1. Click in the **space** between the two slides where you want the slides from the other presentation to appear. The insertion bar will appear between the two slides.

2. Click on **Insert**. The Insert menu will appear.

3. Click on **Slides from Files**. The Slide Finder dialog box will open.

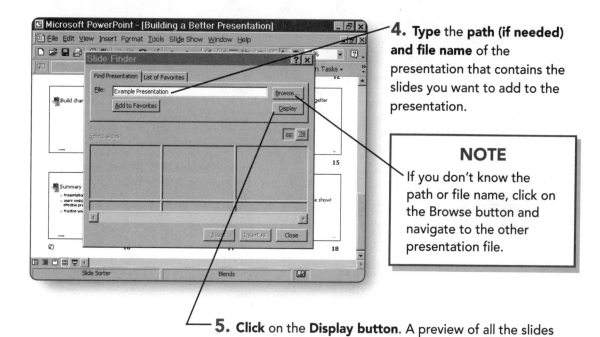

4. Type the **path (if needed) and file name** of the presentation that contains the slides you want to add to the presentation.

NOTE

If you don't know the path or file name, click on the Browse button and navigate to the other presentation file.

5. Click on the **Display button**. A preview of all the slides contained in the presentation will appear in the Select slides: list box.

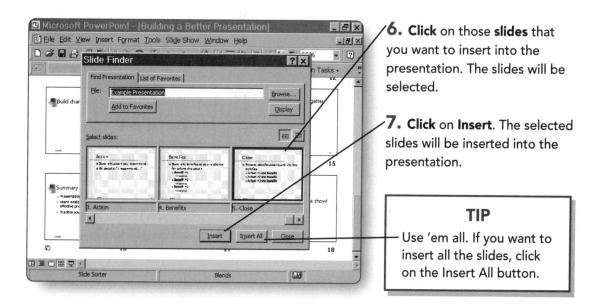

6. Click on those **slides** that you want to insert into the presentation. The slides will be selected.

7. Click on **Insert**. The selected slides will be inserted into the presentation.

TIP

Use 'em all. If you want to insert all the slides, click on the Insert All button.

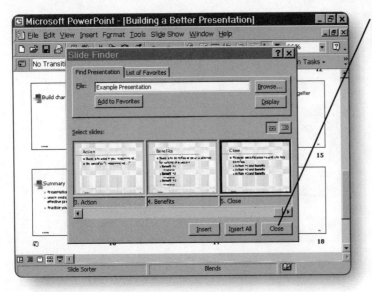

8. Click on **Close**. The Slide Finder dialog box will close.

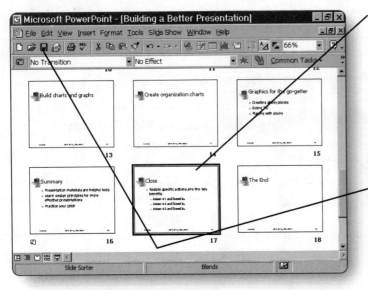

The slide from the other presentation will appear in the selected position and have the same look as the other slides in the presentation in which you are working.

NOTE

Have you been saving your work as you go along? Click on the Save button, or press Ctrl+S.

7

Editing Text

So far, you've learned how to work with text in the Outline view and the Slide Sorter view. Now it's time to take a look at the individual slides that make up your presentation so you can enhance the text that you've already created. In addition to the basic tasks of adding and deleting text, you can use an automated feature to make your presentation look good: the spell checker. Make generous use of the spell checker to be sure that your presentation is the best it can be. In this chapter, you'll learn how to:

- Work with text in the Slide view
- Add formatting to text to make it stand out
- Look for and replace text in your presentation

Working with Text

Before you begin working with the text on each individual slide, you'll need to know how to open a slide, how to move from slide to slide in the presentation, and how to use PowerPoint's text features to add text to a slide more easily.

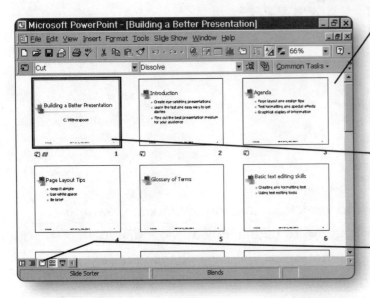

1. Open the **presentation** with which you want to work. The presentation will appear in the PowerPoint window and will appear in the view in which you last worked.

2. Click on the **slide** with which you want to work, if you are in a view other than the Slide view. The slide will be selected.

3. Click on the **Slide View button**. The selected slide will appear in the Slide view.

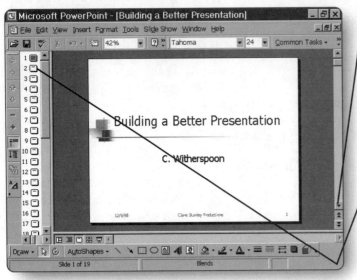

4. Click on the **Next Slide button**. The next slide in your presentation will appear in the Slide pane.

NOTE

You can also click on a slide icon in the Outline pane to move to a different slide.

Adding Text to a Placeholder

When you learned how to add a new slide in the Slide Sorter view, you were introduced to the many slide layouts available in PowerPoint. These slides contain placeholders for text, images, and charts. You can use the text placeholders to add titles, body text, and bulleted lists.

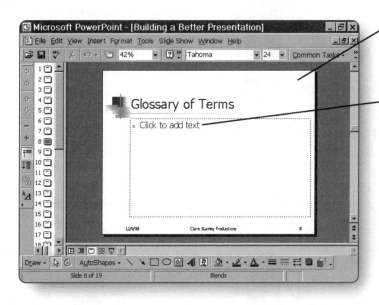

1. Open a **slide** that contains a text placeholder. The slide will appear in the Slide view.

2. Click on the **text** in the placeholder. The placeholder text will disappear and a cursor will appear at the upper-left corner of the placeholder.

NOTE

If you want the text to appear in the outline pane, make sure that you type the text into a placeholder.

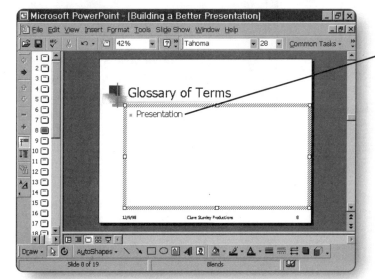

3. Type the **text** that you want to appear in the placeholder.

TIP

What if the text doesn't fit in the placeholder? You may have more text than can be easily viewed on a slide. Create a new slide and add the extra text to that slide.

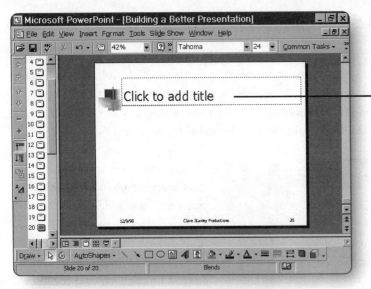

4. Here are a few of the text placeholders that you may encounter:

● The Title placeholder normally appears at the top of the slide and contains a single line of text. Use this placeholder to add text that describes the rest of the content on the slide.

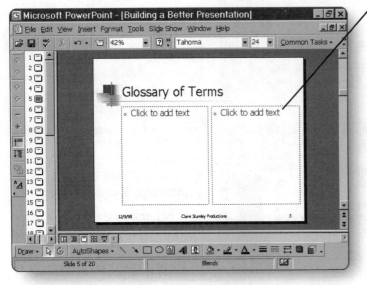

● The Text placeholder can appear anywhere on a slide and can be a range of sizes. Normally, this placeholder displays text in bulleted points.

TIP

Remove bullets by clicking on the Bullets button on the Formatting toolbar.

Creating a Text Box

You may find that you sometimes want to add text to a slide to call attention to something in an image, chart, or table. You can position text boxes any place you want them to appear. You can also use the Fill tool to give the text box a background color, or the Line Color tool to add a border around the text box.

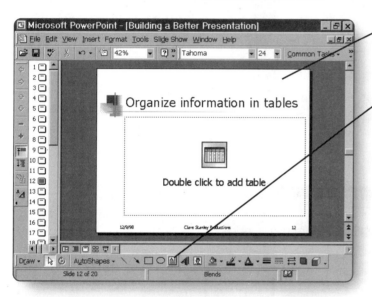

1. **Open** the **slide** with which you want to work. The slide will appear in the Slide view.

2. **Click** on the **Text Box button** on the Drawing toolbar. The cursor will change to an I-beam.

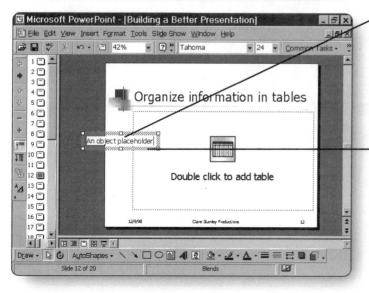

3. **Click** on the **position** where you want to add text, and type the text you want to appear in the text box. If the text box does not appear in the position you want, you can move it.

4. **Click and hold** the **mouse pointer** on the text box border. The mouse pointer will change to a four-pointed arrow.

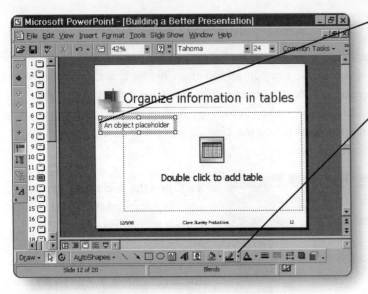

5. **Drag** the **text box** to the new position and release the mouse button. The text box will be moved.

6. **Click** on the **down arrow** (⏷) next to the Line Color button on the Drawing toolbar. A menu of color choices will appear.

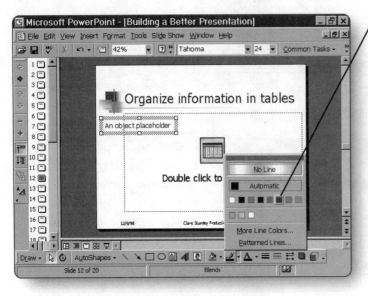

7. **Click** on a **color**. A border will appear around the text box in the color you selected.

NOTE

If you hold the mouse pointer over a color button, a ToolTip will appear that tells you the color scheme element to which the color corresponds.

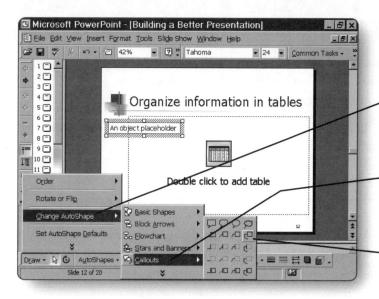

8. Click on the **Draw button** on the Drawing toolbar. The Draw menu will appear.

9. Click on **Change AutoShape**. A submenu will appear.

10. Click on a **shape category**. A list of shapes associated with that category will appear.

11. Click on a **shape**. The shape of the text box outline will change.

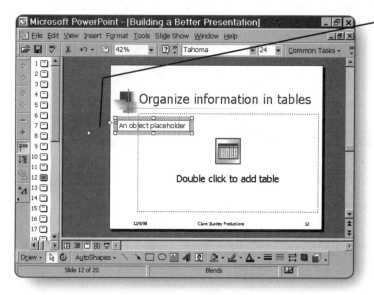

You can move AutoShapes around on the slide. You can also change their size. You'll learn more about AutoShapes in Chapter 9, "Adding Graphics to a Presentation."

Selecting Text with the Keyboard

If you've been a hard-core computer user for long time, you may be noticing a slight discomfort every time you click that mouse button. Here are some more keyboard shortcuts for you to memorize.

TIP

If you have a vision impairment, check out the Magnifier. Begin at the Start button, and then choose Programs, Accessories, and finally Accessibility. You may also want to check out the Accessibility Wizard while you're there.

To execute this command	Do this
Move one character to the right	Press the Shift and Right arrow keys simultaneously (Shift+Right arrow)
Move one character to the left	Press Shift+Left arrow
Go to the end of a word	Press Ctrl+Shift+Right arrow
Go to the beginning of a word	Press Ctrl+Shift+Left arrow
Move up one line	Press Shift+Up arrow
Move down one line	Press Shift+Down arrow

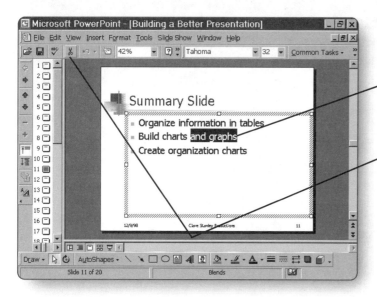

Deleting Text from a Slide

1. Select the **text** that you want to delete. The text will be highlighted.

2. Click on the **Cut button**. The text will be removed from the slide.

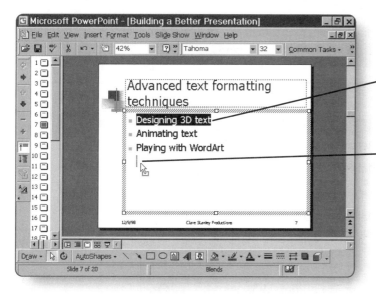

Moving and Copying Text

1. Select the **text** that you want to move or copy. The text will be highlighted.

2. Click and drag the selected **text** to the place where you want it moved.

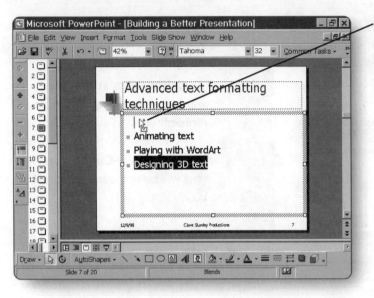

3. Press and hold the **Ctrl key** to copy selected text, and drag the selected text to the place where you want to make a copy.

Using Keyboard Shortcuts to Edit Text

Sometimes it's just easier to use keyboard shortcuts than the mouse to execute commands.

To execute this command	Do this
Delete one character to the left	Press the Backspace key
Delete one word to the left	Press Ctrl+Backspace
Delete one character to the right	Press Delete
Delete one word to the right	Press Ctrl+Delete
Delete the selected object	Press Ctrl+X
Copy the selected object	Press Ctrl+C
Paste an object from the clipboard	Press Ctrl+V
Undo any editing changes	Press Ctrl+Z

Formatting Text

Most of the character and paragraph formatting contained in your presentation has been taken care of by the design template you chose. Sometimes, however, you may want to emphasize a word or group of words. You'll use boldface, italics, or color to accomplish this. You may also want to change the font that is used. You'll need to be sure, of course, that any computer that runs the presentation can read the formatting you choose.

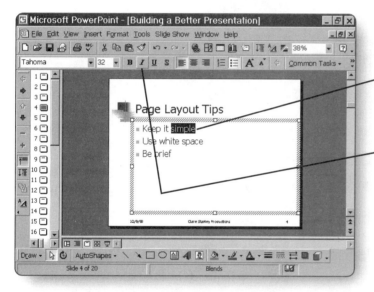

Using the Formatting Toolbar

1. Select the **text** that you want to format. The text will be highlighted.

2. Click on a **Formatting toolbar button**. The text will be formatted in the style selected.

TIP

Toolbars are moveable. Click on the vertical line at the left edge of the toolbar and drag the toolbar to a new position.

Here are a few formatting styles that you may want to apply to your text:

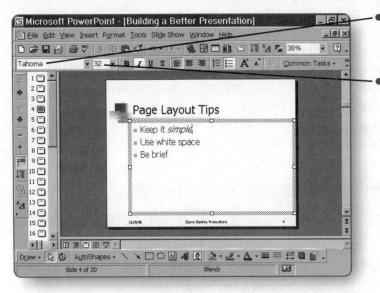

- The Font button changes the style of the type used for the text.

- The Font Size button makes the text larger or smaller.

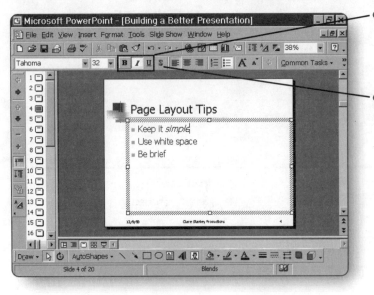

- You can emphasize text so that it stands out from other text by using the Bold, Italic, and Underline buttons.

- The Text Shadow button shouldn't be used on small text sizes or text contained inside a paragraph. It is best used as a special effect to enhance titles.

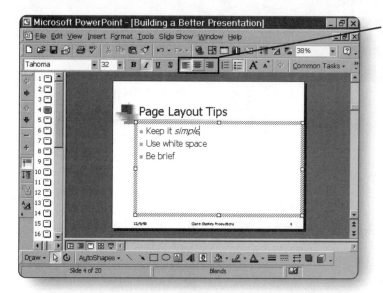

- By default, all placeholder text is left aligned. To change the way paragraphs appear on a slide, use the Align Left, Center, and Align Right buttons.

Copying Text Formatting Attributes

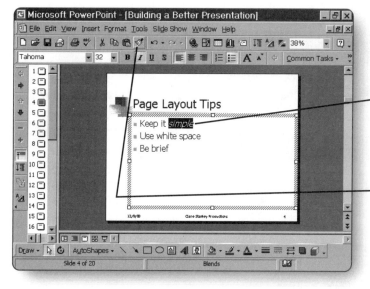

1. **Select** the **text** that is formatted in the style you want to format other text in the presentation slide.

2. **Click** on the **Format Painter button**. The cursor will turn into a paintbrush.

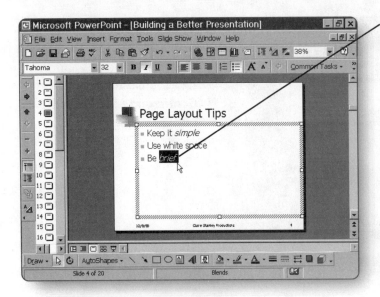

3. Select the **text** to which you want to apply the formatting.

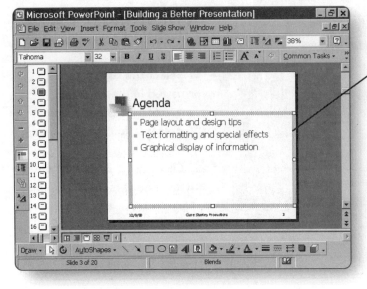

Changing Bullet Characters

1. Click on the **placeholder** that contains the bulleted list with the bullet character that you want to change. The placeholder will be selected.

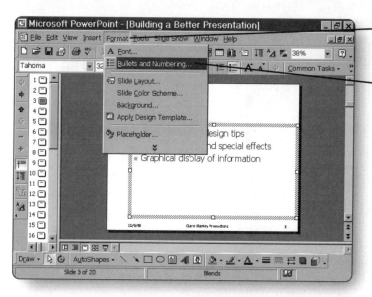

2. Click on **Format**. The Format menu will appear.

3. Click on **Bullets and Numbering**. The Bullets and Numbering dialog box will open, and the Bulleted tab will be on top.

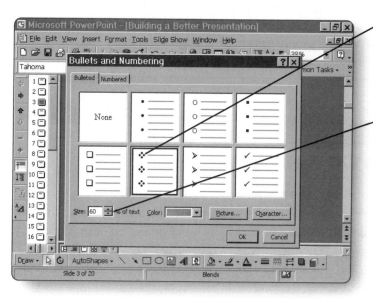

4. Click on the **bullet character** that you want to use in the bulleted list. The bullet character will be selected.

5. Click the **up and down arrows** (⬍) next to the Size: list box to select how large or small the bullet will be compared to the text. The percentage you choose will appear in the list box.

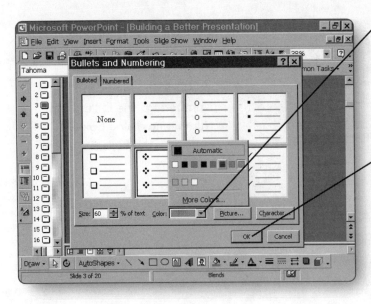

6. Click the **down arrow** (⬇) next to the Color: list box and select a color from the list. The color that appears in the list box will be applied to the bullet character.

7. Click on **OK**. The bullet character and color will be applied to all the bullet points in the placeholder.

TIP

Select additional bullet characters by clicking on the Character button. Or, click on the Picture button to use a bullet that you designed yourself (or maybe a friend did) or downloaded from the Web.

Displaying Text Correctly on Different Computers

If your presentation will be viewed on different computers, you'll want to be sure that the presentation displays on the other computers the same way it did on the computer on which you created it. Not all computers have the same fonts installed. Here's how you can embed fonts into a presentation to ensure that the presentation displays the same on each computer that runs it.

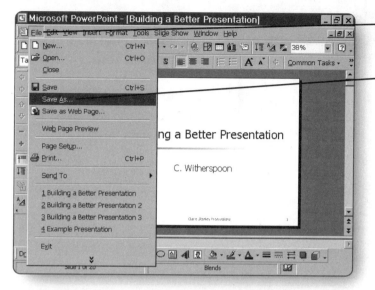

1. Click on **File**. The File menu will appear.

2. Click on **Save As**. The Save As dialog box will open.

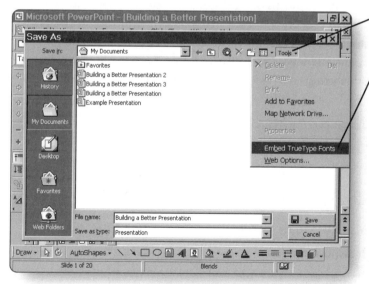

3. Click on **Tools**. The Tools menu will appear.

4. Click on **Embed TrueType Fonts**. The option will be selected.

NOTE

Embedding fonts into your presentation increases the file size. It may increase the file size enough that your presentation may not fit on a floppy disk.

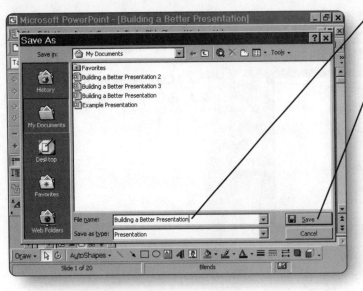

5. Type a new **name** for the presentation, if desired, in the File name: text box.

6. Click on **Save**. The presentation will be saved with the embedded fonts.

Finding Formatting Shortcuts

Formatting text using keyboard shortcuts is easy, and most of these shortcuts are easy to memorize. To format the text, select the text first and then use the appropriate key combination. You'll find these same shortcuts in all Microsoft Office programs and in many Windows programs.

To execute this command	Do this
Change the font	Press the Ctrl, Shift, and F keys simultaneously (Ctrl+Shift+F)
Make the font larger	Press Ctrl+Shift+>
Make the font smaller	Press Ctrl+Shift+<
Make selected text bold	Press Ctrl+B
Underline the selected text	Press Ctrl+U
Italicize the selected text	Press Ctrl+I
Center a paragraph	Press Ctrl+E
Left align a paragraph	Press Ctrl+L
Right align a paragraph	Press Ctrl+R

Searching for Text in a Presentation

You can use Find and Replace to search for any text, such as phrases, words, or characters in a presentation. When you find this text, you can replace it with some other text, or you can delete entirely.

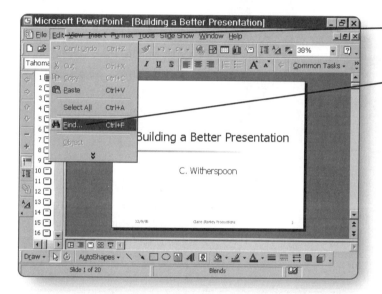

1. Click on **Edit**. The Edit menu will appear.

2. Click on **Find**. The Find dialog box will open.

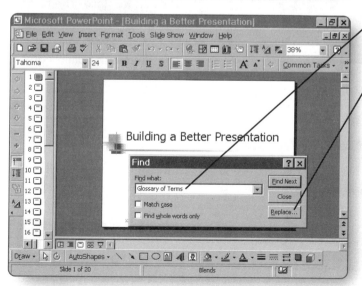

3. Type the **text** you want to find in the Find what: list box.

4. Click on the **Replace button**. The dialog box will expand to display an area in which you can type the replacement text.

5. Type the **text** you want to replace in the Replace with: text box.

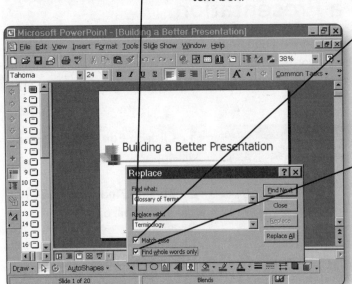

6. Click on the **Match case check box** if you want to find only text that matches the upper- and lowercase letters you type. A ✓ will appear in the box.

7. Click on the **Find whole words only check box** if you want Find to locate only exact word matches, not part of a word. A ✓ will appear in the box.

8. Click on the **Find Next button**. The first occurrence of the word for which you are searching will be highlighted on the slide.

9. Click on **Replace**. The text that is highlighted on the slide will be replaced with the text you specified in the dialog box.

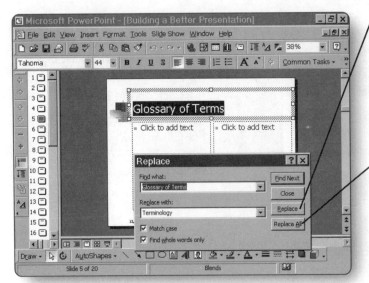

TIP

Replace it all! Click on Replace All to automatically replace all occurrences of the Find text with the Replace text.

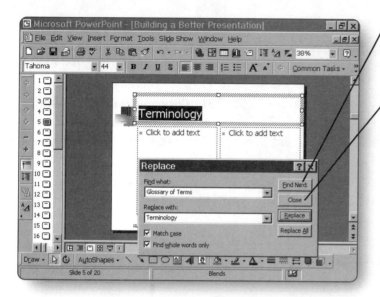

10. **Click** on the **Find Next button**. The next occurrence of the Find text will appear.

11. **Click** the **Close button** when you finish with your search and replace. The dialog box will close, and the changes will be made to your presentation.

Spell Checking Your Presentation

Before you finalize your presentation, you'll want to run a spell check. Nothing can discredit a presentation more than a bunch of misspelled words. Even if you've read through the entire presentation, it's still a good idea to let PowerPoint run a spell check also. PowerPoint will not only help you spot misspellings but also look for repeated words.

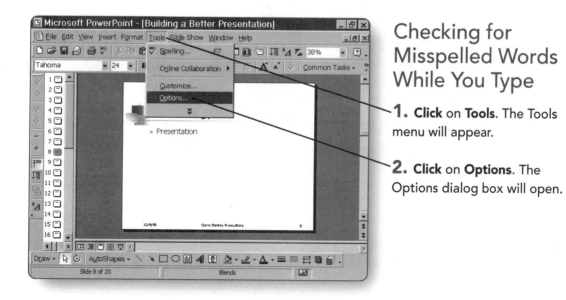

Checking for Misspelled Words While You Type

1. **Click** on **Tools**. The Tools menu will appear.

2. **Click** on **Options**. The Options dialog box will open.

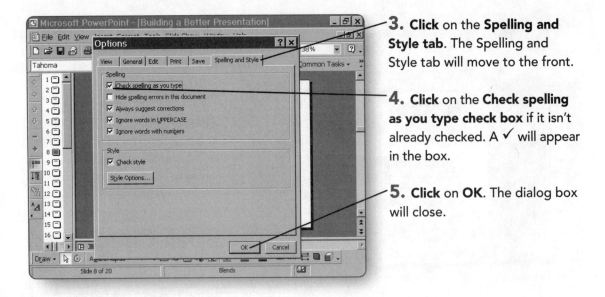

3. Click on the **Spelling and Style tab**. The Spelling and Style tab will move to the front.

4. Click on the **Check spelling as you type check box** if it isn't already checked. A ✓ will appear in the box.

5. Click on **OK**. The dialog box will close.

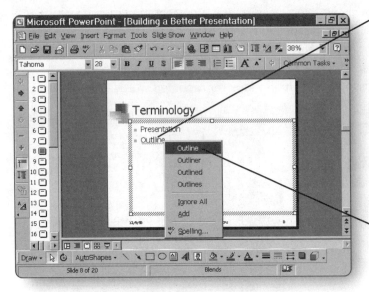

6. Look for a **red, wavy line** while you are adding text to your presentation. The line will appear beneath words that the PowerPoint dictionary does not recognize.

7. Right-click on a **word** that displays a wavy line underneath it. A shortcut menu will appear.

8. Click on the **correct spelling**. The word will be corrected.

Checking the Spelling of an Entire Presentation

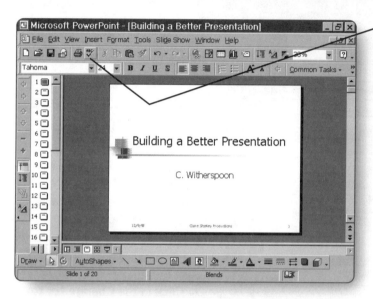

1. Click on the **Spelling button**. The Spelling dialog box will open with the first misspelled word displayed in the Not in Dictionary: text box.

NOTE

The Spell Checker will not check the spelling in charts or text created with WordArt. WordArt is a small Office program that creates artistic text.

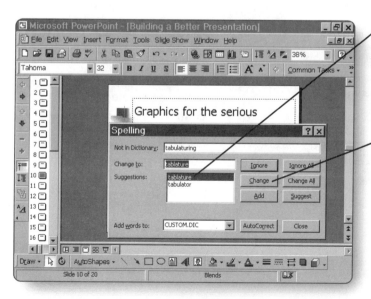

2. Click on the **correct spelling** in the Suggestions: text box. The word will be selected and will appear in the Change to: text box.

3. Click on the **Change button**. The misspelled word will be corrected, and the next misspelled word will appear in the Not in Dictionary: text box.

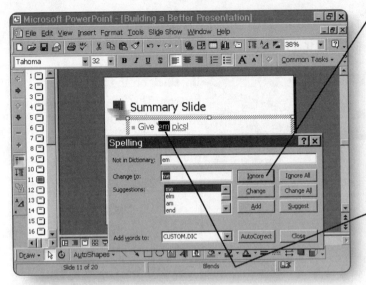

4. Click on the **Ignore button** if you don't want the Spell Checker to correct the word. The word will be left as is, and the next misspelled word will appear in the Not in Dictionary: text box.

TIP

The misspelled word will also be highlighted on the presentation. This will help you determine how to correct the error.

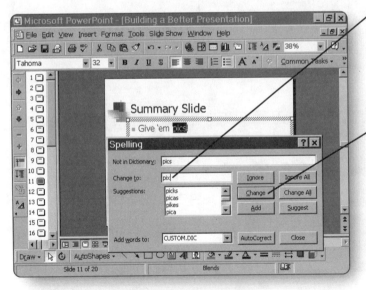

5. Click in the **Change to: text box**. The word in the text box will be selected.

6. Type the correct **word**.

7. Click on the **Change button**. The Spell Checker will finish checking the presentation and a message dialog box will open, confirming that the spell check is complete.

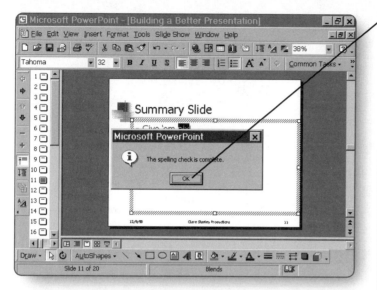

8. Click on **OK**. The spell check will be completed.

TIP

Do you want to check your presentation for design consistency? Turn on the Office Assistant. The Office Assistant will look for consistency errors. When it finds one, you'll see a light bulb appear next to the Assistant. Click on the light bulb for help.

8

Customizing Your Presentation

A few chapters back, you learned how to use the PowerPoint design templates to build a color-coordinated, graphically balanced set of presentation slides. The individual elements that make up a template, such as the background, text formatting, and images, can all be changed. You have the choice of changing the look of an individual slide or the whole set of slides. You can also divide your presentation into parts so that one presentation can be used for a variety of audiences. Not all audiences will see all parts of the presentation. In this chapter, you'll learn how to:

- Give individual slides a different look
- Change the look of the entire presentation
- Create an Agenda slide to customize the delivery of your presentation

Changing the Design of an Individual Slide

Each individual slide gets its design from the Slide Master (which you'll learn about later in this chapter). But you do have the flexibility to change any design element on an individual slide. For example, you may want a blank background on a slide that showcases pictures of your company's products. This section shows you some of your options for changing the look of an individual slide.

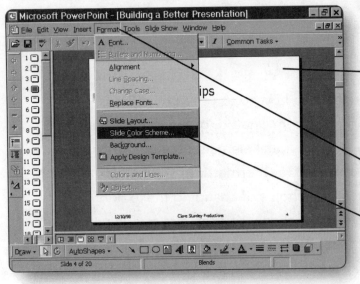

Using a Different Color Scheme

1. Open the **slide** to which you want to apply a different color scheme. The slide will appear in the Slide view.

2. Click on **Format**. The Format menu will appear.

3. Click on **Slide Color Scheme**. The Color Scheme dialog box will open.

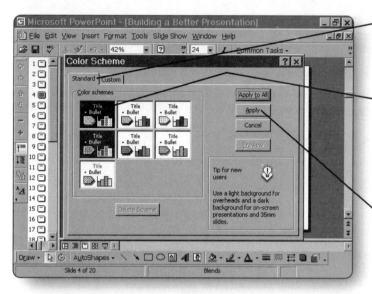

4. Click on the **Standard tab**. The Standard tab will move forward.

5. Change the **color scheme** or create a scheme of your own. For a refresher course, see Chapter 3, "Creating a Quick and Easy Presentation."

6. Click on **Apply**. The changes will affect only the slide that is displayed in the Slide view.

Applying Text Formatting to Individual Slides

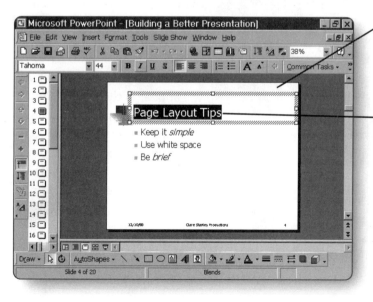

1. Open the **slide** on which you want to make the formatting changes. The slide will appear in the Slide view.

2. Select the **text** that you want to format. The text will be selected.

3. Format the **Title**, **text**, and **bullets** as you want. For some more ideas, see Chapter 7, "Editing Text."

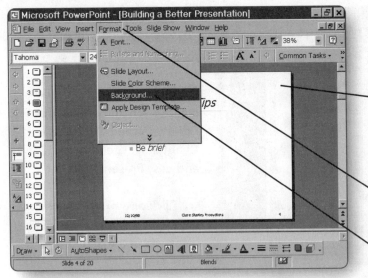

Putting a Different Background on a Slide

1. Open the **slide** on which you want to make the formatting changes. The slide will appear in the Slide view.

2. Click on **Format**. The Format menu will appear.

3. Click on **Background**. The Background dialog box will open.

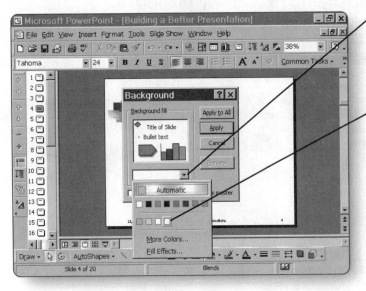

4. Click the **down arrow** (▾) at the bottom of the Background fill section. A menu of colors and effects will appear.

5. Click on a **color**. The color will appear in the list box. You can choose to use just a plain color for a background, or you may want to look through the list of textures and gradients that are also available to you.

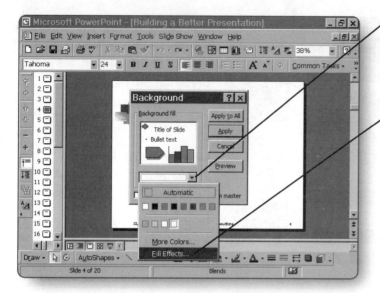

6. Click the **down arrow** (⏷) at the bottom of the Background fill section. A menu of colors and effects will appear.

7. Click on **Fill Effects**. The Fill Effects dialog box will open.

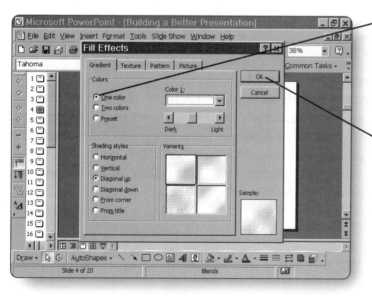

8. Make any **changes** you want. You can click on the different tabs to see all the different choices that are available.

9. Click on **OK**. The background you selected will appear in the list box and in the Background fill preview window.

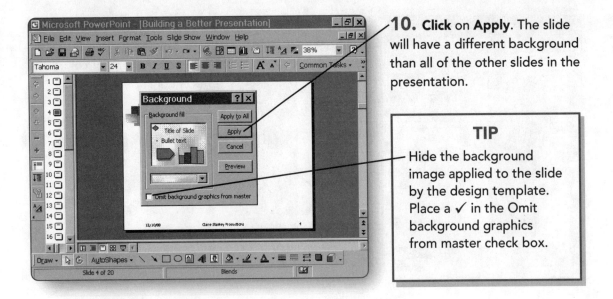

10. **Click** on **Apply**. The slide will have a different background than all of the other slides in the presentation.

TIP

Hide the background image applied to the slide by the design template. Place a ✓ in the Omit background graphics from master check box.

Creating a Slide Master

Are you adventurous? Change all the slides in the presentation at one time. Design templates use the Slide Master to give all the slides in the presentation a uniform look. Here's your chance to customize the Slide Master to give your presentation that personal touch. You can make the same types of changes to the Slide Master as you did with the individual slides. The difference is that this time, the changes you make will be applied to every slide in your presentation.

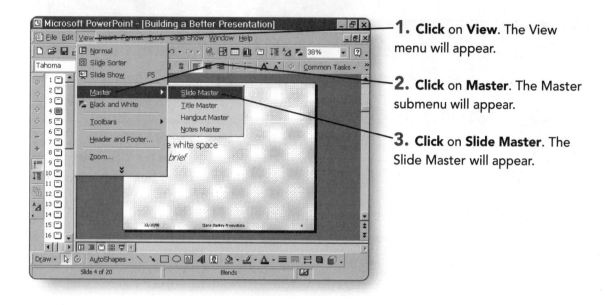

1. **Click** on **View**. The View menu will appear.

2. **Click** on **Master**. The Master submenu will appear.

3. **Click** on **Slide Master**. The Slide Master will appear.

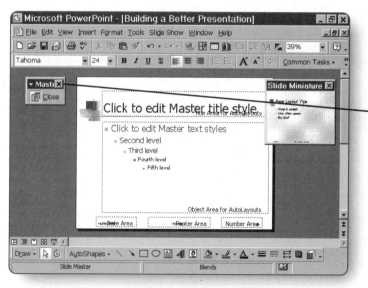

4. **Make changes** as desired. Keep reading to find out how to change the look of the Slide Master.

5. **Click** on the **Close button** (☒) on the Master toolbar when you finish with your changes.

NOTE

The Slide Miniature shows you how your changes affect an individual slide.

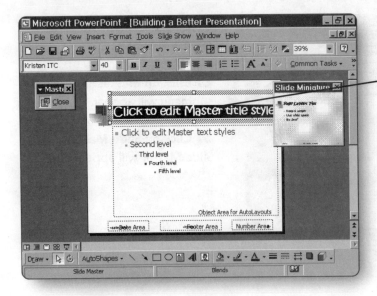

Giving Fonts a Facelift

1. Select the **text** that you want to format. The text will appear highlighted.

2. Format the **Title**, **outline levels**, and **bullets** as you want.

TIP

You can copy and delete objects in the design template.

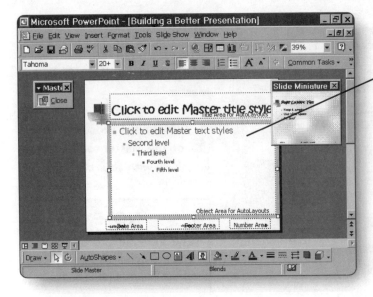

Adjusting Text Placeholders

1. Click on a text **placeholder**. You can change the size of the area allowed for the title, body or bullet text, and any footer placeholder. A border will appear around the placeholder that contains handles at the sides and corners. You'll use these handles to resize the placeholder.

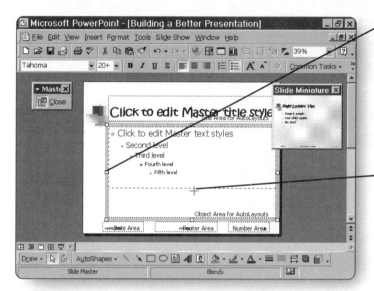

2. **Click and hold** on a **handle,** and then drag the corner or edge to the new position. The mouse pointer will change to a double arrow and a dotted line will appear to show the new size of the placeholder.

3. **Release** the **mouse pointer**. The placeholder will be resized.

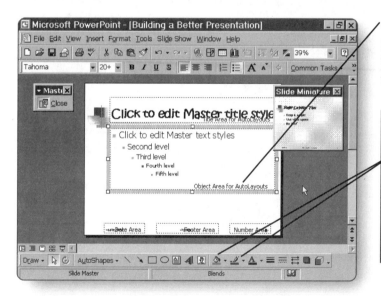

Any text typed into the placeholder will not be allowed to go beyond the boundaries of the placeholder.

TIP

Add a border or a background color to a placeholder. Experiment with the Fill Color and Line Color buttons on the Drawing toolbar.

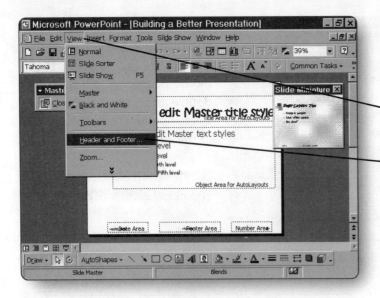

Changing Header and Footer Information

1. Click on **View**. The View menu will appear.

2. Click on **Header and Footer**. The Header and Footer dialog box will open.

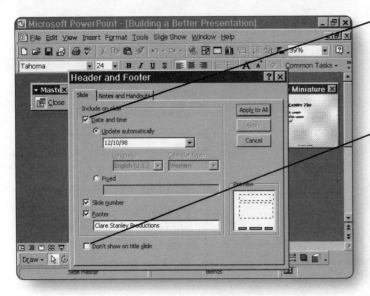

3. Place a ✓ in the check boxes next to those footer items that you want to appear in your presentation. A ✓ will appear in the check boxes.

4. Click on the ✓ to clear it from any check boxes next to footer items that you do not want displayed on all the slides. The check box will appear blank.

5. Click on **Apply to All**. The footer information will be changed.

TIP

Change the text formatting in the footer items. Select the text and change the font style, size, color, and other attributes.

Creating a Backdrop

PowerPoint provides hundreds and hundreds of possibilities for placing images, pictures, shapes, textures, and text in the background of each and every slide in your presentation. Take a look at your options.

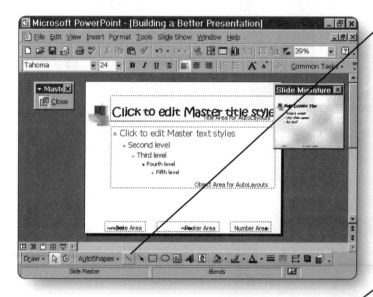

1. **Click** on the **drawing object** or **AutoShape** that you want to add to the Slide Master. The object will be selected.

NOTE

To learn more about drawing objects and AutoShapes, see Chapter 9, "Adding Graphics to a Presentation."

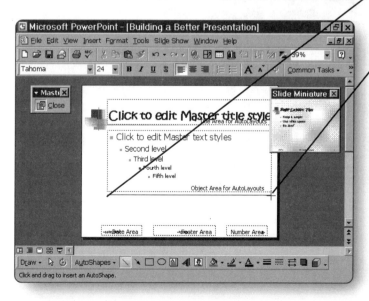

2. **Click and hold** the **mouse pointer** in the position where you want to insert the object.

3. **Drag** the **mouse pointer** down and to the right until the object is the correct size. An outline of the object will appear on the Slide Master.

4. **Release** the **mouse pointer**. The object will be created. In addition to the various shapes that you can add to the Master Slide, you can also add clip art or images you've stored on your computer.

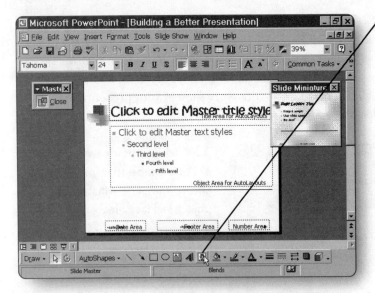

5. Click on the **Insert ClipArt button** on the Drawing toolbar. The Insert ClipArt dialog box will open.

NOTE

Find out how to add other types of images in Chapter 9, "Adding Graphics to a Presentation."

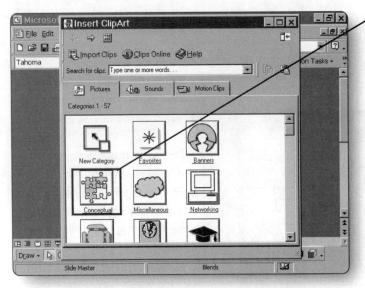

6. Click on a **category**. The clip art images contained in that category will appear.

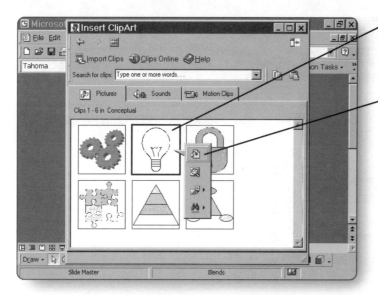

7. Click on the **image** that you want to add to the Slide Master. A shortcut menu will appear.

8. Click on **Insert clip**. The clip art image will be inserted to the Slide Master, and the dialog box will stay open.

9. Click on the **Close** (☒) **button**. The dialog box will close and you can see the image on the Slide Master.

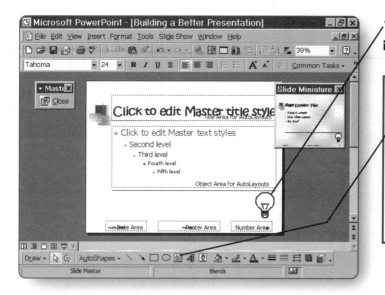

10. Size and **position the image** as needed.

TIP

To add the same text to every slide, use the Text Box button on the Drawing toolbar. Don't place the Text Box inside a text placeholder, however.

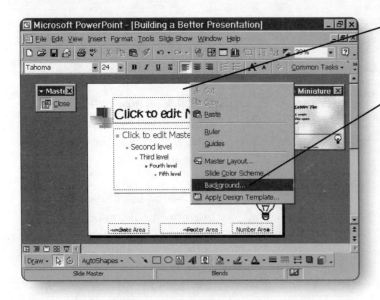

11. Right-click on **an empty area** of the Slide Master. A shortcut menu will appear.

12. Click on **Background**. The Background dialog box will open.

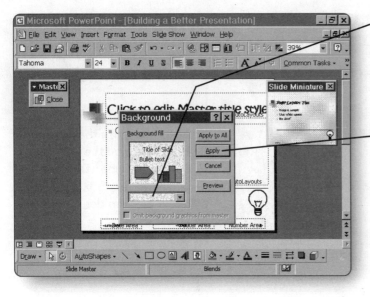

13. Select a **background** color, pattern, gradient, or texture to use. The background will preview in the Background fill section.

14. Click on **Apply**. The background will be applied to all the slides in your presentation.

TIP

Use a different design on all the presentation slides that use the Title Slide layout. Open the View menu and select Master, Title Master. Make changes to the Title Master as wanted.

Getting Organized with the Agenda Slide

A great way to organize your presentation so that you can show different parts to different audiences is to use the Agenda slide. If you're familiar with the way Web pages work, you'll find this method very similar. Several steps are involved in this process, so take your time here. The method used in this section is a quick and simple example of what you can do with Agenda slides and custom shows. Experiment with these features and maybe you'll find some great ways to make efficient use of a single presentation.

Creating a Custom Show

The first step is to divide your presentation into sections. You'll turn each of these sections into a custom show. It is the first slide in each of these custom shows that will be listed on the Agenda slide.

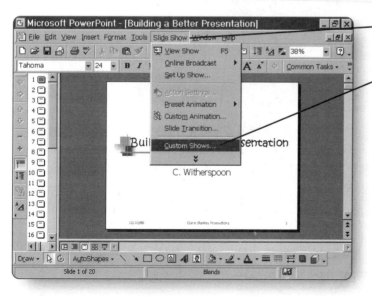

1. Click on **Slide Show**. The Slide Show menu will appear.

2. Click on **Custom Shows**. The Custom Shows dialog box will open.

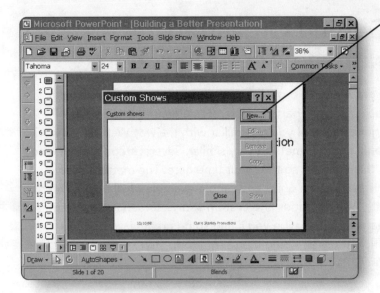

3. Click on **New**. The Define Custom Show dialog box will open.

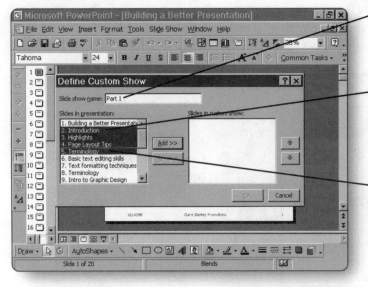

4. Type a **name** for the custom show in the Slide show name: text box.

5. Click on a **slide** in the Slides in presentation: list box that you want included in this custom show. The slide will be selected.

6. Press and hold the **Ctrl key,** and then click on the remaining slides that you want included in the custom show. The group of slides will be selected.

7. Click on **Add**. The slides will be added to the Slides in custom show: list box.

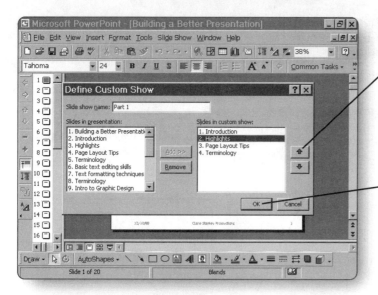

TIP
Change the order of slides in the custom show. Click on a slide and click the up or down arrow to move the slide.

8. Click on **OK**. The name of the custom show you just created will appear in the Custom Shows dialog box.

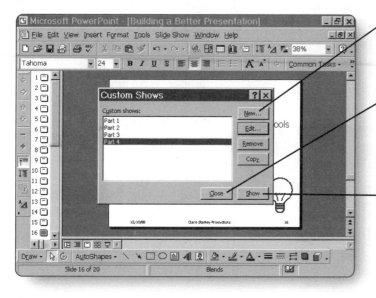

9. Create the remaining **custom shows** that you want to appear on the Agenda slide.

10. Click on **Close**. You're now ready to build the Agenda slide.

NOTE
The Show button runs a screen show of the selected custom show.

Building the Agenda Slide

1. Click on the **Slide Sorter View button**. The presentation will appear in the Slide Sorter view.

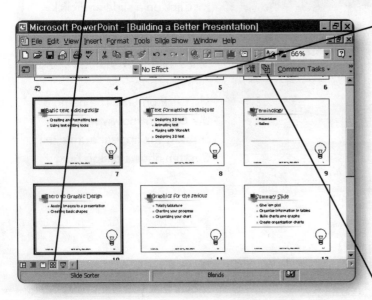

2. Select the first **slide** from each of the custom shows you just created. The slides will be highlighted.

NOTE
Select multiple slides by clicking on the first slide and then holding down the Ctrl key while you click on the other slides.

3. Click on the **Summary Slide button** on the Slide Sorter toolbar. The Summary slide will be added to the list of slides in the Slide Sorter view.

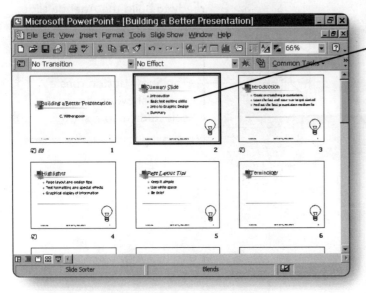

The Summary slide will be added in front of the first selected slide. It contains a bulleted list of the titles of all the selected slides.

Linking to the Agenda

Now you're ready to create hyperlinks that will help you navigate between the Agenda slide and each of the custom shows.

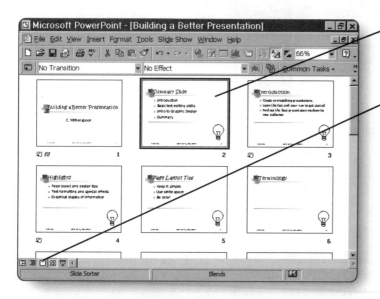

1. Select the **Agenda slide** you just created. The slide will be highlighted.

2. Click on the **Slide View button**. The Agenda slide will appear in the Slide view.

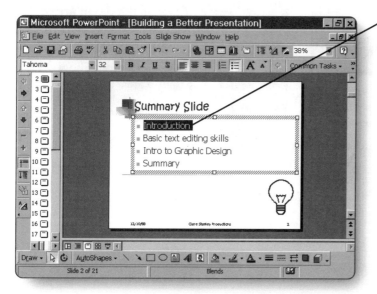

3. Select the first bulleted **item**. The text will be highlighted.

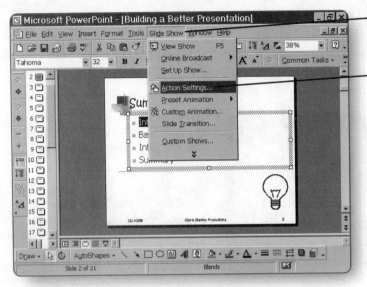

4. **Click** on **Slide Show**. The Slide Show menu will appear.

5. **Click** on **Action Settings**. The Action Settings dialog box will open, and the Mouse Click tab will be on top.

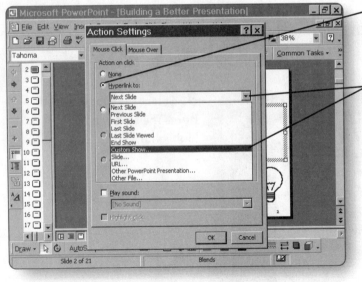

6. **Click** on the **Hyperlink to: option button**. The option will be selected.

7. **Click** on the **down arrow** (▼) next to the Hyperlink to: list box and click on Custom Show. The Link to Custom Show dialog box will open.

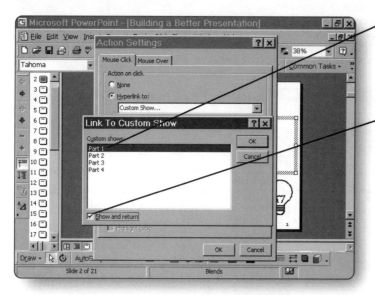

8. Click on the **custom show** that is associated with the selected bulleted item. The custom show will be selected.

9. Click on the **Show and return check box.** This option returns you to the agenda slide when the last slide in the custom show is viewed.

10. Click on **OK**. You will return to the Action Settings dialog box.

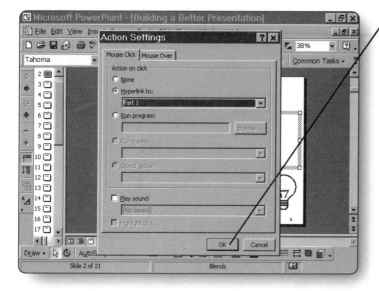

11. Click on **OK**. You will return to the Agenda slide.

You'll notice that the bulleted item is now displayed in a different color and is underlined. If you are familiar with Web browsing, you'll recognize this as a hyperlink.

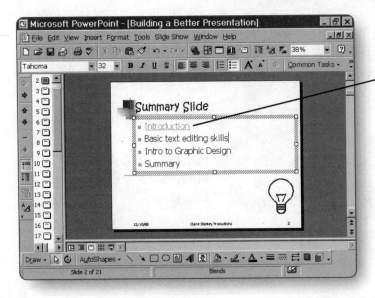

12. Create hyperlinks for the remaining bulleted items.

You can now run a slide show. When you come to the Agenda slide, click on a bulleted item. It will take you to the corresponding custom show. The slide that shows after the last slide in the custom show is the Agenda slide. You can then click on a different custom show.

Part II Review Questions

1. Which toolbar can you display while you're outlining your presentation to make your job easier? See "Editing the Presentation Outline" in Chapter 5

2. Name three keyboard shortcuts you can use to move items within an outline. See "Rearranging Items in an Outline" in Chapter 5

3. Which file formats can PowerPoint read when importing outlines from other applications? See "Sharing Outlines between Applications" in Chapter 5

4. What is the easiest way to add a new slide to a presentation? See "Working with Slide Miniatures" in Chapter 6

5. How does a Summary slide help make organizing your presentation quick and easy? See "Creating a Summary Slide" in Chapter 6

6. How do you turn off the bullet characters in a text placeholder? See "Working with Text" in Chapter 7

7. Which toolbar button allows you to copy the formatting of one word or paragraph to another? See "Formatting Text" in Chapter 7

8. What is the fastest way to replace words and phrases? See "Searching for Text in a Presentation" in Chapter 7

9. How many different elements on an individual slide can be changed to make it different from all other slides? See "Changing the Design of an Individual Slide" in Chapter 8

10. What is the easiest way to change the design of all the slides in a presentation? See "Creating a Slide Master" in Chapter 8

PART III

Enhancing Your Presentation

9

Adding Graphics to a Presentation

You don't need to be a great illustrator to create slides with good-looking pictures. You just need to know how to work with the tools provided in PowerPoint. Myriad clip art images are at your disposal so you can vary the design of your presentation. Change the color, alter the size, delete parts of an image; let your imagination have fun. You'll also find an arsenal of ready-made shapes that you can fill, color, and position anywhere. How creative do you want to be today? In this chapter, you'll learn how to:

- Add clip art and modify it to fit your presentation
- Position images in just the right place
- Use WordArt to create stunning text effects
- Create a variety of quick and easy shapes

Adding Clip Art to Your Presentation

PowerPoint shares a clip art gallery with the other Microsoft Office programs. While you're thinking about the pictures you need for your presentation, you may want to browse through the gallery. Clip art is arranged by categories to help you find pertinent images. You can also perform a search using keywords to help you locate images. If a clip art image isn't exactly what you want, you can change its appearance.

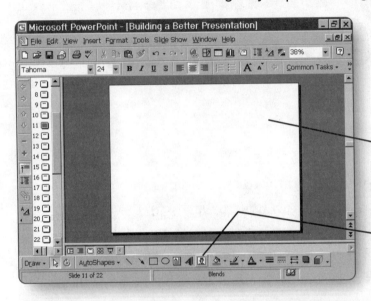

1. Open the **slide** to which you want to add the clip art image. The slide will appear in the Slide view.

2. Click on the **Insert ClipArt button** on the Drawing toolbar. The Insert ClipArt dialog box will open, and the Pictures tab should be at the front.

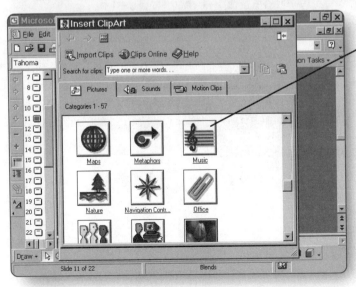

3. Click on a **Category**. The clip art images contained in the category you selected will appear in the dialog box.

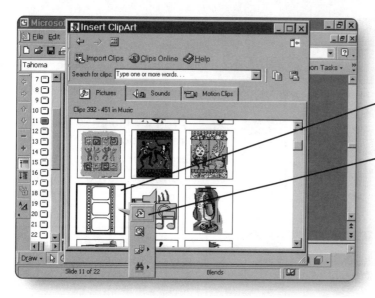

4. Browse through the list of **images** until you find one that fits your needs.

5. Click on a clip art **image**. A shortcut menu will appear.

6. Click on **Insert Clip**. The clip art image will be added to the slide, and the Insert ClipArt dialog box will remain open.

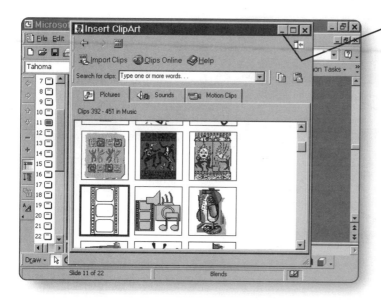

7a. Click on the **Minimize** (■) **button** if you'll be inserting another clip art image. The Insert ClipArt dialog box will become an icon on the Windows taskbar.

OR

7b. Click on the **Close** (☒) **button** if you're finished with the dialog box. The Insert ClipArt dialog box will close.

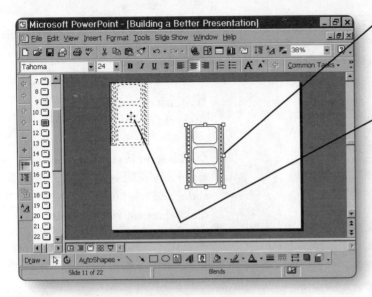

8. To move the clip art images, **click and hold** on the **image**. The mouse pointer will become a four-pointed arrow.

9. Drag the **image** to the desired location and release the mouse button. The clip art image will be moved to the new location.

TIP

To make a copy of the image, press Ctrl while you drag the image.

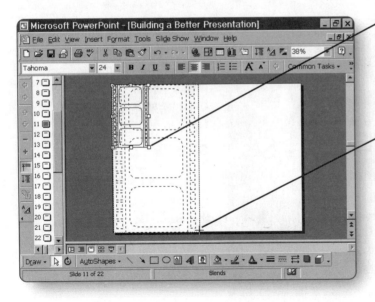

10. Click and hold the image **handles** that appear when the image is selected to change the size of the image. The mouse pointer will turn into a crosshair.

11. Drag the **mouse pointer** away from the image to make it larger or toward the image to make it smaller. An outline of the image will show the change in size.

12. Release the **mouse button**. The image will be resized.

TIP

You can maintain the image width and height ratio. Press the Shift key while you drag the mouse.

Changing Clip Art Image Colors

Now that you've added a few clip art images to your slides and positioned them just where you want them, you may want to make things look a little different. For example, you can change the colors of an image to better match the colors used in your slides. Take some time to experiment and have fun.

Before you begin, display the Picture toolbar to make your task a little easier.

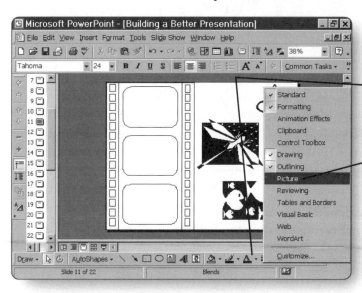

1. Right-click on any **toolbar**. A shortcut menu that lists all the toolbars will appear.

2. Click on **Picture**. The Picture toolbar will appear as a separate, floating toolbar.

NOTE

You can move the toolbar by dragging its Title bar to the position where you want the toolbar to be located.

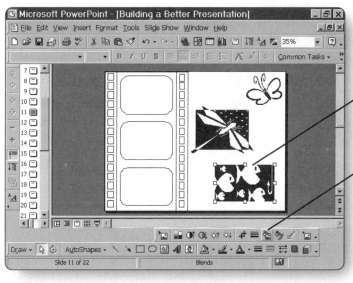

3. Click on the clip art **image** that you want to recolor. The image will be selected.

4. Click on the **Recolor Picture** button on the Picture toolbar. The Recolor Picture dialog box will open.

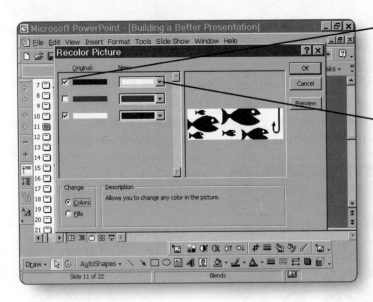

5. Click in the **check box** next to the color that you want to change. A ✓ will appear in the box.

6. Click the **down arrow** (▼) next to the color and select a new color to replace the old one. The new color will appear in the list box.

7. Click on **OK**. The picture will be recolored according to the new colors you chose.

NOTE

Some clip art images are actually an AutoShape and are not recolored using the method used to recolor clip art pictures.

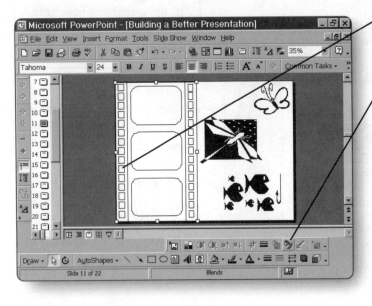

8. Click on the clip art **image** that you want to change. The image will be selected.

9. Click on the **Format AutoShape button** on the Picture toolbar. The Format AutoShape dialog box will open, and the Colors and Lines tab will be at the front.

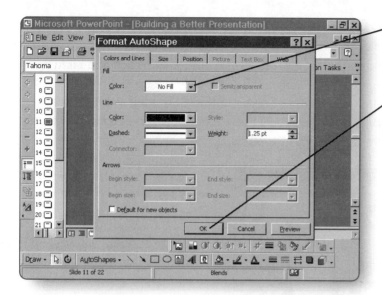

10. Make changes to the fill color, line color, line style, and line weight options.

11. Click on **OK**. The changes will be applied to the clip art image.

Try out some of the other tools on the Picture toolbar:

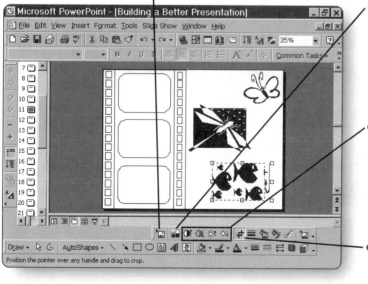

• The Insert Picture from File button inserts a picture that is stored on your computer into a slide.

• The Image Control button can turn color images into black and white, or make an image suitable as a watermark that works great as a background image.

• Use the More Contrast, Less Contrast, More Brightness, and Less Brightness buttons to adjust brightness and contrast to enhance how the image appears.

• The Crop button will eliminate unwanted parts of an image.

Positioning Graphics on a Slide

It's not always easy to look at something (such as a picture hanging on a wall) and be able to line it up straight. That's when you need to break out the tools, such as a T-square, a level, or a ruler. You'll find all the tools you need to do the job in the PowerPoint toolbox.

Using Guides to Position Images

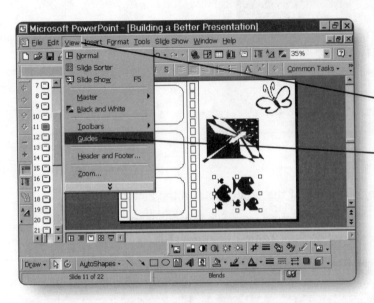

1. Click on **View**. The View menu will appear.

2. Click on **Guides**. Two guides will appear as dotted, perpendicular lines.

NOTE

Depending on how you work with PowerPoint, the adaptive menus that you see on your screen may be different. To display the other commands in the menu, click on the down arrow at the bottom of the menu list.

---

3. Click and drag the **guides** to the position where you want to align the image. The guides will be moved.

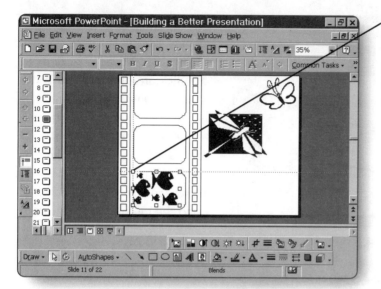

4. Drag the **image** so that the edges are aligned with the guides and release the mouse button. The image will be lined up with the guides.

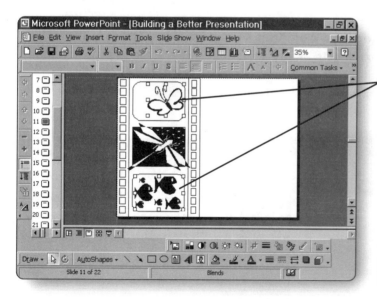

Aligning Images with Other Images

1. Select the **images** that you want to align with each other. The objects will be selected.

NOTE

To select more than one image, press and hold the Shift key while clicking on the images you want to select.

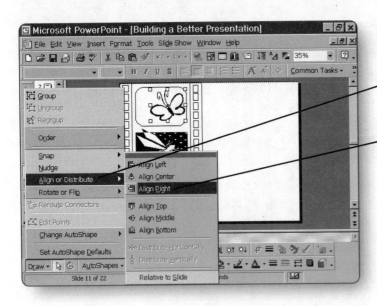

2. Click on **Draw**. The Draw menu will appear.

3. Click on **Align or Distribute**. A submenu will appear.

4. Click on the **method** that you want to use to align the objects. The objects will be aligned relative to each other using the method you specified.

Playing with WordArt

WordArt is another tool common to all Microsoft Office programs. WordArt is an easy way to create wavy and 3-D text effects. Here's another chance for you to play. But don't get too carried away; overdone text effects can be a distraction, and you don't want to distract a good audience.

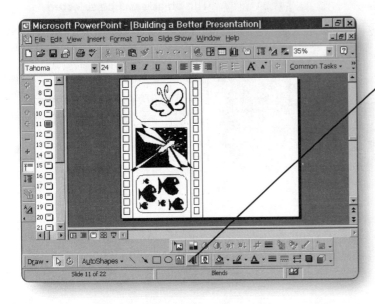

Creating the WordArt Object

1. Click on the **Insert WordArt button** on the Drawing toolbar. The WordArt Gallery dialog box will open.

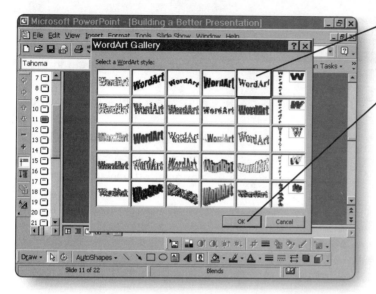

2. **Click** on the **WordArt style** that you want to use. The style will be selected.

3. **Click** on **OK**. The Edit WordArt Text dialog box will open.

4. **Click** on the **down arrow** (⏷) next to the Font: list box, and click on the font that you want to use in the WordArt object. The font name will appear in the list box.

5. **Click** on the **down arrow** (⏷) next to the Size: list box and click on the size you want to apply to the text. The size will appear in the list box.

6. **Click** on the **Bold** or **Italic** **buttons** as desired to apply these styles to the text.

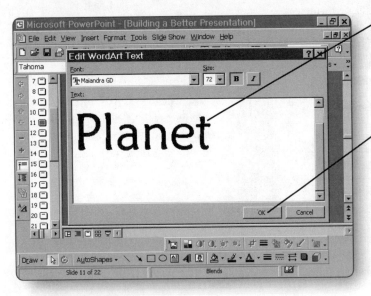

7. Select the existing **text** in the Text: text box, and type the text you want to appear in the WordArt object. The new text will appear in the Text: text box.

8. Click on **OK**. The WordArt object will appear on the slide along with the WordArt toolbar.

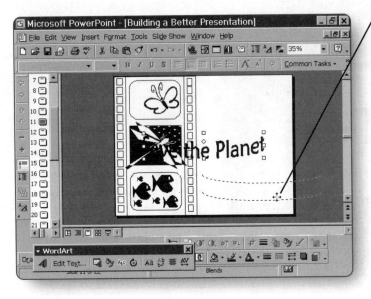

9. Click and drag the **WordArt object** to the place where you want it to appear on the slide. The WordArt object will be moved.

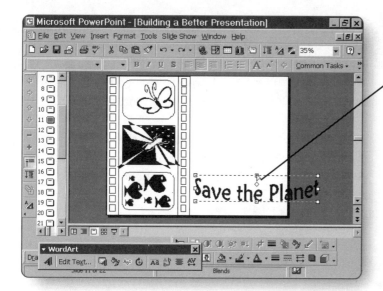

Making Changes to the WordArt Object

1. Click and drag the **resize handle** up and down or right and left. The text will slant in a different direction or will become a different size.

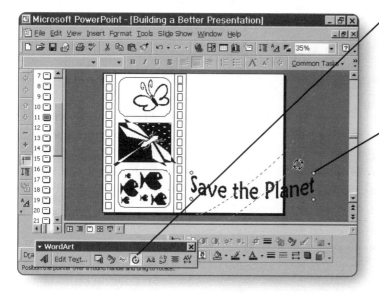

2. Click on the **Free Rotate button** on the WordArt toolbar. Circular rotate handles will appear at the edges of the WordArt object.

3. Click and drag the **mouse pointer** in the direction you want to rotate the WordArt object. The WordArt object will be turned in the direction you specified.

4. Click on the **WordArt Shape button**. A set of shapes will appear from which you can choose to change the shape of the existing WordArt object.

5. Click on a **shape**. The WordArt object will change to the new shape you selected.

Here are some more editing tricks you can play on your WordArt object:

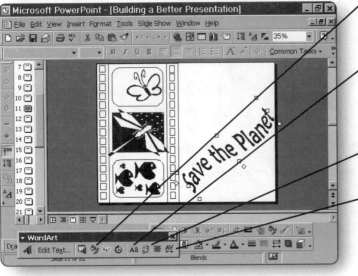

● Change the color of the WordArt object by clicking on the Format WordArt button.

● Make all the letters in the WordArt object the same height by using the WordArt Same Letter Heights button.

● Turn text vertical with the WordArt Vertical Text button.

● Change the spacing between letters using the WordArt Character Spacing button.

Using AutoShapes

When you need a box, a circle, arrows, or callouts, you'll find a variety of ready-made styles from which to choose. When you're looking for banners and stars, or some irregular shape, there's probably an AutoShape that can do the job. AutoShapes are easy to create: Just a few mouse clicks and you have a shape you can make almost any way you'd like.

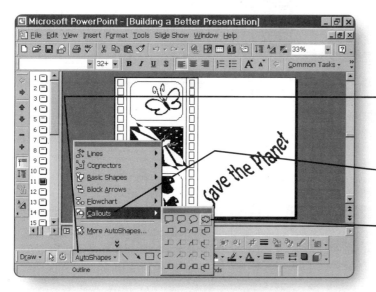

Creating a Basic Shape

1. **Click** on the **AutoShapes button**. A menu of AutoShape categories will appear.

2. **Click** on a **category**. The category's submenu will appear.

3. **Click** on a **shape**. The mouse pointer will turn into a crosshair.

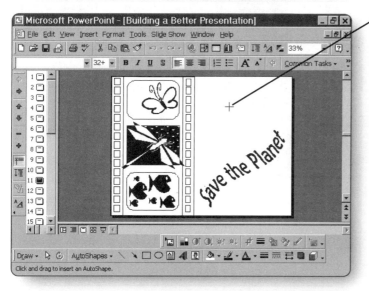

4. **Click** on the **place** on the slide where you want the shape to appear. The shape will appear in its default size.

NOTE

Some shapes can include text. If the cursor appears inside a shape, you can type text that will appear inside the shape. If you don't see a cursor, click inside the shape.

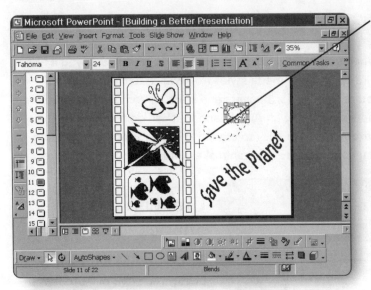

5. Resize the **shape** by dragging the size handles. Remember to press the Shift key if you want to maintain the shape's original proportions.

TIP

You can Move the shape to a different position by simply dragging the shape to the new place.

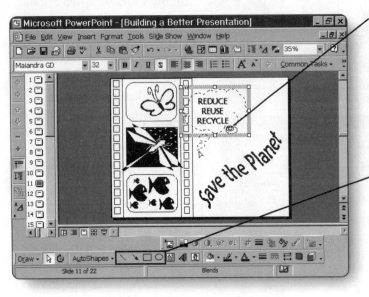

6. When you see a diamond on a shape, this means that part of the shape is moveable. **Click and drag** the **diamond mouse pointer** to a new position.

TIP

You can also draw simple shapes using the Line, Arrow, Rectangle, and Oval buttons on the Drawing toolbar.

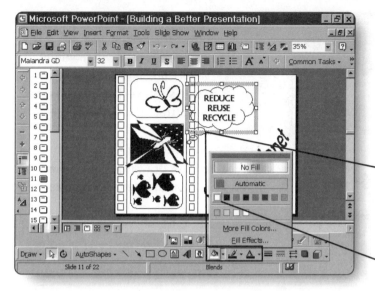

Enhancing Shapes

You can change the color with which a shape is filled, the color of the line that surrounds the shape, or the text contained inside the shape.

1. Click on the **down arrow** (▼) next to either the Fill Color, Line Color, or Font Color buttons. A menu of colors will appear.

2. Select a **color** from the menu. The color will be applied to shape.

You can change the thickness of the line that surrounds the shape.

1. Click on the **Line Style button**. A menu of line choices will appear.

2. Click on the **style** that you want to apply to the shape. The line thickness on the shape will change.

Sometimes, adding a shadow effect to a shape makes it appear to stand out from the slide. This is an easy way to make subtle enhancements that will attract the audience's eye.

1. **Click** on the **Shadow button** on the Drawing toolbar. A menu of shadow styles will appear.

2. **Click** on a **shadow style**. The shadow will be applied to the shape.

TIP

You can customize the shadow. Click on Shadow Settings. A toolbar will appear that you can use to adjust the position of the shadow.

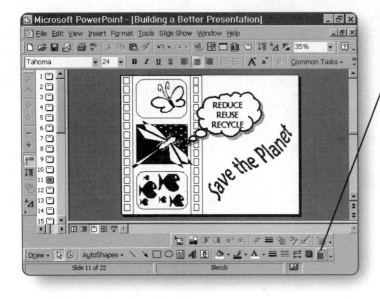

NOTE

You can also use the 3-D button to make your shapes stand out from the slide.

10
Displaying Special Effects

In the last chapter, you learned how to add clip art, WordArt, and shapes to your presentation. After you placed the images on the slide and lined them all up; did they look a little flat? You might be looking for a way to make your pictures come alive. Try some of the special effects included in PowerPoint to give your pictures depth, dimension, and freedom to sing and dance. In this chapter, you'll learn how to:

- Add shadow effects to text and images
- Create and customize 3-D images
- Animate text, objects, and slides for moving presentations
- Enhance a presentation with sound

Adding a Shadow to an Image or Text

One of the easiest ways to give your flat objects dimension is to add a shadow. Shadows are also a great way to make your text more readable.

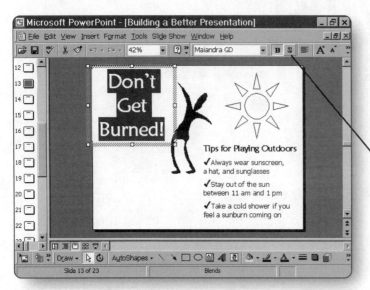

Creating an Easy Text Shadow

1. **Select** the **text** to which you want to add a shadow. The text will be highlighted.

2. **Click** on the **Text Shadow button** on the Formatting toolbar. A shadow will be applied to the text.

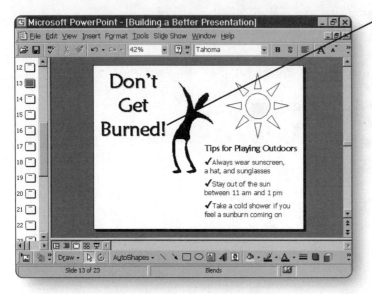

This shadow can be applied only to text, not images or shapes, and you can't customize the shadow. That is, you cannot change the shadow color or the position of the shadow in relation to the text.

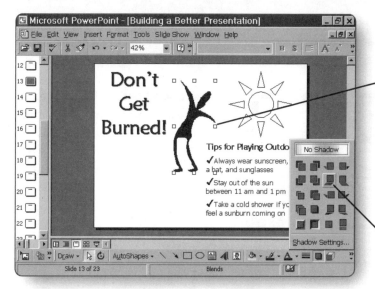

Customizing Object Shadows

1. Click on the **object** to which you want to add the shadow. The object will be selected.

2. Click on the **Shadow button** on the Drawing toolbar. A menu of shadow styles will appear.

3. Click on the **shadow style** that you want to apply to the object. The shadow will be applied to the object. If the shadow isn't positioned exactly as you'd like, you can make a few adjustments.

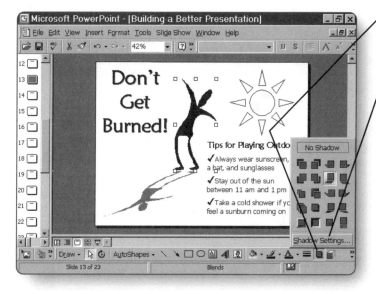

4. Click on the **Shadow button**. A menu of shadow styles will appear.

5. Click on **Shadow Settings**. The Shadow Settings toolbar will appear.

You have several options for repositioning the shadow and changing the shadow color. Try out these buttons on the Shadow Settings toolbar until the shadow looks just perfect.

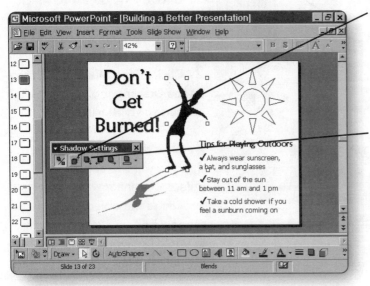

- **Nudge Shadow Up**. Moves the shadow toward the top of the slide. Keep clicking this button until you have moved the shadow up as far as you want.

- **Nudge Shadow Down.** Moves the shadow toward the bottom of the slide. Keep clicking this button until you have moved the shadow down as far as you want.

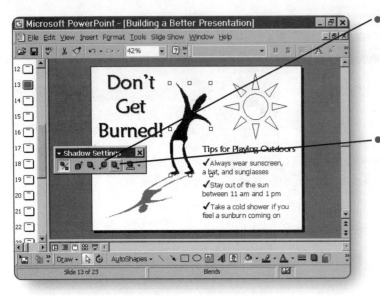

- **Nudge Shadow Left.** Moves the shadow toward the left side of the slide. Keep clicking until the shadow is moved to the desired position.

- **Nudge Shadow Right**. Moves the shadow toward the right side of the slide. Keep clicking until you've got the shadow where you want it.

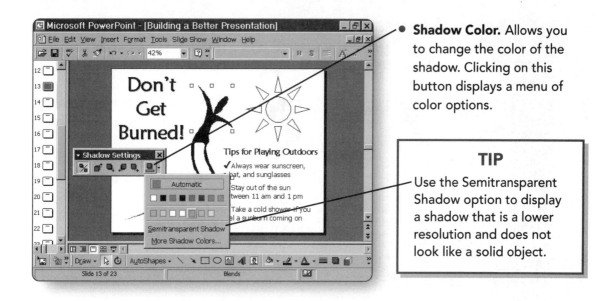

Shadow Color. Allows you to change the color of the shadow. Clicking on this button displays a menu of color options.

TIP

Use the Semitransparent Shadow option to display a shadow that is a lower resolution and does not look like a solid object.

6. Click on the **Close (⊠) button** on the Shadow Settings toolbar. The toolbar will close.

Creating 3-D Images

Up to this point, the images you've placed on your slides have been 2-D, or two-dimensional. This means that they have a height and a width. Give your images a life-like appearance by adding depth to the image, thereby making it 3-D. This third dimension makes it possible to rotate images so that you see not only an image's face (2D) but also its sides (3-D). This 3-D effect works best when applied to basic shapes (such as circles and squares) and the AutoShapes.

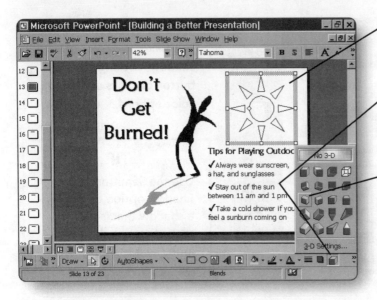

1. Click on the **object** to which you want to apply a 3-D effect. The object will be selected.

2. Click on the **3-D button** on the Drawing toolbar. A menu of 3-D effects will appear.

3. Click on the **3-D effect** that you want to apply to the object. The object will turn into a 3-D image.

TIP

You can apply the same 3-D effect to several objects at once. Select all the objects to which you want to have the same 3-D effect applied.

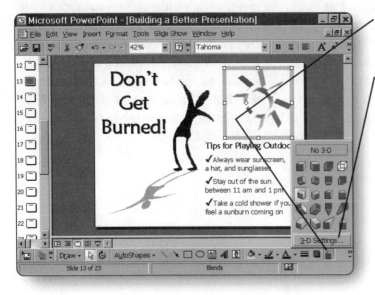

4. Click on the **3-D button**. A menu of 3-D options will appear.

5. Click on **3-D Settings**. The 3-D Settings toolbar will appear.

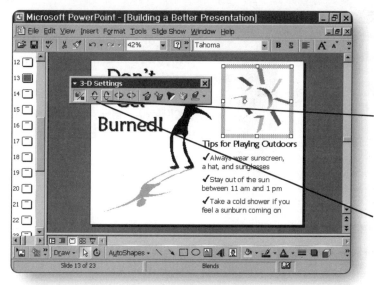

You can rotate the image by clicking on the following buttons until the image faces in the direction that shows the 3-D effect to the best advantage.

- **Tilt Up**. Rotates the object so that the top of the object moves away from you and you can see the bottom of the object.

- **Tilt Down**. Rotates the object so that the bottom edge moves away from you and you can see the top of the object.

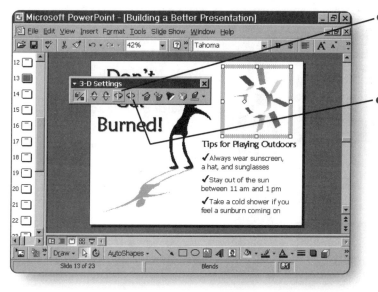

- **Tilt Left**. Rotates the object so that the left edge moves away and the right side becomes visible.

- **Tilt Right.** Rotates the object so that the right edge moves away and the left side becomes visible.

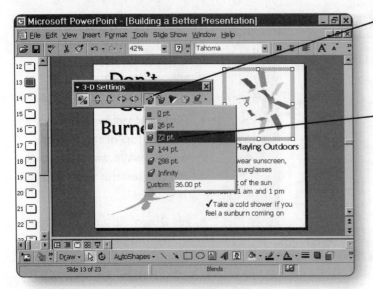

6. **Click** on the **Depth button**. A menu of sizes will appear that allow you to select how deep to make the 3-D effect.

7. **Click** on a **size**. The depth of the 3-D effect will be changed.

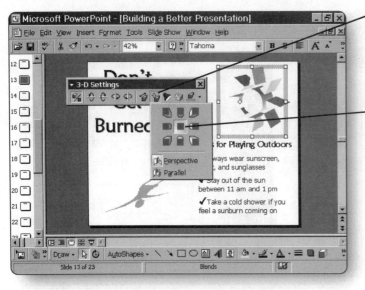

8. **Click** on the **Direction button**. A menu of directions in which you can face the 3-D image will appear.

9. **Click** on a **direction**. The direction that the 3-D image faces will be changed.

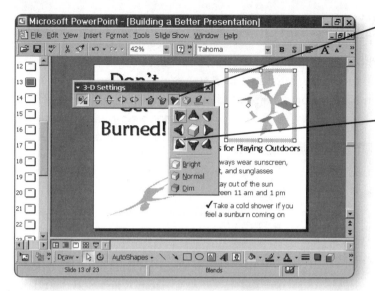

10. Click on the **Lighting button**. A menu of directions from which the 3-D effect can be illuminated will appear.

11. Click on a **lighting direction**. The shadow effect displayed on the 3-D portion of the image will be changed.

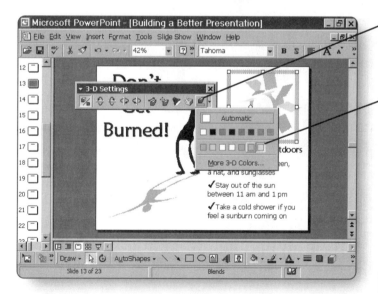

12. Click on the **3-D Color button**. A menu of color choices will appear.

13. Click on the **color** in which you want the 3-D portion of the image to appear. The color will be applied to the 3-D object.

NOTE

To remove the 3-D effect, click on the 3-D button and select the No 3-D option.

Animating Text

When out-standing shadowed and 3-D text and images are still too static for your tastes, try your hand at animation. You can easily apply a number of customizable animation effects so that objects fly, slide, flip, and dissolve right before your eyes. You can also organize a series of objects so that they perform object by object.

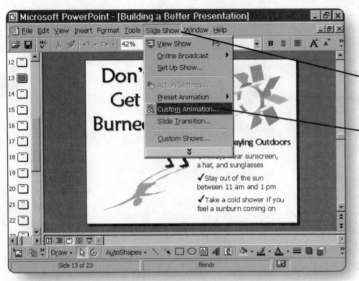

1. Click on **Slide Show**. The Slide Show menu will appear.

2. Click on **Custom Animation**. The Custom Animation dialog box will open, and the Order & Timing tab will be at the front.

3. Click in the **check box** next to those items that you want to animate. A ✓ will appear in the box, and the selected item will be highlighted in the Preview pane.

4a. Click on the **On mouse click option button** if you want the animation to play when you click on a slide during a slide show. The option will be selected.

OR

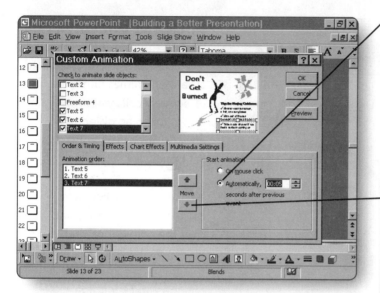

4b. Click on the **Automatically option button** if you want the animation to play automatically after a specified amount of time has elapsed. The option will be selected.

NOTE

Change the order in which animated objects will appear on the slide. Select the object and click on the Move up and down arrows.

5. Click on the **Effects tab**. The Effects tab will move to the front.

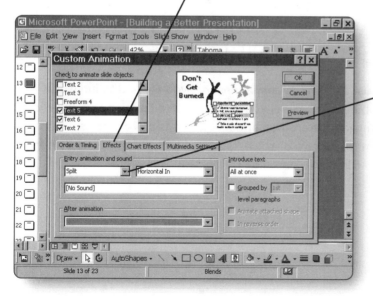

6. Click on the **object** to which you want to apply the animation. The object will be selected.

7. Click the **down arrow** (▾) next to the Entry animation and sound list box and click on the animation effect you want to apply to the object. The animation effect will appear in the list box, and the other list boxes will contain options for controlling different aspects of the effect.

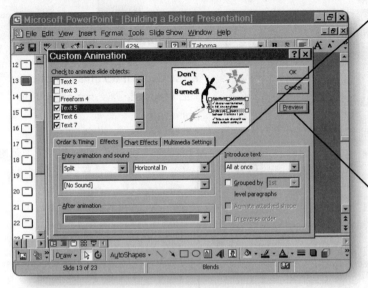

8. Click the **down arrows** (▾) next to the remaining list boxes and apply the effect options to create an animation that effectively calls the proper attention to an object. The effect options will appear in the list boxes.

9. Click on the **Preview button**. The Preview pane will play the animations that you set up. If you are not satisfied with the animation, make a few changes and try it again.

10. Click on **OK**. The animations will be applied to the objects in the slide.

Applying Transitions between Slides

Just as with the animations that you applied to individual objects on a slide, you can apply an animation to a slide (also known as transition effect). The transition effect causes the entire slide to dissolve, fade, or break up into pieces when moving from one slide to the next.

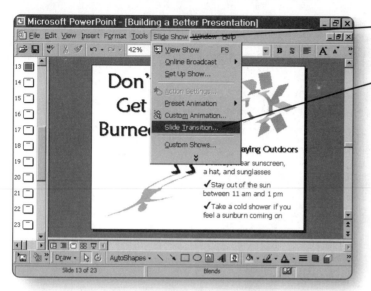

1. Click on **Slide Show**. The Slide Show menu will appear.

2. Click on **Slide Transition**. The Slide Transition dialog box will open.

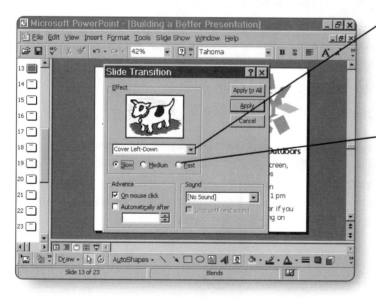

3. Click on the **down arrow** (▼) next to the Effect list box and select a transition effect from the list. The transition effect will appear in the list box.

4. Click on the **Slow**, **Medium**, or **Fast option button** to select the amount of time the transition effect will last. The option will be selected.

5. Click on the **Apply button**. The transition effect will be applied to the slide.

Inserting Music and Sound into a Presentation

If your presentation won't have a speaker or narration during its showing, you may want to add some background music. Music is another good way to keep your audience's attention on your presentation.

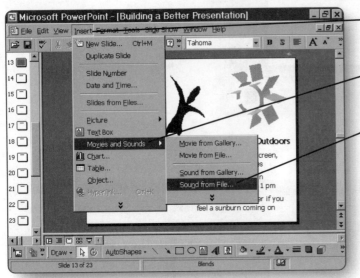

1. Click on **Insert**. The Insert menu will appear.

2. Click on **Movies and Sounds**. A submenu will appear.

3. Click on **Sound from File**. The Insert Sound dialog box will open.

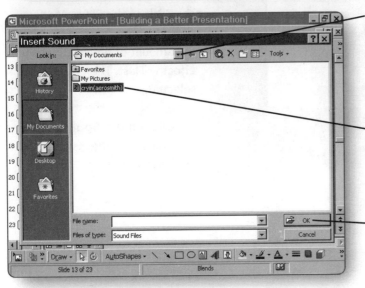

4. Open the **folder** that contains the sound file that you want to add to the slide. The folder name will appear in the Look in: list box.

5. Click on the **sound file** that you want to add to the presentation slide. The file will be selected.

6. Click on **OK**. A confirmation dialog box will open.

7a. **Click** on **Yes** if you want the sound to play when the slide is displayed during a slide show.

OR

7b. **Click** on **No** if you want the sound to play only when you click on the sound icon during a slide show.

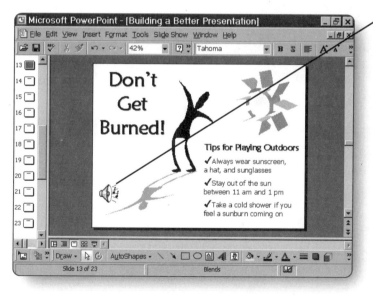

A sound icon for the sound file will appear on the slide. You can resize this icon by dragging the size handles that appear when the icon is selected. If you want to hear the sound, double-click on the icon. You can also move the icon to any place on the slide that you want.

11

Adding Tables

You've probably seen tables used in spreadsheets and word processing documents. Tables are a great way to organize information. When you want to organize information into neat little rows and columns, tables provide an easy format with which to start. Your tables can be very simple, or you can make them more complex with designer lines and colors. In this chapter, you'll learn how to:

- Create the beginnings of a table
- Add and format text in a table
- Add and delete rows, columns, and cells
- Apply background fills to selected cells in a table

Creating the Basic Table

Before you begin building your table, you should have an approximate idea of the size of the table you want. If you aren't exactly sure, don't fret. You can always add and delete rows and columns later.

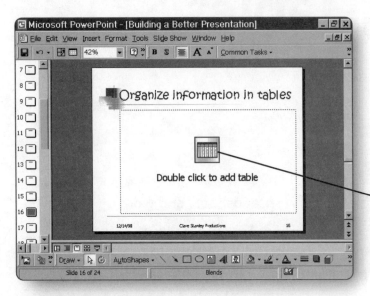

Getting Started with the Table Slide Layout

Probably the easiest way to get started with a table is to create a new slide using the Table slide layout.

1. **Double-click** on the **table placeholder**. The Insert Table dialog box will open.

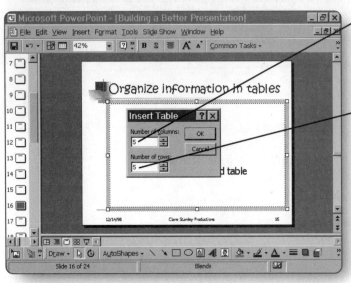

2. **Click** in the **Number of columns: text box** and type the number of columns you want to appear in the table.

3. **Click** in the **Number of rows: text box** and type the number of rows you want to appear in the table.

4. **Click** on **OK**. The table will appear and will match the size of the placeholder.

Creating a Table on Your Own

If you want to place a table on a page that doesn't contain a table placeholder, you'll have to start the process yourself. The result is the same as if you had used a Table slide layout.

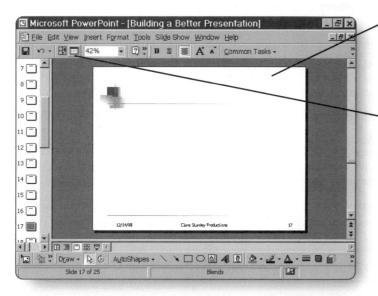

1. Open the **slide** on which you want to insert the table. The page will appear in the Slide view.

2. Click on the **Insert Table button**. A table palette will appear.

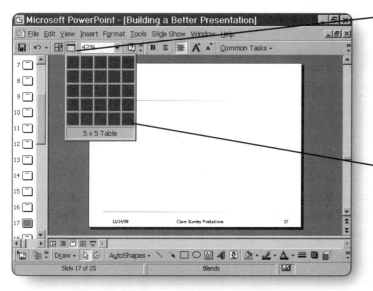

3. Click and hold the **mouse button** on the upper-left cell of the table palette. The table size will appear at the bottom of the table palette, showing you the number of rows and columns that will be created.

4. Drag the **mouse pointer** down and to the right. The table size will grow.

5. Release the **mouse button** when the table is the desired size. A blank table will appear on the slide.

Moving Around in a Table

It's easy to get around a table with a mouse. Just one click and you're there! Moving around with the keyboard isn't as intuitive. Here's a short list of key combinations to help you get around.

To perform this action	Do this
Go to the next cell	Press the Tab key
Go to the preceding cell	Press Shift+Tab
Move to the next row	Press the Down arrow
Move to the preceding row	Press the Up arrow
Add a new row to the end of a table	Press Tab at the end of the last row

TIP

Another way to make working with a table easier is to use the Tables and Borders toolbar. Click on the Tables and Borders button on the Standard toolbar to display this toolbar.

Adding Text to a Table

After you have built a structure for your table, you can begin to add some words. You can also format the text just as you would text within a slide.

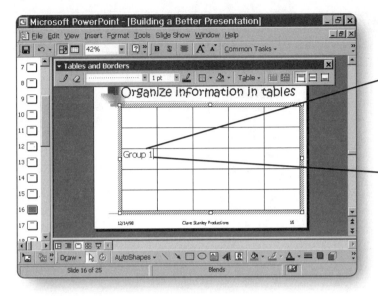

Inserting Text into a Table

1. Click in the **cell** where you want to place the text. The insertion bar will appear in the cell.

2. Type the **text**.

TIP

To add a second row of text to a cell, press the Enter key for a separate paragraph. Or, press Shift+Enter to keep the lines within a single paragraph.

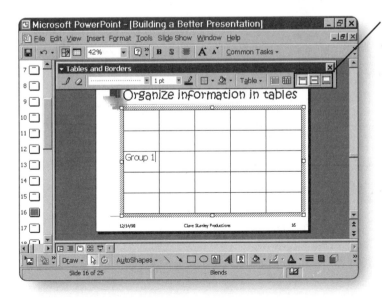

3. Click on a **paragraph alignment button**. The text will be aligned in the cell.

- **Align Top** places the text at the top of the cell.

- **Center Vertically** places the text in the middle of the cell.

- **Align Bottom** places the text at the bottom of the cell.

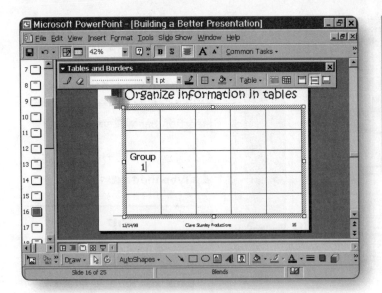

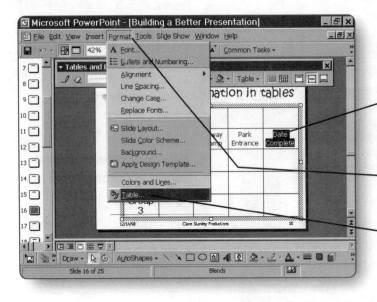

Changing the Text Orientation in a Table

1. Click in the **cell** containing the text that you want to rotate. The cell will be selected.

2. Click on **Format**. The Format menu will appear.

3. Click on **Table**. The Format Table dialog box will open.

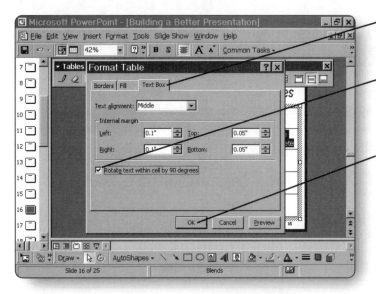

4. Click on the **Text Box tab**. The tab will move to the front.

5. Click in the **Rotate text within cell by 90 degrees check box**. A ✓ will appear in the box.

6. Click on **OK**. The text will changed from a horizontal orientation to a vertical orientation.

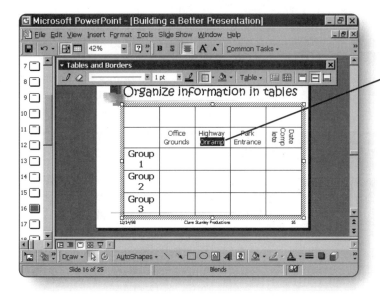

Deleting Text from a Cell

1. Select the **text** that you want to delete. The text will be highlighted.

2. Press the **Delete key**. The cell contents will be cleared but the cell itself will remain.

Adding and Deleting Rows and Columns

If you find that your table doesn't contain enough cells, you may need to add a few rows or columns. Or, if you got carried away and have more table than you need, start deleting those extra cells.

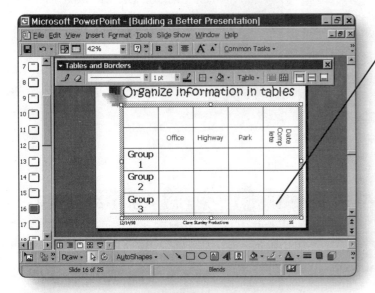

Adding a New Row

1. Click in the **row** under which you want to create the new row. The insertion bar will appear in the row.

> ### TIP
>
> Add multiple rows at one time. Select several rows before executing the Insert Rows command. The same number of rows will be inserted into the table as you selected.

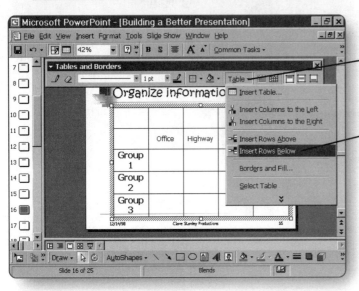

2. Click on the **Table button** in the Tables and Borders toolbar. The Table menu will appear.

3. Click on **Insert Rows Below**. A new row will be added to the table and will appear below the selected row.

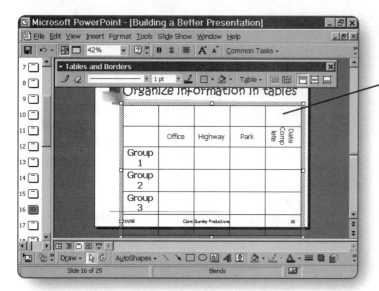

Adding a New Column to a Table

1. Click in the **column** to the left of which you want to create the new column. The insertion bar will appear in the column.

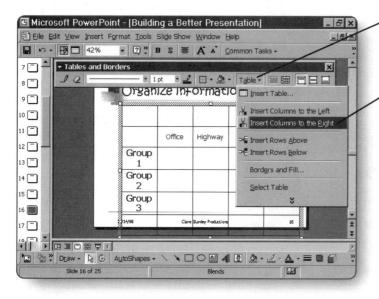

2. Click on the **Table button** in the Tables and Borders toolbar. The Table menu will appear.

3. Click on **Insert Columns to the Right**. A new column will be added to the table and will appear to the right of the selected row.

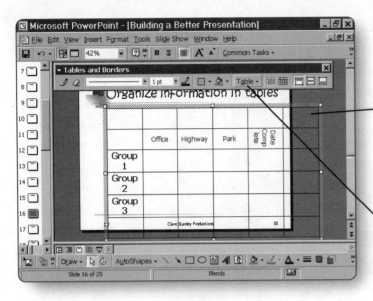

Removing Rows and Columns from a Table

1. Click in a **cell** that is contained in the row or column that you want to delete. The insertion bar will appear in the cell.

2. Click on the **Table button** on the Tables and Borders toolbar. The Table menu will appear.

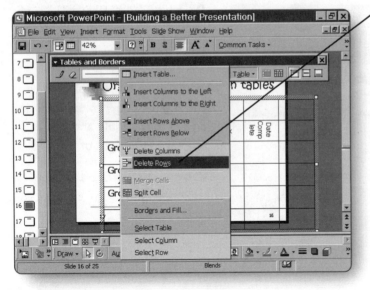

3a. Click on **Delete Rows**. The row in which the cursor was positioned will be deleted.

OR

3b. Click on **Delete Columns**. The column in which the cursor was positioned will be deleted.

Merging and Splitting Cells

If you want to create a space to place a table heading, you can combine several cells and turn them into a single cell. You can also split a cell into several cells to make space for additional information.

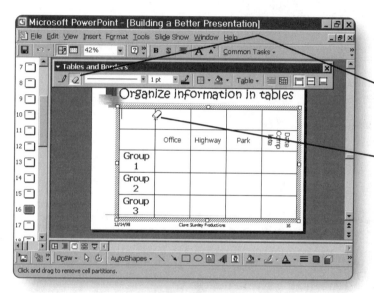

Merging Two Cells into One

1. **Click** on the **Eraser button**. The mouse pointer will turn into an eraser.

2. **Click** on the **cell border** located between the two cells that you want to merge in the row. The border between the two cells will be deleted.

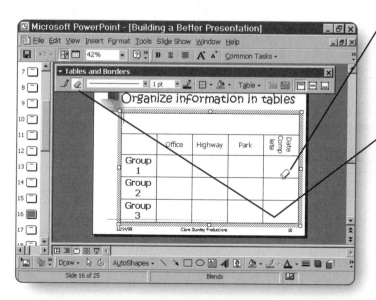

3. **Click** on the **cell border** located between the two cells that you want to merge in the column. The border between the two columns will be deleted.

4. **Click** on the **Eraser button**. The merge function will be turned off.

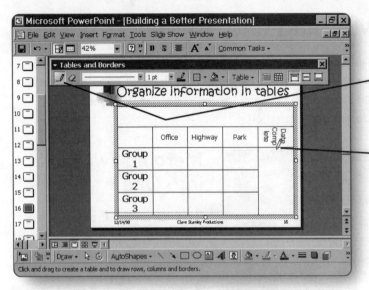

Splitting One Cell into Many

1. Click on the **Draw Table button**. The mouse pointer will turn into a pencil

2. Press and hold the **mouse button** on the location where you want to start the new cell.

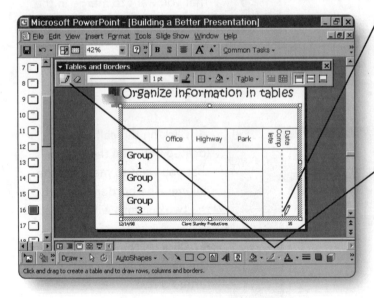

3. Drag the **mouse pointer** to the location where you want to end the new cell.

4. Release the **mouse button**. A new cell or group of cells will be added to the table.

5. Click on the **Draw Table button**. The cell-drawing feature will be turned off.

Resizing the Table

You'll notice that the table you inserted onto the slide takes up the maximum allowable space on the screen. You can change the total size of the table to fit on the slide better.

You'll also notice that rows and columns are of equal height and width. These measurements can also be changed.

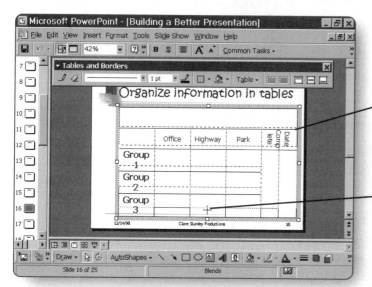

1. **Click** on the **table**. The table placeholder and handles will appear around the outside border of the table.

2. **Click and drag** the **mouse** in the direction in which you want the table to be resized.

3. **Release** the **mouse button**. The table will be resized.

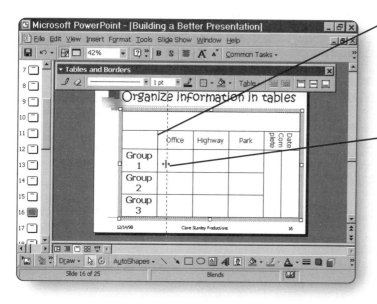

4. **Position** the **mouse pointer** on the line between the two columns you want to change. The mouse pointer will turn into two arrowheads.

5. **Click** and **drag** the **line** to the left or to the right to change the size of the columns.

6. **Release** the **mouse button**. The two columns will change to different widths.

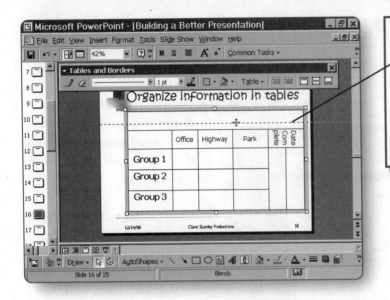

TIP

You can change the row height by positioning the mouse pointer on a line and holding the mouse button while dragging up or down.

Detailing the Table

After you have created a table and added some text, you may decide that the table lacks color. You can spruce up your tables by adding background colors, and by changing the color and style of the border lines.

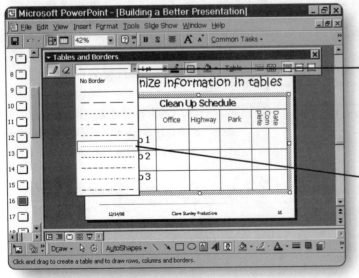

Formatting Table Borders

1. Click on the **down arrow** (▾) next to the Border Style button on the Tables and Borders toolbar. A list of line styles will appear.

2. Click on the **line style** that you want to apply to a table border. The line style will appear in the list box.

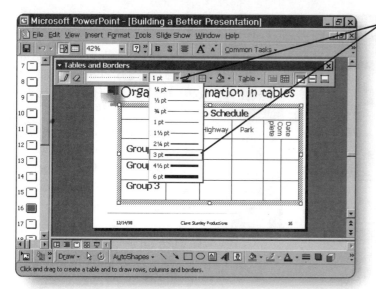

3. **Click** on the **down arrow** (◘) next to the Border Width button and click on the size that you want to use for the table border. The size will appear in the list box.

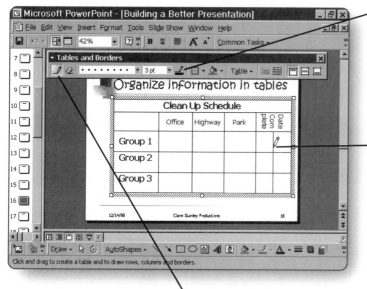

4. **Click** on the **Border Color button** and click on the color that you want to use for the table border. The color will appear at the bottom edge of the button.

5. **Click** on the **lines** on the table to which you want to apply the new border. The border lines will be changed to reflect the choices you made on the Tables and Borders toolbar.

6. When you finish, **click** on the **Draw Table button**. The table drawing function will be turned off.

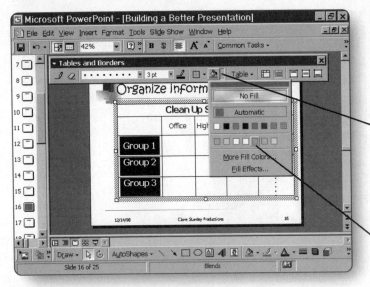

Colorizing Cells

1. Select the **cells** to which you want to add a background fill color. The cells will be selected.

2. Click on the **down arrow** (▼) next to the Fill Color button on the Tables and Borders toolbar. A list of colors from which you can choose will appear.

3. Click on a **color**. The selected cells will appear with the color you chose.

12

Building Charts

Charts and graphs are the visual representation of a relationship between two or more items. They can show a trend over a period of time or an item's size in relation to the total. All these relationships can be displayed with bars, pies, lines, and scattered dots. Your charts can be flat or 3-D. PowerPoint can create some complex charts, but you need to remember your audience. Ease of understanding should be your major goal. In this chapter, you'll learn how to:

- Begin building a simple chart
- Apply a different format and color to chart elements
- Reorganize the contents of a chart
- Add motion to a chart

Starting Your Chart

Before you begin building your chart, you need to organize all the data that you'll be plotting. Most charts compare two types of data; for example, the amount spent on a specific item during a range of time periods. PowerPoint provides a small example to get you started. You can just replace the sample data with your own. If there isn't enough space, just add information to the blank cells.

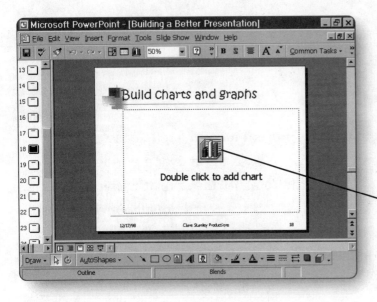

Getting Started with the Chart Slide Layout

The easiest way to get started with a chart is to create a new slide using the Chart slide layout.

1. Double-click on the **chart placeholder**. The chart datasheet will open.

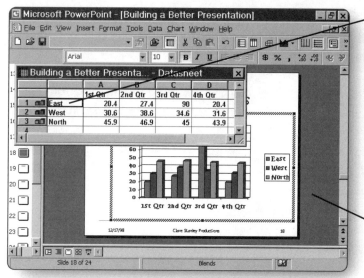

2. **Click** in a **cell** on the datasheet. The cell contents will be selected.

3. **Type** the **information** that you want to appear in the chart. If your chart will contain more data than is used by the sample chart, add your data to the blank cells.

4. **Click** on an area **outside** the datasheet window. You will return to the slide where you can see the chart you just built.

Creating a Chart on Your Own

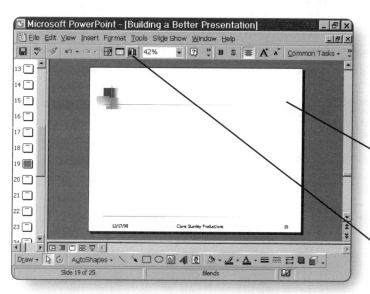

If you want to place a chart on a page that doesn't contain a chart placeholder, you'll have to start the process yourself. The result is the same as if you had used a Chart slide layout.

1. **Open** the **slide** on which you want to insert the chart. The page will appear in the Slide view.

2. **Click** on the **Insert Chart button**. The chart datasheet will appear.

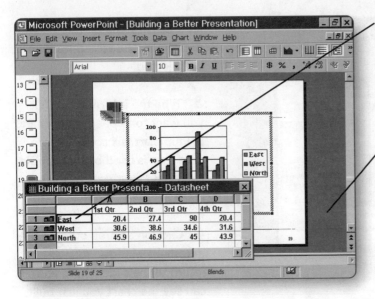

3. **Click** in a **cell** on the datasheet. The cell contents will be selected.

4. **Type** the **information** that you want to appear in the chart.

5. **Click outside** the datasheet window. The chart will appear on the slide.

Switching Between the Chart and the Datasheet

Now that you've taken a quick look at your chart, you may decide that you want to make more changes to its information. It's easy to switch between the chart and the datasheet.

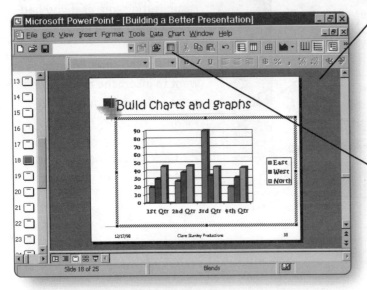

1. **Double-click** on a **blank area** inside the chart boundary. The chart will be selected and additional chart toolbar buttons will be added to the Standard toolbar. There will also be additional menu items.

2. **Click** on the **View Datasheet button**. The datasheet window will appear.

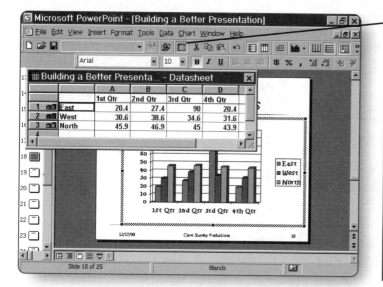

3. Click on the **View Datasheet button**. The datasheet window will disappear.

TIP

Find commands for working with the chart. Right-click on a cell, row heading, or column heading. You can add rows and columns, copy and clear data in cells, and format datasheet text.

Formatting Your Information

After you have entered all your data into the datasheet, it's time to create charts that will most effectively display the relationship between the two types of data you are comparing.

Changing the Chart Type

PowerPoint uses the bar chart as the default chart type. You can also choose from an assortment of pie charts, line charts, scatter charts, and much, much more. After you select the type of chart you want to use, you can further customize the chart to make it look the way you want.

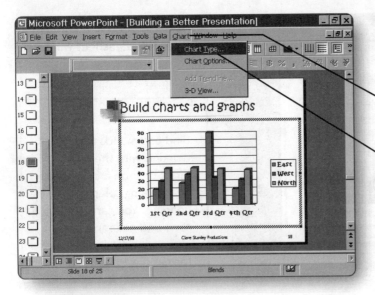

1. Double-click on a **blank space** inside the chart boundary. The chart will be selected.

2. Click on **Chart**. The Chart menu will appear.

3. Click on **Chart Type**. The Chart Type dialog box will open, and the Standard Types tab will appear in front.

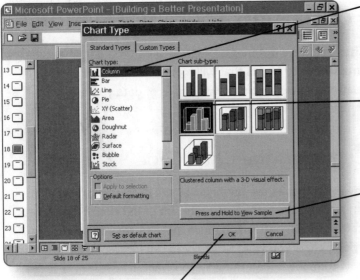

4. Click on the **type** of chart in the Chart type: list box that you want to use. The chart type will be selected.

5. Click on the **style** of chart in the Chart sub-type: area that you want to use. The chart sub-type will be selected.

6. Click and hold the **Press and Hold to View Sample button**. A preview of the chart will appear in the Sample: pane.

7. Click on **OK**. The chart type will be changed.

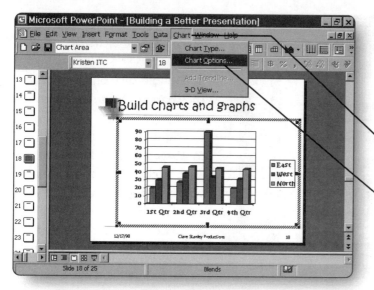

Giving Your Chart a Title

1. Double-click on the **chart**. The chart will be selected.

2. Click on **Chart**. The Chart menu will appear.

3. Click on **Chart Options**. The Chart Options dialog box will open.

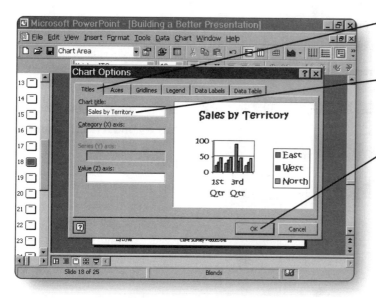

4. Click on the **Titles tab**. The Titles tab will move to the front.

5. Click in the **Chart title: text box** and type a title for your chart.

6. Click on **OK**. The title will be added to the top of the chart.

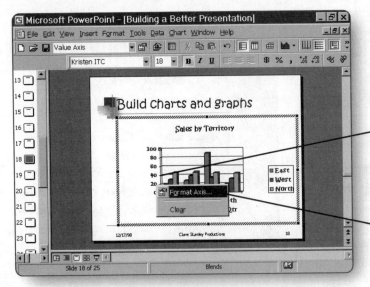

Formatting the Axis Text

1. Double-click on the **chart**. The chart will be selected.

2. Right-click on the **axis** containing the text that you want to change. A shortcut menu will appear.

3. Click on **Format Axis**. The Format Axis dialog box will open.

TIP

Format the Legend text. Right-click on the legend and select Format Legend from the shortcut menu.

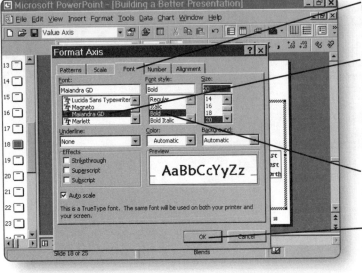

4. Click on the **Font tab**. The Font tab will move to the front.

5. Click on the **font** in the Font: list that you want to apply to the text on the selected axis. The font name will appear in the list box.

6. Change other font **formatting options** as desired.

7. Click on **OK**. The new font formatting will be applied to the text on the selected axis.

TIP

Change the axis line. Click on the Patterns tab and choose a new line style.

Colorizing Your Chart

PowerPoint uses the color scheme that you applied to your presentation to color the different parts of your chart. You can colorize your charts by changing the color of the individual bar or pie pieces, giving the entire chart area a background, or just adding a background to the area where the data is plotted.

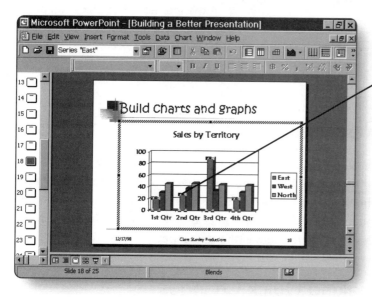

1. Double-click on the **chart**. The chart will be selected.

2. Double-click on the **chart element** that you want to change. A Format dialog box for the chart element will open, and the Patterns tab will be on top.

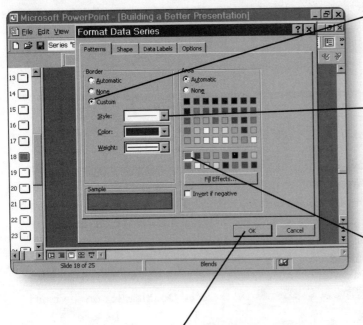

3. Click on the **Custom option button** to apply a different border to the chart element. The option will be selected.

4. Click on the **down arrow** (🔽) next to the Style:, Color:, and Weight: list boxes and select a design for the border line. The selected options will appear in the list boxes.

5. Click on a **color** in the Area section to change the color of the element. The color will be selected.

6. Click on **OK**. The changes will be applied to the chart.

Reorganizing Your Information

There are several things you can do to give your chart a different look and try out other ways of presenting your data. The Standard toolbar contains a few buttons that will change the look of a chart. You can also delete data series from a chart but leave them in the datasheet.

Making Quick Changes from the Standard Toolbar

When the chart is selected, the Standard toolbar gains a number of new buttons. These buttons help you change the way the chart looks. Many of these buttons act as toggle switches, which means that they turn a feature on and off.

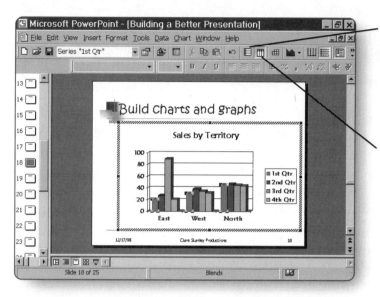

- **By Row.** Uses the data contained in the datasheet rows as the data series items in the chart. Data series items are individual bars or pie pieces.

- **By Column.** Uses the data contained in the datasheet columns as the data series items in the chart.

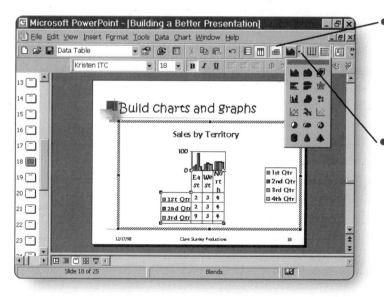

- **Data Table**. Adds the datasheet to the bottom of the chart. Click on the Data Table button a second time and the datasheet will disappear.

- **Chart Type.** Allows you to change the type of chart that is used to display the data. For example, you can easily change from a bar to a pie chart.

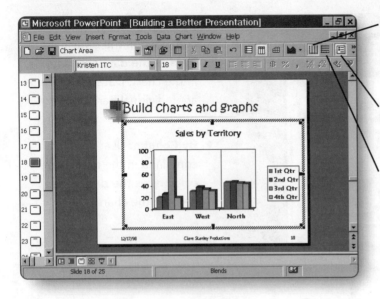

● **Category Axis Gridlines.** Adds (or hides) a vertical line between each of the categories in your chart.

● **Legend.** Hides or displays the legend shown to the right of the chart.

● **Value Axis Gridlines.** Adds (or hides) a horizontal line between each of the values in your chart.

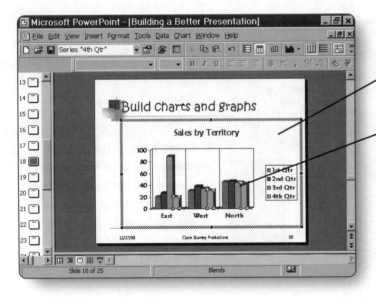

Hiding Data Used in a Chart

1. Double-click on the **chart**. The chart will be selected.

2. Click on the **data series** that you want to delete. The data series will be selected.

3. Press the **Delete key**. The data series elements will be deleted.

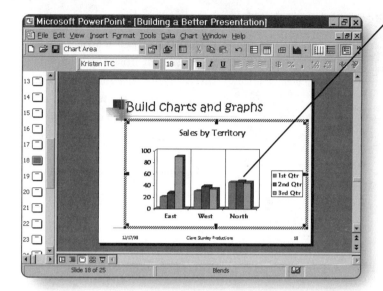

The data will be removed from the chart but will still be available in the datasheet.

Animating Chart Elements

In Chapter 10, "Displaying Special Effects," you learned about animating objects found on a slide. You can also animate the different elements in a chart so that they appear on the slide one by one in a defined pattern.

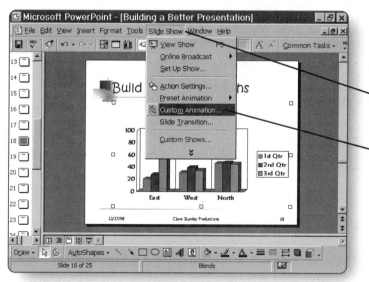

1. Click on the **chart** that you want to animate. The chart will be selected.

2. Click on **Slide Show**. The Slide Show menu will appear.

3. Click on **Custom Animation**. The Custom Animation dialog box will open, and the Chart Effects tab should be on top.

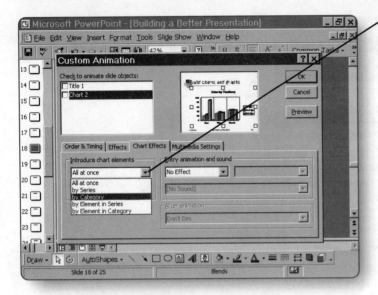

4. Click on the **down arrow** (▼) next to the Introduce chart elements list box, and click on the grouping method that you want to use to animate the chart. The method will appear in the list box, and other options in the dialog box will change depending on the method you choose.

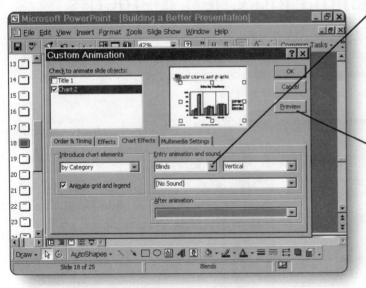

5. Click on the **down arrows** (▼) in the Entry animation and sound area and select those options that you want to apply to the chart animation. The options will be selected.

6. Click on the **Preview button**. The chart will display in the Preview pane using the animation you selected.

7. Click on **OK**. The animation will be applied to the chart, and you will see it in action when you run the slide show.

13

Creating an Organizational Chart

For those times when you need to diagram the hierarchy of a group of people, PowerPoint can access an Office feature separate from PowerPoint called Microsoft Organization Chart. This feature helps you create a structure that shows the different reporting levels within a workgroup, division, or company. You can show the people who are subordinate to a manager, the people who function as assistants and are not in the direct chain of command, and the interaction of co-workers with one another. In this chapter, you'll learn how to:

- Create a basic organization chart
- Give the organization chart a title
- Add more people to an organization chart
- Format different elements in the organization chart

Starting Microsoft Organization Chart

Before you begin creating the organization chart, you'll need the list of people who will be represented in the chart, their job titles, or other information related to the group.

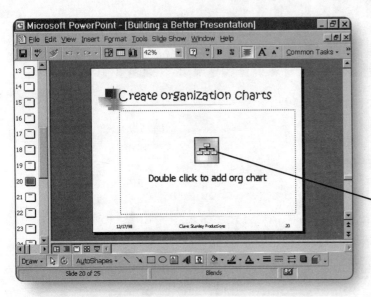

Getting Started with the Organization Chart Slide Layout

The easiest way to get started with an organization chart is to create a new slide using the Organization Chart slide layout.

1. Double-click on the **organization chart placeholder**. Microsoft Organization Chart will open, and a sample organization chart will be started for you.

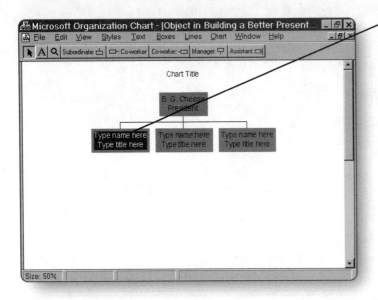

2. Click in a **box** on the organization chart. The box contents will be selected.

3. Type the **information** that you want to appear in the organization chart.

Creating an Organization Chart on Your Own

If you want to place an organization chart on a page that doesn't contain a placeholder, you'll have to start the process yourself. The result is the same as if you had used the Organization Chart slide layout.

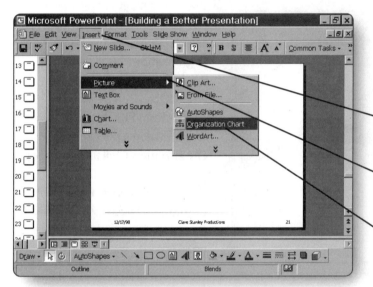

1. Open the **slide** on which you want to insert the organization chart. The page will appear in the Slide view.

2. Click on **Insert**. The Insert menu will appear.

3. Click on **Picture**. A submenu will appear.

4. Click on **Organization Chart**. Microsoft Organization Chart will appear.

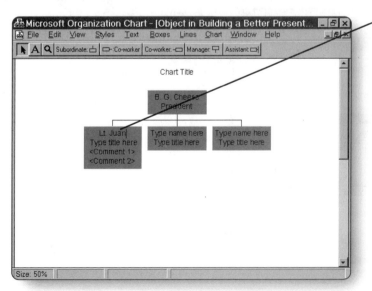

5. Click in a **box** on the organization chart. The box contents will be selected.

6. Type the **information** that you want to appear in the organization chart.

Switching Between the Organization Chart and PowerPoint

You've made a few changes to Microsoft Organization Chart. If you want to see how your organization chart looks in PowerPoint, you'll need to switch between the programs. Then, after you've taken a quick look at your organization chart, you may decide that you want to make some changes. It's easy to switch between Organization Chart and PowerPoint.

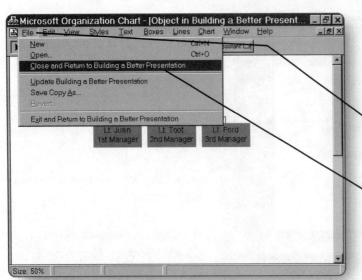

1. **Click** on **File** in the Organization Chart window. The File menu will appear.

2. **Click** on **Close and Return to [name of your presentation]**. A confirmation dialog box will open.

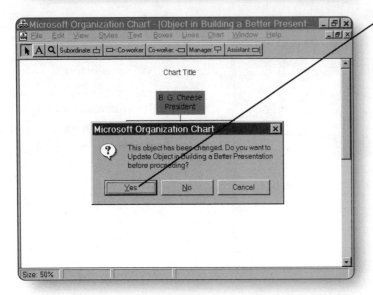

3. **Click** on **Yes**. The information that you created in Microsoft Organization Chart will be updated in PowerPoint. Organization Chart will close, and you'll see your organization chart on the slide.

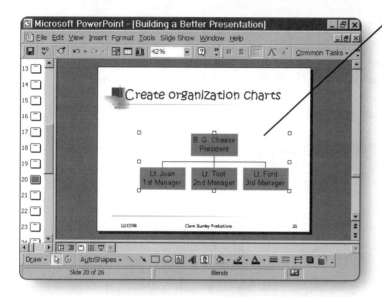

4. **Double-click** on the **organization chart**. Organization Chart will open, and you can begin making changes to your organization chart.

Giving the Organization Chart a Title

Above the organization chart, there is a placeholder (indicated by the words "Chart Title") where you can add a title to the chart. If you choose not to use this title, the placeholder will remain but no title will appear on the PowerPoint slide. If you plan to give your organization chart a title, use this placeholder. The size of the title will always stay proportional to the size of the organization chart, and the title will not overlap with the chart.

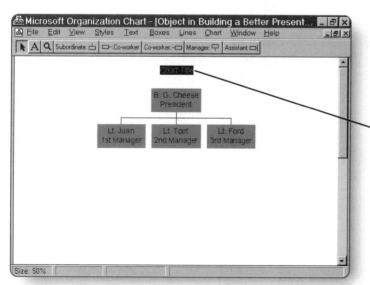

Creating the Title

1. **Select** the words **Chart Title**. The title placeholder will be selected.

2. **Type** a **title** for the organization chart.

Formatting the Title Text

The title text can be formatted in different ways. You can change the paragraph alignment and the font style.

1. Select the chart **title text**. The text will be highlighted.

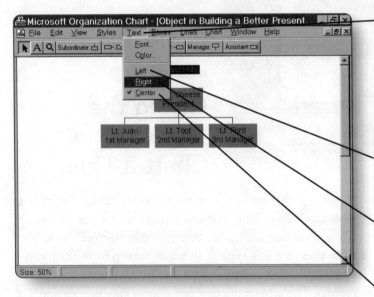

2. Click on **Text**. The Text menu will appear.

3. Click on a paragraph **alignment**. The paragraph will be aligned according to your selection.

- **Left** positions the title text so that it lines up on the left side of the chart.

- **Right** positions the title text so that it lines up on the right side of the chart.

- **Center** positions the title text so that it lines up in the middle of the chart.

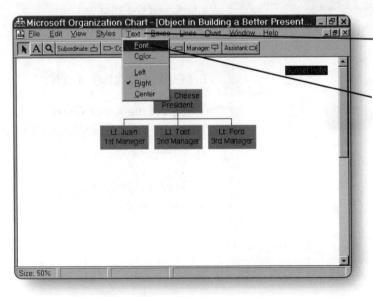

4. Click on **Text**. The text menu will appear.

5. Click on **Font**. The Font dialog box will open.

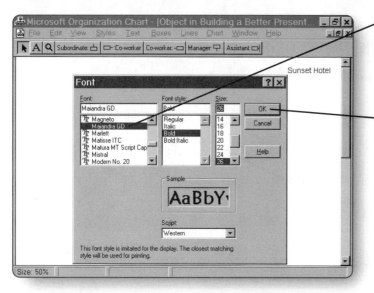

6. Click on the **font**, **font style**, and **font size** to change these as desired. The options will be selected.

7. Click on **OK**. The new font will be applied to the title.

Adding Members to the Chart

The sample organization chart with which you started probably won't fit your needs. You'll want to add more boxes so that all the important people in your workgroup, department, company, or organization are represented.

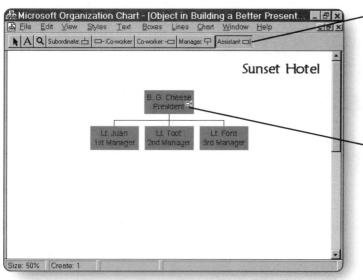

1. Click on the **box button** that best matches the position within the organization where the box will be placed. The mouse pointer will turn into a connecting box.

2. Click on the **box** to which you want the new box to be attached. A new box will be created and will be attached to the selected box.

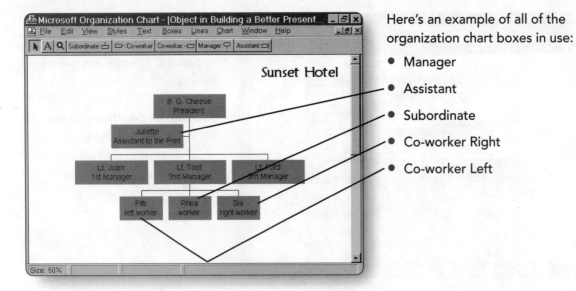

Here's an example of all of the organization chart boxes in use:

- Manager
- Assistant
- Subordinate
- Co-worker Right
- Co-worker Left

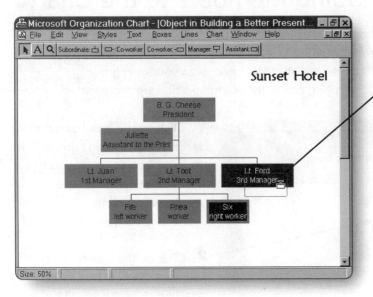

It's easy to move a box after you've attached it to another box.

1. **Click and drag** a **box** over the box to which you want the first box attached. The mouse pointer will change.

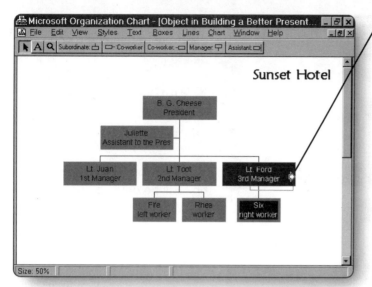

2. Move the **mouse pointer** toward the right or left side of the box to which it will be attached to place the box at the same level. The mouse pointer will change to an arrow.

3. Release the **mouse button**. The box will move to the new position.

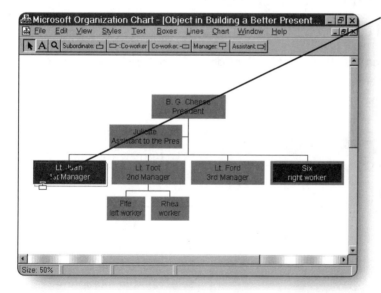

4. Move the **mouse pointer** toward the bottom of the box to which it will be attached, to place the box at a subordinate level. The mouse pointer will change to a connection box.

5. Release the **mouse button**. The box will move to the new position.

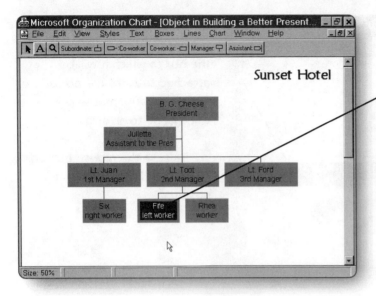

If you mistakenly placed a box in the organization chart, you can delete it.

1. **Click** on the **box** that you want to delete. The box will be selected.

2. **Press** the **Delete key**. The box will be deleted.

Formatting Text in a Member Box

The text that you typed inside each box can be formatted in many ways. You might want to format a person's name in bold text and that person's title in italics.

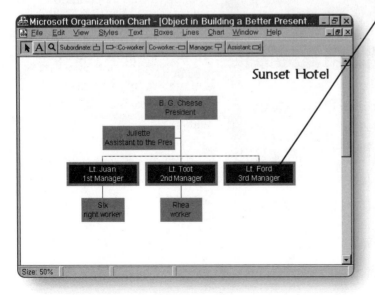

1. **Select** the **text** that you want to format. The text will be highlighted.

NOTE

To select all the text in a box, click on the box. To select text in multiple boxes, press and hold the Shift key while you click on the boxes you want to select.

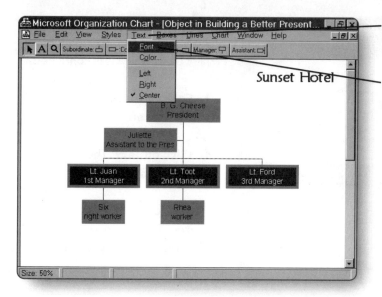

2. Click on **Text**. The Text menu will appear.

3. Click on **Font**. The Font dialog box will open.

4. Click on the **font** in the Font: list box that you want to use for the selected text. The font name will appear in the list box.

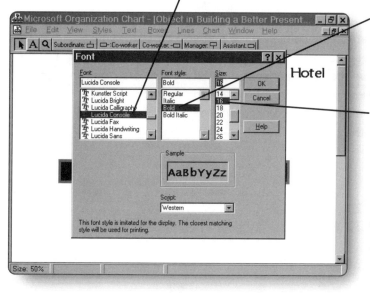

5. Click on the **font style** that you want to apply to the selected text. The font style will appear in the list box.

6. Click on the **font size** that you want to apply to the selected text. The size will be selected.

7. Click on **OK**. The new text formatting will be applied to the selected text.

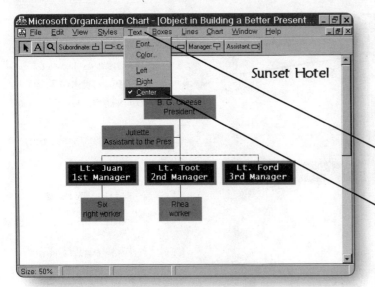

You can also change the alignment of the text relative to the box in which it is contained.

1. **Select** the **text**. The text will be highlighted.

2. **Click** on **Text**. The Text menu will appear.

3. **Click** on **Left**, **Right**, or **Center**. The alignment of the selected text will be changed.

Formatting Member Boxes

When you see your chart in the PowerPoint slide, the colors used by the color scheme that you chose for your presentation will be applied to the organization chart. You do have the option of choosing different colors. You can change the color and style of the line that borders a box. You can also give a different color to the box background or add a shadow to the box.

Changing the Line Style of a Box

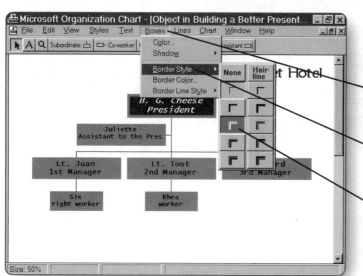

1. Select the **box or boxes** that you want to change. The boxes will be selected.

2. Click on **Boxes**. The Boxes menu will appear.

3. Click on **Border Style**. A submenu will appear.

4. Click on the **line style** that you want to use for the border that appears around the box. The border style will be changed.

TIP

To change the line color, click on the Border Color command.

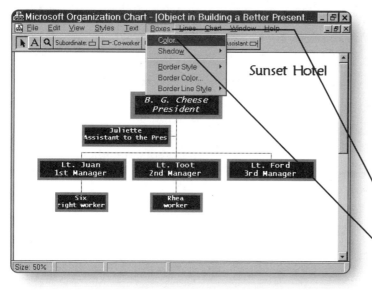

Changing the Color of a Box

1. Select the **boxes** for which you want to change the background color. The boxes will be selected.

2. Click on **Boxes**. The Boxes menu will appear.

3. Click on **Color**. The Color dialog box will open.

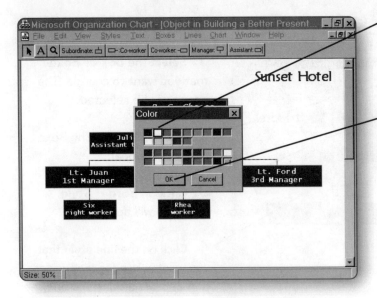

4. Click on the **color** that you want to apply to the background of the box. The color will be selected.

5. Click on **OK**. The color will be applied to the background.

Adding a Shadow to a Box

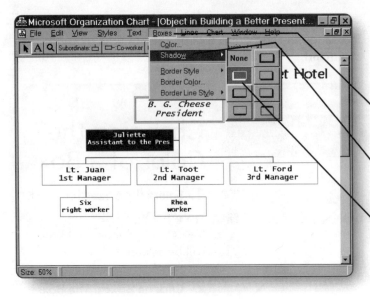

1. Select the **boxes** to which you want to add a shadow effect. The boxes will be selected.

2. Click on **Boxes**. The Boxes menu will appear.

3. Click on **Shadow**. A submenu will appear.

4. Click on a **shadow style**. The shadow style will be applied to the selected boxes.

Part III Review Questions

1. *What can you do to clip art images to make them look different?*
   See "Adding Clip Art to Your Presentation" in Chapter 9

2. *Which tools are available to help you line up images?*
   See "Positioning Graphics on a Slide" in Chapter 9

3. *Name two ways that you can add a shadow to an object.*
   See "Adding a Shadow to an Image or Text" in Chapter 10

4. *How do you give a flat image some depth? See "Creating 3-D Images" in Chapter 10*

5. *What are the two different methods you can use to start a new table? See "Creating the Basic Table" in Chapter 11*

6. *Name three ways in which you can format text inside a table.*
   See "Adding Text to a Table" in Chapter 11

7. *What is the fastest way to make a chart look different?*
   See "Reorganizing Your Information" in Chapter 12

8. *How can you give the chart and its elements movement on a slide?*
   See "Animating Chart Elements" in Chapter 12

9. *What are the different levels that you can add to an organization chart? See "Adding Members to the Chart" in Chapter 13*

10. *How do you change the color and line style of boxes in an organization chart? See "Formatting Member Boxes" in Chapter 13*

PART IV

Collaborating with PowerPoint

14

Working on a Presentation with a Group

You've been working away at your presentation, all by yourself. It's easy to control a project if you're the only person you have to manage. But what do you do when several people are involved? You need a method for managers and reviewers to give input. PowerPoint allows you to place comments on a slide and navigate between comments. You also need to route the presentation, or parts of the presentation, to the various workgroup members. E-mail, whether on the Internet or your company intranet, is a common and easy way to share information. In this chapter, you'll learn how to:

- Add comments to a presentation and move between comments
- E-mail a presentation to an individual
- Route a presentation to a group

Commenting on a Presentation

If your presentation is going to be a group effort, you'll need a method for making comments about the content or design of the presentation. PowerPoint allows you to add comment boxes to a slide. In addition to adding comments, you can move between comments, delete comments, or hide comments.

Placing Comments on PowerPoint Slides

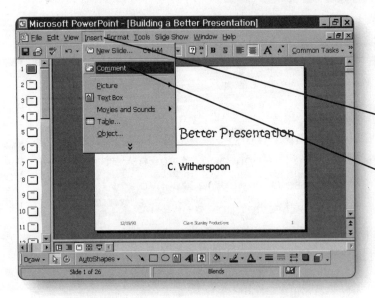

1. Open the **slide** to which you want to add the comments. The slide will appear in the Slide view.

2. Click on **Insert**. The Insert menu will appear.

3. Click on **Comment**. A yellow comment box will appear at the upper-left corner of the slide, and the Reviewing toolbar will also appear.

NOTE

If you don't see the Comment command, click on the down arrow at the bottom of the menu.

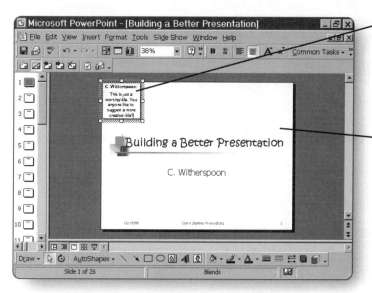

4. Type your **comments**. Your comments will appear inside the box and are preceded by your name so that the comments are identified as coming from you.

5. Click outside the comment box. Your comments will be added to the presentation and will appear in the upper-left corner of the slide. You may want to move the comment box to be closer to the item about which you made the comments.

NOTE

You can leave the comment box as it is, or you can format text, move the box, change the size of the box, or apply a different color to the box.

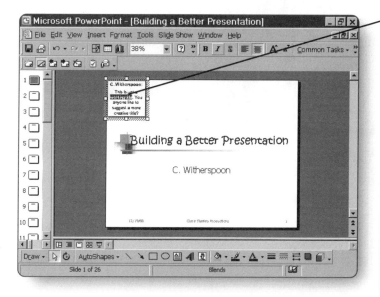

6. Select the **text** that you want to format. The text will be highlighted.

7. Make any desired **changes** to the text. You can change the font or its size, add bold and italic effects, or change the color.

NOTE

To change how a paragraph displays in a comment box, use the paragraph alignment buttons.

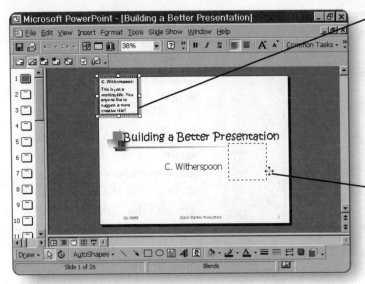

8. **Click and drag** the **border** around a comment box to the position where you want it to be placed on the slide. The mouse pointer will turn into a four-pointed arrow, and an outline of the comment box will appear while the box is being moved.

9. **Release** the **mouse button**. The comment box will appear in the new position.

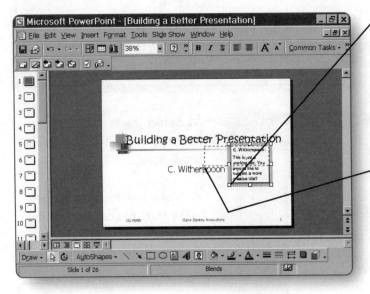

10. **Click and drag** an **image handle** in the direction that you want to resize the comment box. The mouse pointer will turn into a double arrowhead, and an outline of the resized comment box will appear.

11. **Release** the **mouse button**. The comment box will be resized.

Navigating Between Comments

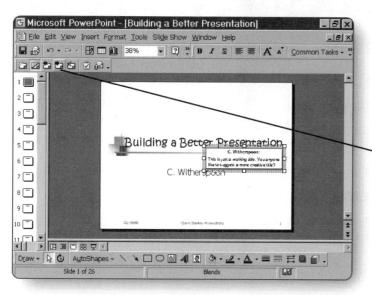

You don't need to look through each slide in a presentation to view all the comments that have been added to the presentation. Use the Reviewing toolbar to make this task easier.

1. **Click** on the **Next Comment button**. The next slide in the presentation that contains a comment will appear in the Slide view, and the comment will be selected.

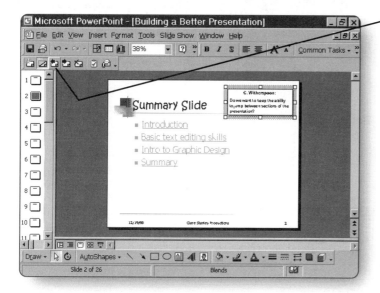

2. **Click** on the **Previous Comment button**. The previous slide that contains a comment will appear in the Slide view.

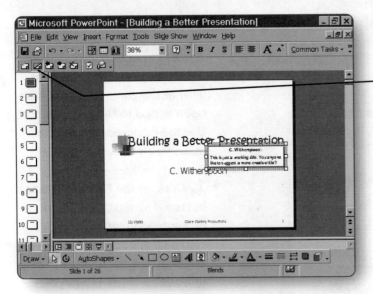

Showing and Hiding Revisions

1. Click on the **Show/Hide Comments button** on the Reviewing toolbar. All the comment boxes contained in the presentation will disappear from view.

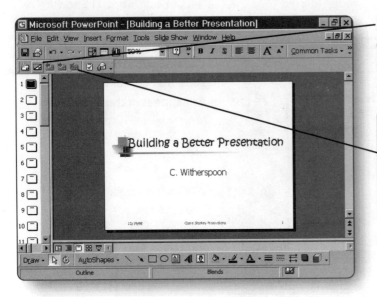

2. Click on the **Show/Hide Comments button**. All the comments will be displayed on all the slides in the presentation.

TIP

If you don't want the comment to appear in the presentation, select the comment and click on the Delete Comment button.

Recording a Comment onto a Slide

Another method you can use to make comments on a slide is to record them. Before you can do this, your computer must be equipped with a microphone, speakers, and a sound card.

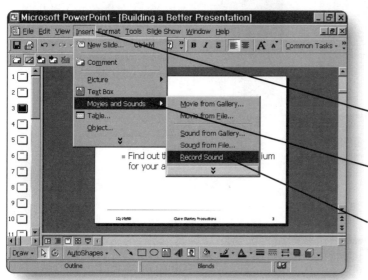

1. Open the **slide** onto which you want to record a comment. The slide will appear in the Slide view.

2. Click on **Insert**. The Insert menu will appear.

3. Click on **Movies and Sounds**. A submenu will appear.

4. Click on **Record Sound**. The Record Sound dialog box will open.

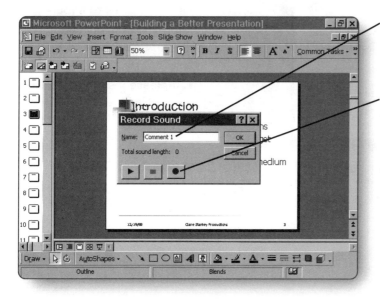

5. Select the **text** in the Name: text box, and type a name for the recorded comment.

6. Click on the **Record button**. The recorder will begin.

7. Speak into the **microphone**. Your comment will be recorded.

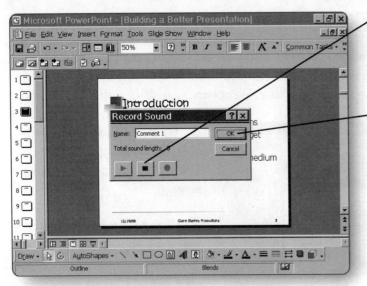

8. Click on the **Stop button** when you finish recording the comment. The recorder will stop recording.

9. Click on **OK**. A sound icon will appear on the slide.

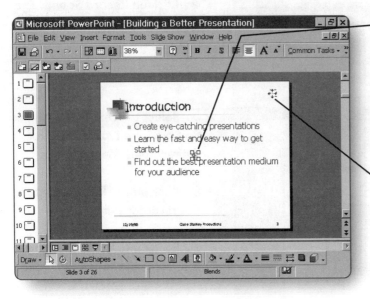

10. Click and drag the **sound icon** to another position on the slide. You can move this icon to any position you like. The mouse pointer will turn into a four-pointed arrowhead, and an outline of the icon will display.

11. Release the **mouse button**. The sound icon will be moved.

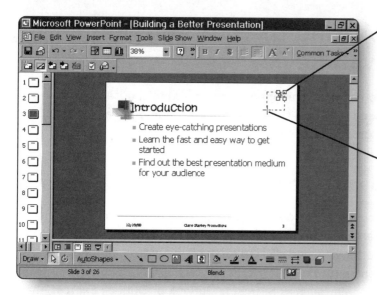

12. **Click and drag** an **image handle** in the direction that you would like to size the icon. The mouse pointer will turn into a crosshair and, an outline of the image box will show the size.

13. **Release** the **mouse button**. The sound icon will be resized.

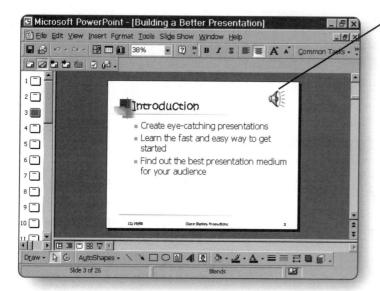

14. **Double-click** on the **sound icon**. The recorded comment will play.

Sharing the Presentation with Reviewers

You have several options from which to choose when you need to send a slide or entire presentation to an individual or a group of people.

Sending a Single Slide

You can e-mail a single slide from a presentation to another person. It's a simple task of selecting the slide in the Slide Sorter view and clicking on the Send button. Before you can send e-mail from PowerPoint you must be using an e-mail program, such as Microsoft Outlook or Outlook Express, that can send attachments and display HTML Web pages.

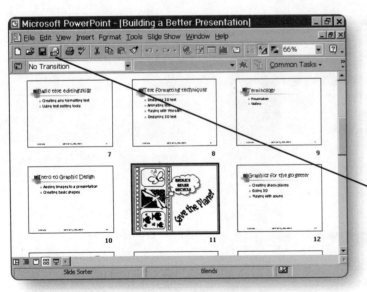

1. Click on the **Slide Sorter View button**. The Slide Sorter view will appear.

2. Click on the **slide** that you want to send as an attachment in an e-mail message. The slide will be selected.

3. Click on the **E-mail button**. The PowerPoint window will change, and a new message window for your default e-mail program will be incorporated. You'll see the entire set of slides, but only the selected slides will be attached to the e-mail message.

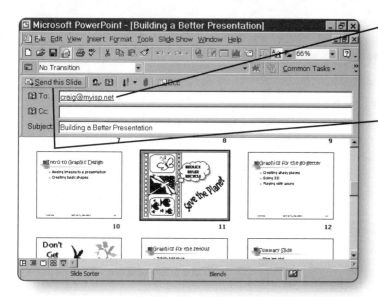

4. Click in the **To:** and **Cc: text boxes** and type the e-mail address of those people to whom you want to send the slide.

5. Click on the **Send this Slide button**. The message will be sent to your default e-mail program. You can connect to your Internet Service Provider or company network and send the message.

NOTE

To learn more about e-mail, read the chapters on Outlook Express in Prima Tech's *Internet Explorer 5 Fast & Easy*.

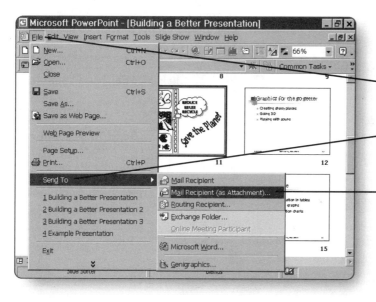

E-mailing the Entire Presentation

1. Click on **File**. The File menu will appear.

2. Click on **Send To**. A submenu will appear.

3. Click on **Mail Recipient (as Attachment)**. A new message window for your default e-mail program will open, and the presentation file will be shown as an attachment.

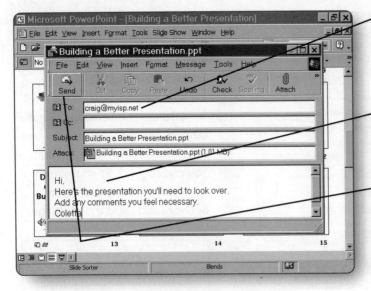

4. Click in the **To:** and **Cc: text boxes** and type the e-mail addresses of people you want to review the presentation.

5. Click in the **message area** and type any message that you want the reviewers to read.

6. Click on the **Send button**. The message will be stored in your e-mail program until you connect to the Internet or your company network.

Routing a Presentation to a Group

If you have several people who need to review a presentation, you can create a routing list to help automate this task.

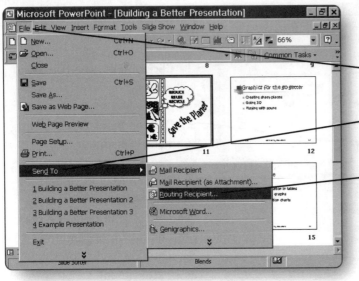

Starting the Routing Process

1. Click on **File**. The File menu will appear.

2. Click on **Send To**. A submenu will appear.

3. Click on **Routing Recipient**. The Add Routing Slip dialog box will open.

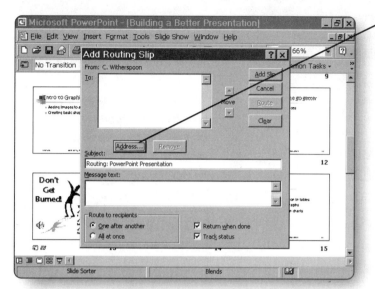

4. **Click** on the **Address button**. The address book for your default e-mail program will open.

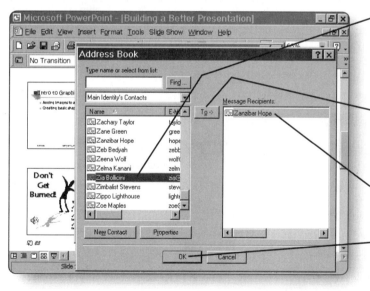

5. **Click** on the **name** of the first person that you want to be listed on the routing slip. The name will be selected.

6. **Click** on the **To button**. The name will be added to the Message Recipients: list.

7. **Add** other **people** to the list as needed.

8. **Click** on **OK**. The names will appear in the To: list box of the Add Routing Slip dialog box.

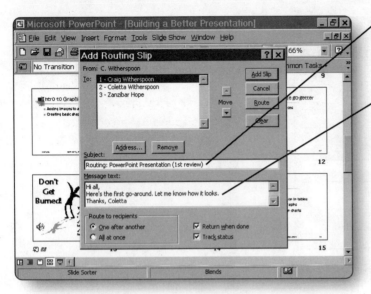

9. Select the **text** in the Subject: text box and type a subject for the e-mail message.

10. Click in the **Message text: text box** and type the message that you want your recipients to read.

NOTE

The following text also appears by default in the message text: "The attached presentation has a routing slip. When you are done reviewing this presentation, choose Next Routing Recipient from the Send To menu on the File menu to continue routing."

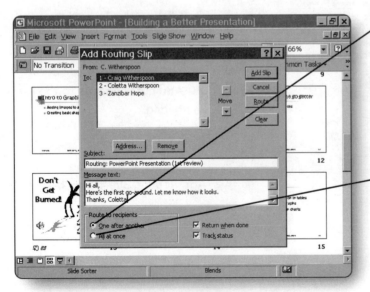

11a. Click on the **One after another option button** if you want each reviewer to look at the presentation in succession and then send it on. The option will be selected.

OR

11b. Click on the **All at once option button** if you want each reviewer to review his or her individual copy of the presentation and then send it back to you. The option will be selected.

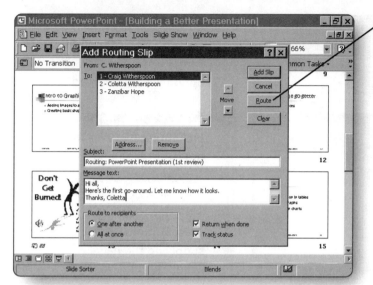

12. **Click** on **Route**. The message will be sent along with the presentation as an attachment to your default e-mail program from which you can send the messages.

Continuing the Routing Process

After a reviewer has finished looking over the presentation, that reviewer needs to send it on to the next person listed on the routing slip.

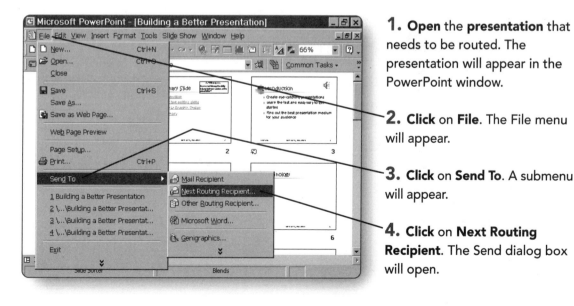

1. Open the **presentation** that needs to be routed. The presentation will appear in the PowerPoint window.

2. Click on **File**. The File menu will appear.

3. Click on **Send To**. A submenu will appear.

4. Click on **Next Routing Recipient**. The Send dialog box will open.

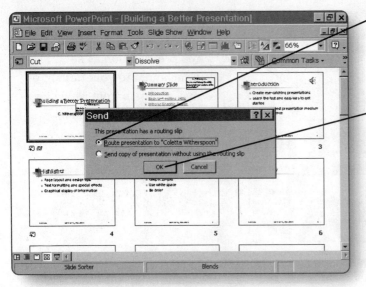

5. Click on the **Route presentation to [recipient name] option button**. The option will be selected.

6. Click on **OK**. The presentation will be routed to the next person on the list. A message will be sent to the originator of the routing slip letting that person know the presentation was routed and supplying the name of the sender and the receiver.

15

Sharing Files with Office Applications

Taking items that you've created in one program (such as text or graphic images) and using them in another program became a reality with the invention of OLE (Object Linking and Embedding). Now this may sound like a complex concept, but it allows you to copy an item, for example a spreadsheet created in Excel, and place it on a PowerPoint slide. The easy part is that you don't need to know anything about converting file formats. You have several options from which to choose when sharing information between Office applications. In this chapter, you'll learn how to:

- Copy items using the Office Clipboard
- Change text formatting when copying an item
- Drag and drop items between Office applications
- Link and embed items

Cutting and Pasting from the Clipboard

The Office Clipboard is an enhanced version of the Windows Clipboard. Instead of being able to store only one item at a time, the Office Clipboard stores 12 items that you can copy among all Office programs (not just within PowerPoint).

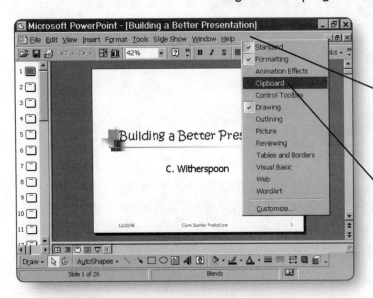

Displaying the Clipboard Toolbar

1. Right-click on an **empty area** of the menu bar or a toolbar. The Toolbars menu will appear.

2. Click on **Clipboard**. The Clipboard toolbar will appear as a floating toolbar on your screen.

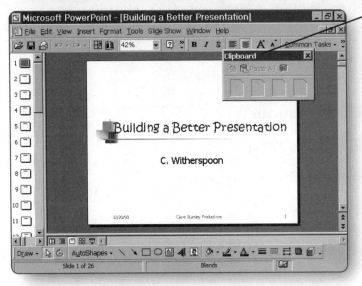

3. Click and drag the toolbar **title bar** toward the toolbars at the top of the PowerPoint window. When you reach the toolbars, the Clipboard toolbar will attach itself to the other toolbars.

4. Release the **mouse button**. The Clipboard toolbar will be docked to the other toolbars.

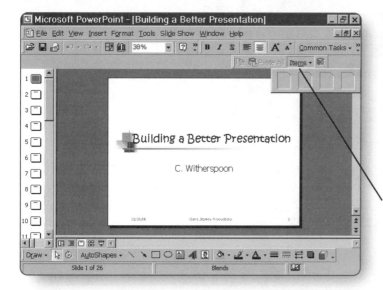

NOTE

You'll notice that the blank icons that were located along the bottom of the toolbar are missing when you dock the Clipboard toolbar.

5. **Click** on the **Items button**. You'll see those missing blank icons. These icons are the placeholders for the items that you will be copying to the Clipboard.

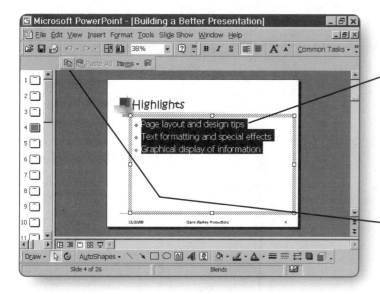

Adding Items to the Clipboard

1. **Select** the **item** that you want to have added to the Clipboard. You can select a few words, a paragraph, a bulleted list, a picture, or a drawing object. The item will be selected.

2. **Click** on **Copy** on the Clipboard toolbar. An icon for the item will appear on the toolbar.

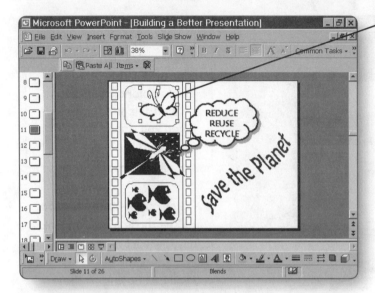

3. **Copy** the **other items** that you want to appear on the Clipboard. The items will appear as icons on the toolbar.

NOTE

You can place up to 12 items at one time on the Clipboard.

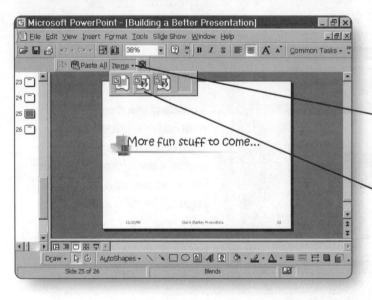

4. **Click** in the **place** where you want to insert an item from the Clipboard. The insertion bar will appear on the slide.

5. **Click** on the **Items button**. A list of the items you have copied to the Clipboard will appear.

6. **Click** on the **Clipboard icon** for the item that you want to insert. A copy of the item will appear on the slide.

NOTE

If you are unsure of which Clipboard icon to choose, hold the mouse pointer over an icon in the Items list to display the first 50 characters of text contained in that item. If the item does not contain any text, a note describing the item as a "Picture" or "Item" will appear.

After you have copied an item from the Clipboard onto a slide, you can change the size, reformat the text, or make any other changes you might want.

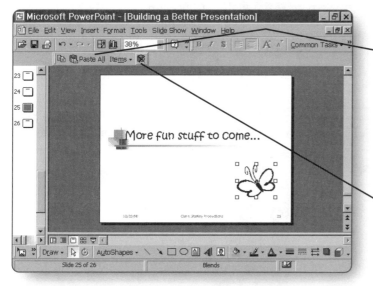

TIP

Copy the entire contents of the Clipboard. Click on the Paste All button, and each item on the Clipboard will be copied to the slide.

7. Click on the **Clear Clipboard button**. The contents of the Clipboard will be emptied.

Formatting Data When Pasting

There may be times when you want to copy information, but the way the text is formatted will not work in the document you are creating. For example, you may want to copy some text you created in a Web page, but you don't want the HTML formatting in your presentation. You can use a special command to make this task easy.

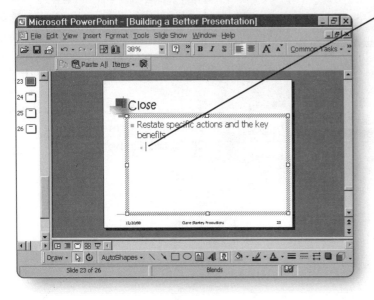

1. Select the **text** that you want to copy. The text will be highlighted.

2. Press Ctrl+C. The selected text will be copied to the Clipboard.

3. Click in the **place** where you want to insert the copied text. The insertion bar will appear in the selected place.

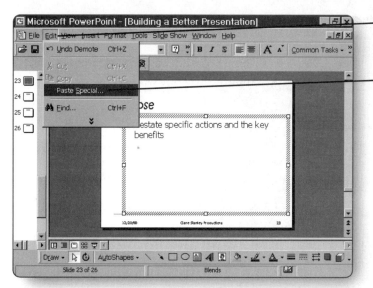

4. Click on **Edit**. The Edit menu will appear.

5. Click on **Paste Special**. The Paste Special dialog box will open.

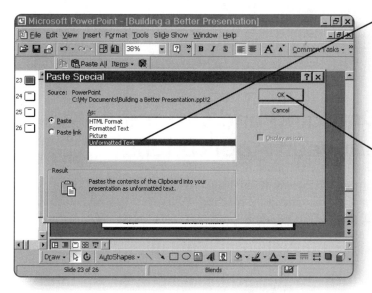

6. Click on the **formatting option** in the As: list box that you want to apply to the copied item when it is pasted into the new place. The option will be selected.

7. Click on **OK**. The pasted text will appear in the selected format.

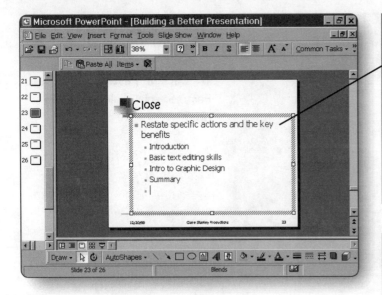

NOTE

The text or images you paste into your PowerPoint slides do not need to have originated from another PowerPoint slide. You can easily copy and paste items from any Office application.

NOTE

Unformatted text will take on the formatting of the paragraph into which it is inserted.

Dragging and Dropping between Applications

The fastest way to move items between two programs is to use the drag-and-drop method. When you use this method, the formatting of any copied text will also be copied.

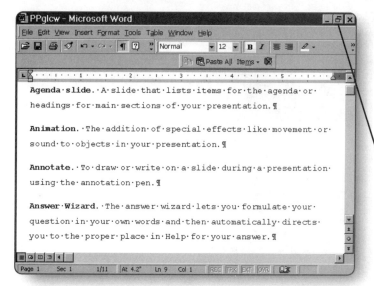

1. Open the **program and file** containing the information that you want to copy and scroll to the place in the file where you want to insert the items from PowerPoint.

2. Click on the **Restore button** located at the top right of the program window. The program window will decrease so that you can see more of your screen behind it.

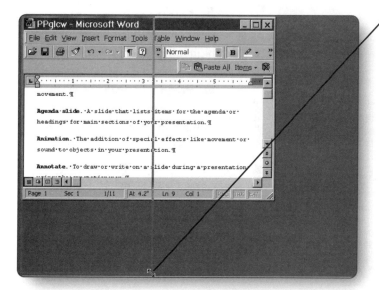

3. Resize the **program window** so that it takes up only half of your monitor screen. Click and drag the corner of the window to the desired location.

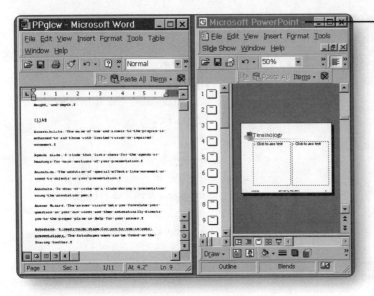

4. Restore and resize the **PowerPoint program window** so that it takes up the other half of your monitor screen.

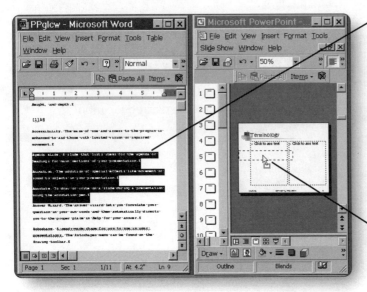

5. Select the **items** that you want to copy. The items will be highlighted.

6. Press and hold the **right mouse button** on the selected items and drag to the location where you want to copy the items. The mouse pointer will have a box attached to it.

7. Release the **mouse button** at the desired location in PowerPoint. A shortcut menu will appear.

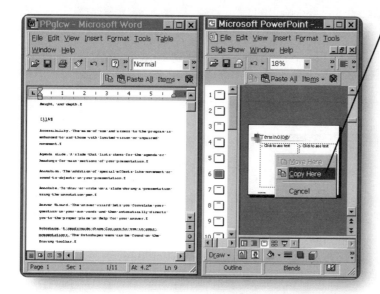

8. Click on **Copy Here**. The items will be copied to the new location within PowerPoint.

Linking and Embedding Documents

Linking and embedding are methods of copying objects (such as files or images) into another file so that the linked or embedded objects can be edited from the program in which they were created (not the program into which they were copied). When a linked file is modified in the program in which it was created, the changes to the file will be seen in PowerPoint. When an embedded file is modified in the program in which it was created, the information in PowerPoint does not change.

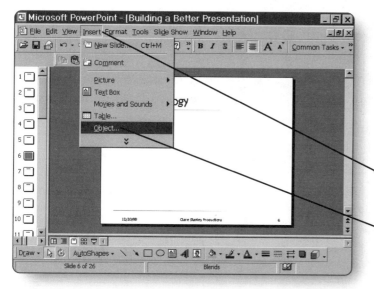

Linking a File to a PowerPoint Slide

1. Open the **slide** in which you want to create a link to an object. The slide will appear in the Slide view.

2. Click on **Insert**. The Insert menu will appear.

3. Click on **Object**. The Insert Object dialog box will open.

TIP

If you want to see the entire list of commands in a menu, double-click on the menu name.

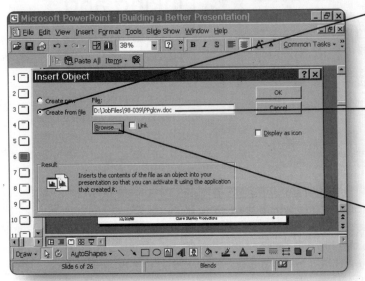

4. Click on the **Create from file option button**. The option will be selected, and the Insert Object dialog box will change.

5. Click in the **File: text box** and type the name of the file that you want to link to the slide.

NOTE

If you don't know the path and filename, click the Browse button and search for the file.

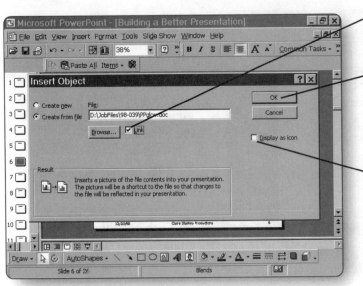

6. Click in the **Link check box**. A ✓ will appear in the box.

7. Click on **OK**. The object will be linked to your presentation.

TIP

You can display the object as an icon by placing a ✓ in the Display as icon check box.

Embedding Documents

To embed an object into a PowerPoint slide, you'll follow almost the same steps as you did to link the object. The only difference is that you can ignore the Link checkbox in the Insert Object dialog box.

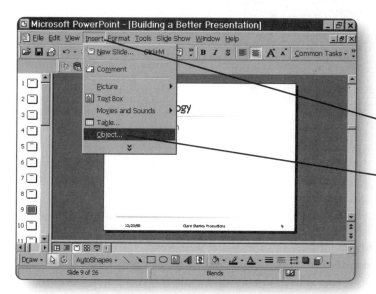

1. Open the **slide** in which you want to embed an object. The slide will appear in the Slide view.

2. Click on **Insert**. The Insert menu will appear.

3. Click on **Object**. The Insert Object dialog box will open.

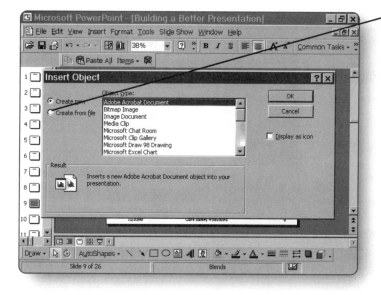

4. Click on the **Create from file option button**. The option will be selected and the Insert Object dialog box will change.

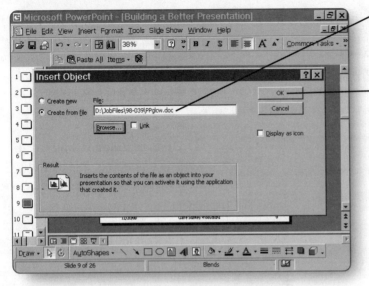

5. Click in the **File: text box** and type the name of the file that you want to link to the slide.

6. Click on **OK**. The object will be embedded in your presentation.

Creating a New Embedded Object

You can embed an object that you haven't created yet. You can create this object in PowerPoint, using toolbars and menus found in the program installed on your computer that is the default program for the file type of the object.

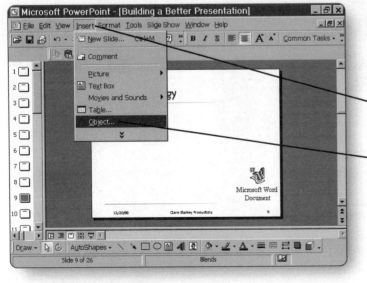

1. Open the **slide** in which you want to create an embedded object. The slide will appear in the Slide view.

2. Click on **Insert**. The Insert menu will appear.

3. Click on **Object**. The Insert Object dialog box will open.

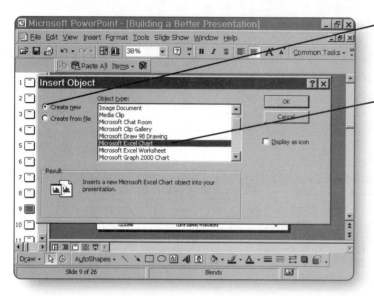

4. Click on the **Create new option button**. The option will be selected.

5. Click on the **type of object** you want to create. The object type will be selected.

6. Click on **OK**. The application installed on your computer that will create the type of file you selected will open in a small window within the PowerPoint slide.

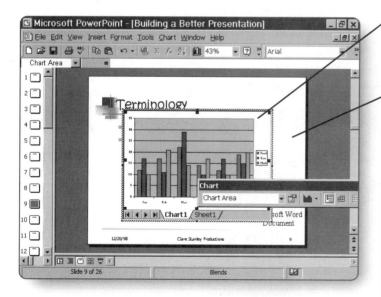

7. Create the **object**. The new object will be displayed in the other program window.

8. Click outside the PowerPoint slide. The object will be added to the slide.

NOTE

If a separate application opened, click on the Close button after you create the desired object. The program will close, and the object you just created will appear on the PowerPoint slide.

Embedding a Portion of an Existing File

If you have a file that contains more information than you want to embed into your presentation, you can elect to embed only part of the file.

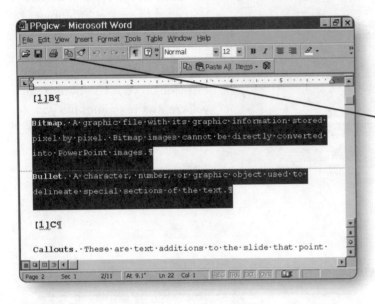

1. Select the **items** that you want to embed into your PowerPoint presentation. The items will be selected.

2. Click on **Copy**. The items will be copied to the Windows Clipboard.

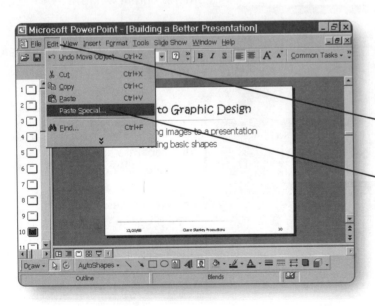

3. Display the PowerPoint **slide** into which you want to embed the items. The slide will appear in the Slide view.

4. Click on **Edit**. The Edit menu will appear.

5. Click on **Paste Special**. The Paste Special dialog box will open.

6. Click on the **Paste option button**. The option will be selected.

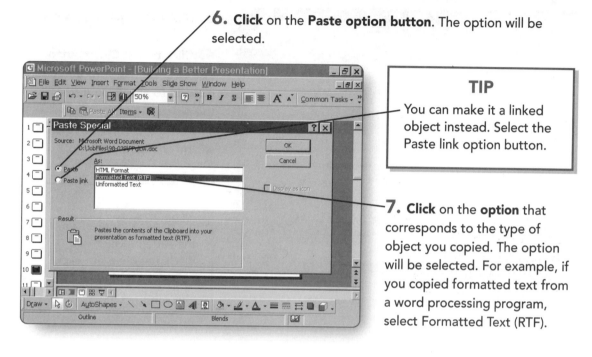

7. Click on the **option** that corresponds to the type of object you copied. The option will be selected. For example, if you copied formatted text from a word processing program, select Formatted Text (RTF).

8. Click on **OK**. The selected items will be embedded into your presentation.

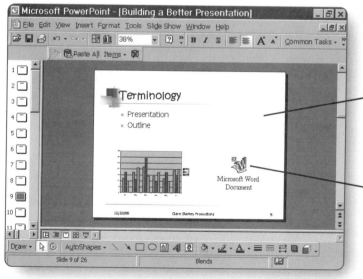

Modifying a Linked or Embedded Object

1. Open the **slide** that contains the linked or embedded object you want to modify. The slide will appear in the Slide view.

2. Double-click on the **object**. The object will appear in the program in which it was created. For some Office programs, a small window in which you can make your changes will appear on the slide.

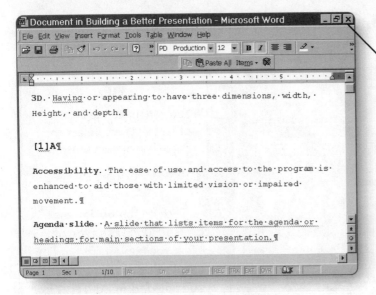

3. **Make changes** as needed.

4. **Click** on the **Close button** (☒) to close the program that opened to allow you to modify the object. The program will close and the object on the slide will be changed.

NOTE

If a window opened on the slide in which you made the changes, click outside the window to close it.

Part IV Review Questions

1. *What is the easiest way to read through comments placed on various slides? See "Commenting on a Presentation" in Chapter 14*

2. *Is it possible to make voice comments rather than written comments on a slide? See "Commenting on a Presentation" in Chapter 14*

3. *Can you e-mail a single slide in a presentation? See "Sharing the Presentation with Reviewers" in Chapter 14*

4. *When would you create a routing list? See "Sharing the Presentation with Reviewers" in Chapter 14*

5. *How does one person on a routing list send the presentation to the next person on the routing list? See "Sharing the Presentation with Reviewers" in Chapter 14*

6. *How many items can you place on the Office Clipboard? See "Cutting and Pasting from the Clipboard" in Chapter 15*

7. *Can you copy text without copying the text formatting? See "Formatting Data When Pasting" in Chapter 15*

8. *What is the fastest way to move data between applications? See "Dragging and Dropping between Applications" in Chapter 15*

9. *What is the difference between a linked object and an embedded object? See "Linking and Embedding Documents" in Chapter 15*

10. *Can you use an icon to represent an embedded object rather than display the object itself? See "Linking and Embedding Documents" in Chapter 15*

PART V

Completing Your Presentation

16

Adding the Final Touches to Your Presentation

You've finished creating the presentation. It's now time to add a few items that will help you when you deliver your presentation. If you'll be delivering the presentation in front of an audience, you'll want to use notes and handouts. You'll also need to practice. To help answer potential questions from the audience, you may want to hide a few slides up your sleeve. Self-running presentations (such as kiosks) that use voice-over narration are more effective than those without accompanying sounds. In this chapter, you'll learn how to:

- Prepare notes and handouts for your use and to give to your audience
- Use hidden slides to your advantage
- Rehearse and set timings
- Narrate a presentation

Using Notes and Handouts

When you're giving a presentation, cue cards and handouts are a handy item. They not only help relieve anxiety caused by stage fright (your audience will be looking at the handouts and not you) but also enhance a presentation. You can develop notes and print them with a copy of the slide. You can use the notes to help keep your presentation on course. To provide an audience with more information, print a notes page that your audience can take home. Or, print the entire set of slides as handouts.

Adding Notes to a Slide

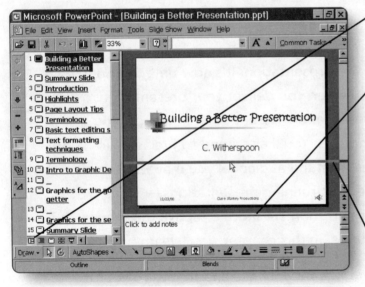

1. **Click** on the **Normal View button**. Your slide will appear Normal view.

2. **Click and drag** the **bar** up to the middle between the Slide pane and the Notes pane. The mouse pointer will turn into a double arrow, and an outline of the bar will show how the pane size will be changed.

3. **Release** the **mouse button**. The two panes will be resized, and you'll have more room with which to work in the Notes pane.

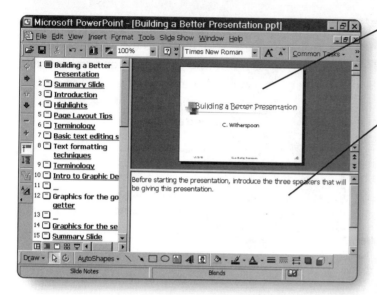

4. Display the **slide** to which you want to add the notes. The slide will appear in the Slide pane.

5. Type notes as desired. These notes can be anything that will help you remember what you need to say, or provide additional background if it is needed during the presentation.

TIP

When a presentation is displayed as Web pages, notes can be shown on a page along with the corresponding slide.

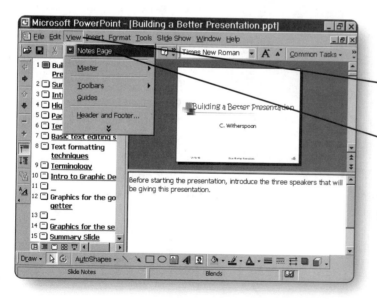

Using Images with Your Notes

1. Click on **View**. The View menu will appear.

2. Click on **Notes Page**. The Notes page for the slide will appear. This is actually a preview of what the Notes page will look like when printed.

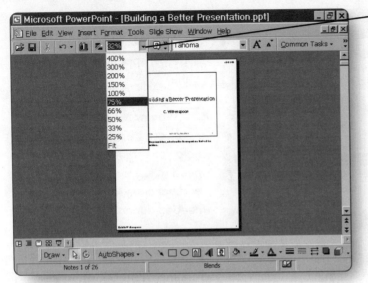

3. Click on the **down arrow** (▼) next to the Zoom button and select a magnification level. You may want to see the notes section of the Notes page better.

TIP

You can also format the text in the notes section.

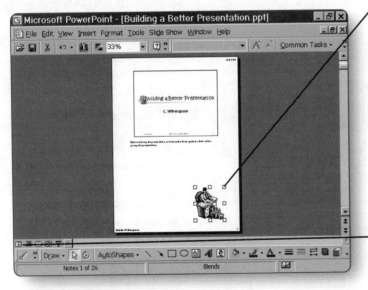

4. Insert an **image or other object** into the notes section. You can add any item to the notes section, as you can to a slide. Part III, "Enhancing Your Presentation," showed you how to insert clip art, pictures stored on your computer, drawing objects, tables, and charts into a slide. You can do the same on the Notes page.

5. Click on the **Normal View button**. The selected slide will appear in the Normal view. You won't see the images that you added to the Notes Page in the Notes pane.

Working with the Notes Master

You worked with the Slide Master in Chapter 8, "Customizing Your Presentation." Like the Slide Master, the Notes Master is where you can set the basic format and look for all the Notes pages in your presentation.

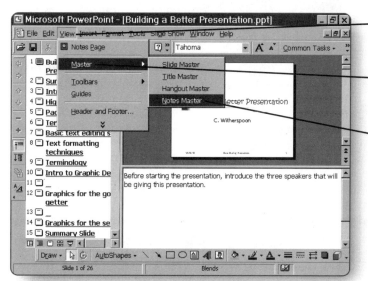

1. Click on **View**. The View menu will appear.

2. Click on **Master**. A submenu will appear.

3. Click on **Notes Master**. The Notes Master page will appear. There are six different elements on the Notes Master that you can change: Header, Date, Notes Body, Footer, and Number areas. You can also change the size of the slide.

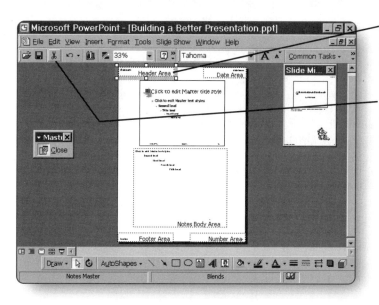

4. To remove an area from the Notes Master, **click** on the **area**. The area will be selected.

5. Click on the **Cut button**. The area will not appear on the Notes pages.

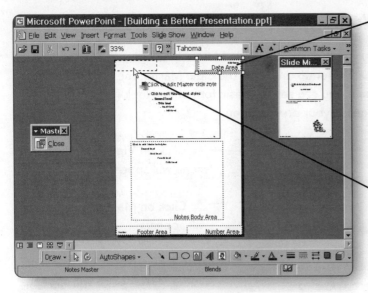

6. To move an area, **click and drag** the **mouse pointer** to the location where you want to place the area. The mouse pointer will turn into a four-pointed arrowhead and an outline of the area will show you the selected position.

7. **Release** the **mouse button**. The area will move to the new location.

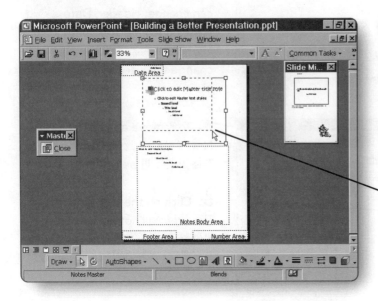

8. To change the size of an area box (including the slide), **click** on the **area** to select it, and click and drag an image handle in the direction that you want to size the area. The mouse pointer will turn into a double arrow, and an outline will show the new size.

9. **Release** the **mouse button**. The area box will be resized.

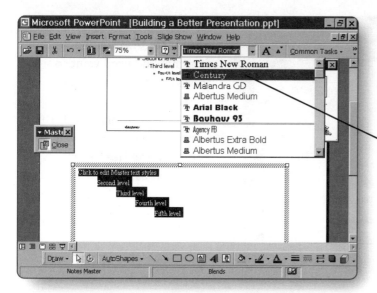

10. To apply new text styles to the text that appears on the Notes Pages, **select** the **text** that you want to reformat. The text will be highlighted.

11. Apply the desired **formatting** changes. You can change the font style and size, as well as add attributes like bold and italic.

TIP

If you want an image, such as a company logo, to appear on all the Notes pages, insert the logo onto the Notes Master.

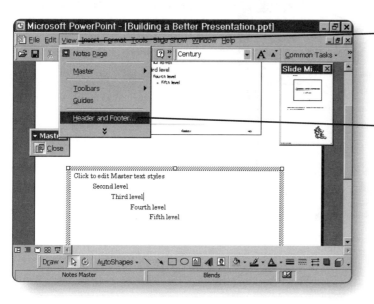

1. Click on **View** to add information to the Header and Footer areas. The View menu will appear.

2. Click on **Header and Footer**. The Header and Footer dialog box will open, and the Notes and Handouts tab will be on top.

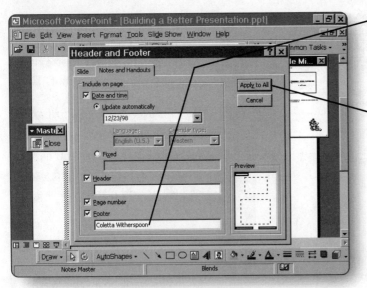

3. Click in the **Header and Footer text boxes** and type the text that you want to appear in those areas.

4. Click on **Apply to All**. The information you typed will appear in the Header and Footer areas.

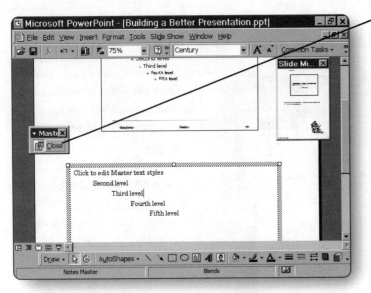

5. Click on the **Close button** on the Master toolbar when you finish making changes to the Notes Master. You will return to the view you were using previously.

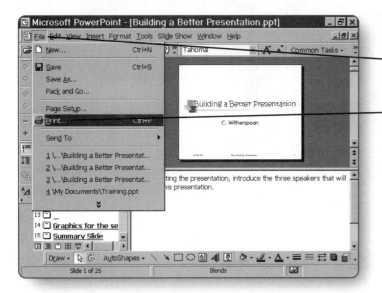

Printing Your Notes

1. **Click** on **File**. The File menu will appear.

2. **Click** on **Print**. The Print dialog box will open.

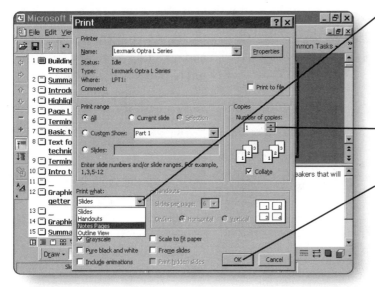

3. **Click** on the **down arrow** (⬜) next to the Print what: list box and click on Notes Pages. The option will appear in the list box.

4. **Change** any **other options** as needed.

5. **Click** on **OK**. The Notes pages will be printed.

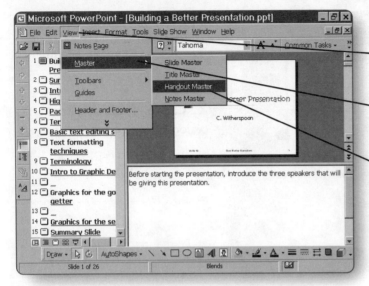

Printing Handouts

1. Click on **View**. The View menu will appear.

2. Click on **Master**. A submenu will appear.

3. Click on **Handout Master**. The Handout Master will appear. The Handout Master can help you decide how you want the printed pages to appear.

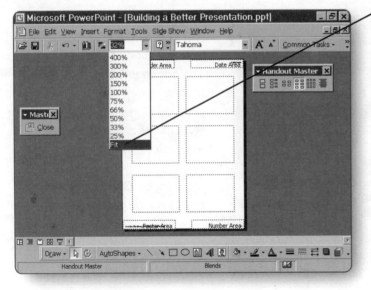

4. Click on the **down arrow** (⏷) next to the Zoom list box and click on Fit to view the entire page on your screen. The entire page will appear.

NOTE

If you don't see the Handout Master toolbar or the Master toolbar, right click on any toolbar and select them from the list of toolbars.

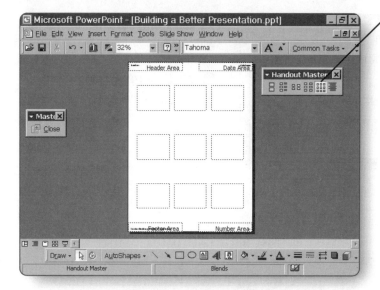

5. Click on a **button** on the Handout Master toolbar. You will have the option to print two, three, four, six, or nine slides per page. You can also use this view to print an outline of the presentation. The number of slides that will appear on the Handout pages will change.

TIP

To change the look of the Handout Master, you can change the various elements on the Handout Master just as you can with the Slide and Notes Masters.

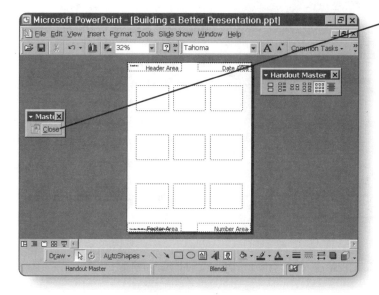

6. Click on the **Close button** on the Master toolbar when you have decided on the look you want to use for your handouts. The presentation will appear in the previous view in which you were working.

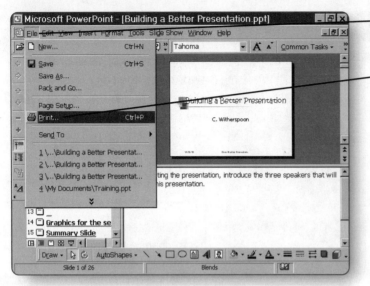

7. **Click** on **File**. The File menu will appear.

8. **Click** on **Print**. The Print dialog box will open.

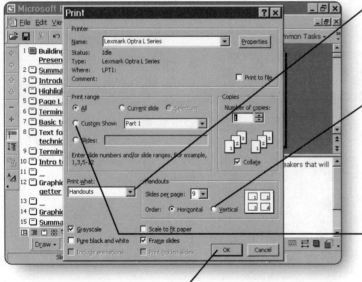

9. **Click** the **down arrow** (▾) next to the Print what: list box and click on Handouts. The option will appear in the list box.

10. **Click** on the **Vertical option button** to change the orientation of the printed page. The option will be selected, and the orientation of the slides on the page will be changed.

11. **Change** any **other options** as needed.

12. **Click** on **OK**. The handouts will be printed.

Using Hidden Slides

Sometime during a presentation, you'll probably receive questions from your audience. Before you deliver your presentation, try to anticipate some of the questions you'll be asked. Make slides that will answer the questions, or maybe provide additional background information in the notes. Your audience will think that you're brilliant!

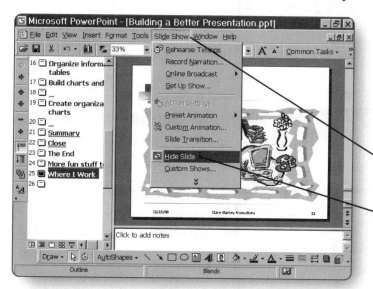

Hiding a Slide

1. Display the **slide** that you want hidden in the Normal or Slide views. The slide will appear in the Slide view.

2. Click on **Slide Show**. The Slide Show menu will appear.

3. Click on **Hide Slide**. The slide will be hidden until you ask for it during your slide show.

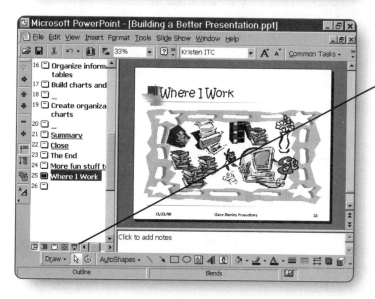

Using Hidden Slides During a Slide Show.

1. Click on the **Slide Show button**. A Slide show of the screens in your presentation will begin.

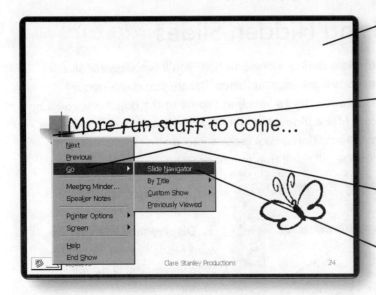

2. Move through the **slide show**. The presentation slides will display in the Slide Show.

3. When you want to display a hidden slide, **right-click** on the **slide** that is showing. A shortcut menu will appear.

4. Click on **Go**. A submenu will appear.

5. Click on **Slide Navigator**. The Slide Navigator dialog box will open.

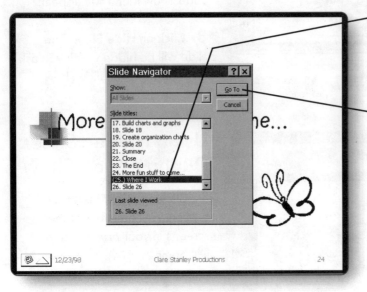

6. Click on the **hidden slide** that you want to view. A number in parenthesis indicates a hidden slide. The slide will be selected.

7. Click on **Go To**. The hidden slide will appear during the slide show.

Rehearsing for the Slide Show

Practice, practice, practice. Be prepared. These and other sayings that we heard repeatedly in our younger years are still good advice today. One way to make sure that your presentation fits within an allotted time frame is to set timings to each slide. You have two choices: 1) you can go through the list of slides and set an amount of time that each slide will display, applying a specific amount of time to a single slide or group of slides; 2) you can set the slide timing while you rehearse the slide show.

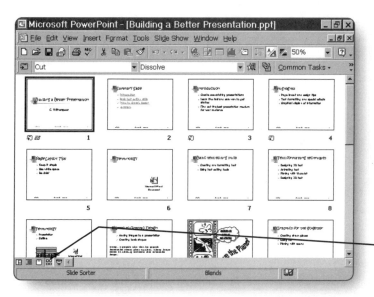

Applying Slide Show Timing to Selected Slides

1. Click on the **Slide Sorter View button**. The presentation will appear in the Slide Sorter view.

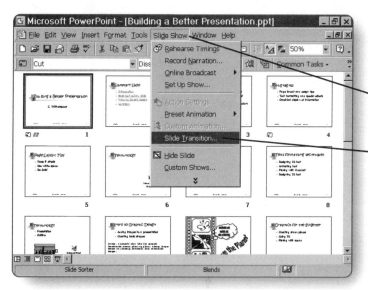

2. Select the **slides** to which you want to set the timing. The slides will be selected.

3. Click on **Slide Show**. The Slide Show menu will appear.

4. Click on **Slide Transition**. The Slide Transition dialog box will open.

5. Click in the **Automatically after check box**. A ✓ will appear in the box, and the time in the text box will be selected.

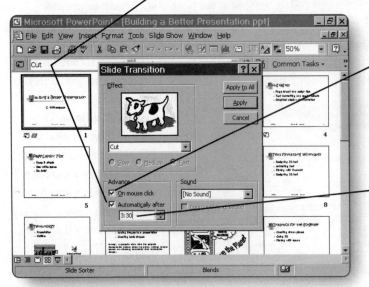

TIP

To preserve the ability to advance through a slide show using the mouse, leave a ✓ in the On mouse click check box.

6. Type the number of **minutes or seconds** that you want the slide to display on the screen before the next screen appears.

7. Click on **Apply**. The timing will be applied to the selected slides.

You'll notice that the timing appears below the slide. If you want to change this timing, right-click on the slide and select Slide Transition from the shortcut menu that appears.

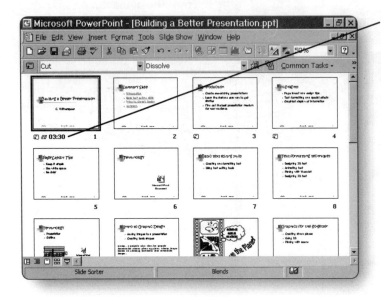

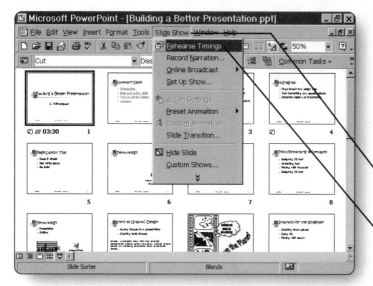

Setting the Timing While You Rehearse

1. Click on the **first slide** that you want to appear when you start the slide show. The slide will be selected.

2. Click on **Slide Show**. The Slide Show menu will appear.

3. Click on **Rehearse Timings**. The slide show will start with the selected slide, and the Rehearsal toolbar will appear on the screen.

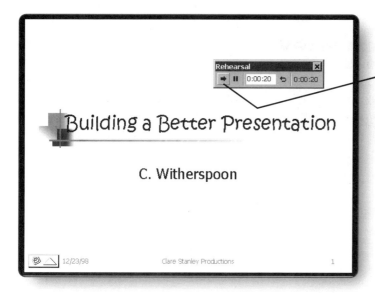

4. Practice your **delivery** for the first slide.

5. When you have finished with the first slide, **click** on the **Next button** on the Rehearsal toolbar. The time spent on the first slide will be recorded, and PowerPoint will begin tracking the timing for the second slide.

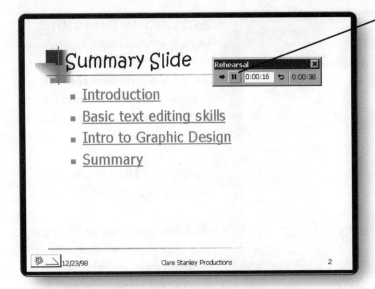

6. Click on the **Pause button** if you need to take a break from the rehearsal. The timer will stop until you are ready to begin again.

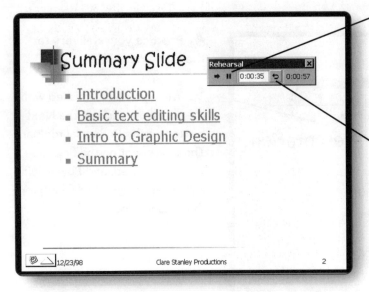

7. Click again on the **Pause button**. The time will begin recording at the place where you left off.

TIP

If you want to erase the time spent on a slide and start the timing over for the slide, click on the Repeat button. The time counter will be cleared, and you can start over with the rehearsal for the slide.

9. Click on the **Close button** (⊠) on the Rehearsal toolbar when you finish rehearsing the last slide. The slide show will close, and a confirmation dialog box will open.

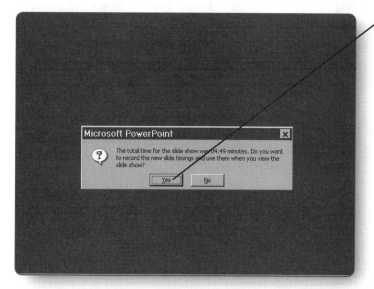

10. Click on **Yes**. Your timings will be applied to each slide in the presentation.

Adding Voice-Over Narration

Voice-over narration works great in presentations for which a live speaker will not be present. If the presentation will be used on the Internet or your company intranet, narration can take the place of the speaker. You might also want to record the actual presentation so that you have a permanent record. If you will be showing the presentation in a kiosk (on an unattended computer that runs a presentation on a continuous basis), you might want to consider narration.

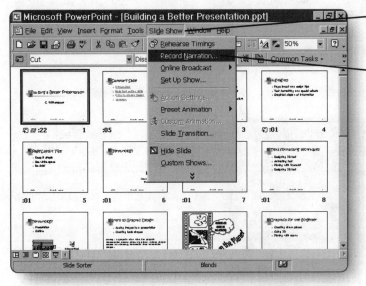

1. **Click** on **Slide Show**. The Slide Show menu will appear.

2. **Click** on **Record Narration**. The Record Narration dialog box will open. Be sure to make a note of your free disk space and how long you can record.

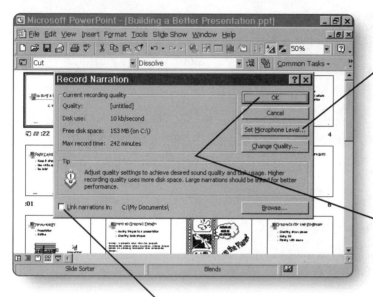

NOTE

If this is the first time you'll be using this feature, click on the Set Microphone Level button and follow the wizard instructions.

3. Click on **OK**. The slide show will start and you can begin recording.

TIP

You can link the narration to the presentation file. Place a ✓ in the Link narrations in: check box. Change the location of the narration file by clicking on the Browse button.

4. Work your way **through the presentation** until you come to the end of the presentation. The screen will go black, and a confirmation dialog box will appear.

TIP

You can pause the narration. Right-click on a slide show screen and select Pause Narration. Start again by right-clicking and selecting Resume Narration.

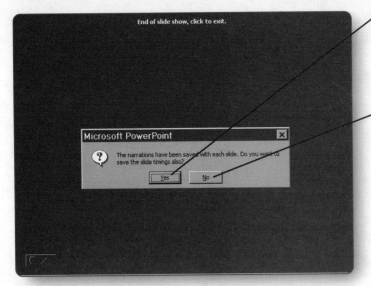

4a. Click on **Yes**. The timing of the slide show will be saved along with the narration.

OR

4b. Click on **No**. Only the narration will be saved.

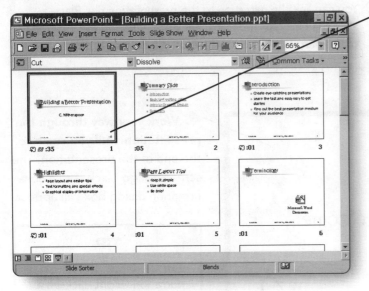

You'll see a sound icon located at the bottom-right corner of each slide. To listen to the narration, double-click on the icon.

17

Delivering Your Presentation

When you first started building your presentation, you probably had a good idea how you wanted to deliver it. You probably told the AutoContent wizard just how you wanted to do this. Even if you set up a presentation one way, this doesn't mean that you can't change your mind later. Or maybe you need multiple options for delivering the presentation. In this chapter, you'll learn how to:

- Change a color presentation to grayscale
- Select a different method of displaying a slide show
- Use the Pack and Go wizard to display a presentation wherever you need

Working in Shades of Gray

You've created a great-looking presentation, in color of course, and now you need to distribute paper copies. If you can only print your presentation in black and white, you'll still want your presentation to look good. PowerPoint will automatically convert your presentation to *grayscale*. You can then go through and adjust any images that may not print clearly.

> **NOTE**
>
> When you convert a color picture to grayscale, the darkest areas of the picture will be black, lighter colors will turn to shades of gray (depending on the darkness of the color), and areas of white or very pale color will contain no color.

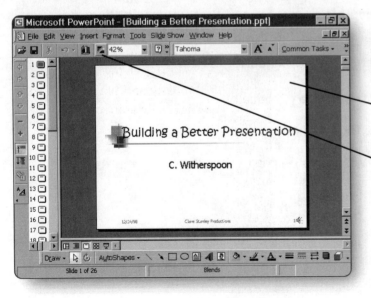

Converting Color Slides into Grayscale

1. Open the **presentation** in Slide view or Normal view.

2. Click on the **Grayscale Preview button** on the Standard toolbar. The displayed slide will turn from color to various shades of gray.

3. Navigate to a **slide** that contains an object that doesn't appear correctly. The slide will display in the view.

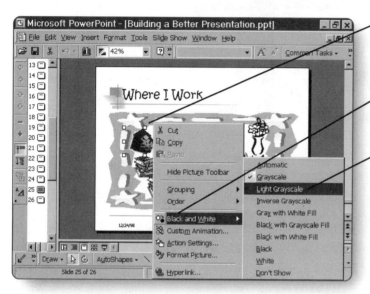

4. Right-click on the **object** that you want to adjust. A shortcut menu will appear.

5. Click on **Black and White**. A submenu will appear.

6. Click on an **option** to change the color of the selected object. If an image is too dark and you want to lighten it, select Light Grayscale or Inverse Grayscale. The selected Black and White command will be applied to the object.

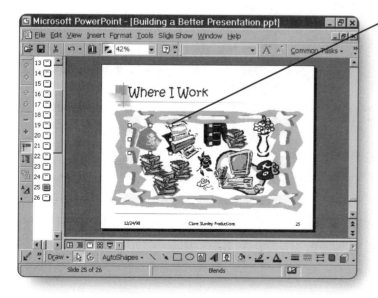

7. If you do not like the enhancement that was made to the image, **right-click** to reopen the **Black and White menu** and select a different option.

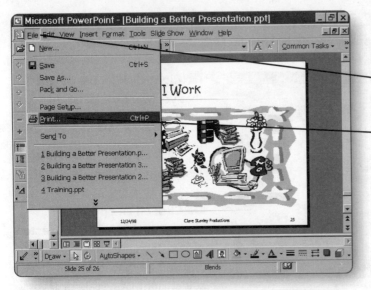

Printing Slides in Grayscale

1. Click on **File**. The File menu will appear.

2. Click on **Print**. The Print dialog box will open.

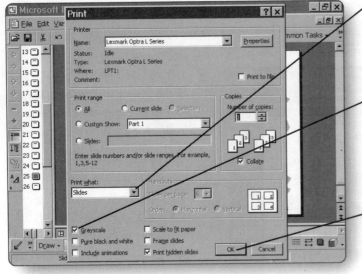

3. Click the **down arrow** (⬝) next to the Print what: list box and click on Slides. The option will appear in the list box.

4. Click in the **Grayscale check box**. A ✓ will appear in the box.

5. Change other **options** as needed.

6. Click on **OK**. The slides will print.

TIP

To change slides back to color, click on the Grayscale Preview button (it's located on the Standard toolbar, and is a box that is divided across the diagonal with the top being a color pattern and the bottom a black and white pattern). You'll notice that changes you made to an image in the Grayscale Preview mode have no effect on the color image.

Setting Up the Slide Show

Regarding control when running a slide show, you have three options. You can give complete control to the speaker who advances through the slides, makes notes on slides, or records narration. You can give control to your audience, who watches the presentation over the Internet or a company network. Your last option is to have the presentation run unattended (as in a kiosk) in a continuous loop.

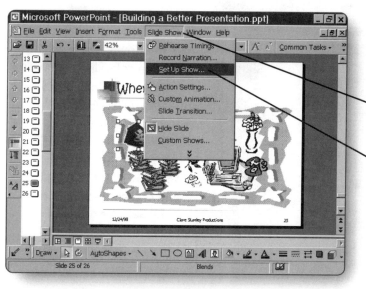

Using a Speaker to Deliver a Presentation

1. Click on **Slide Show**. The Slide Show menu will appear.

2. Click on **Set Up Show**. The Set Up Show dialog box will open.

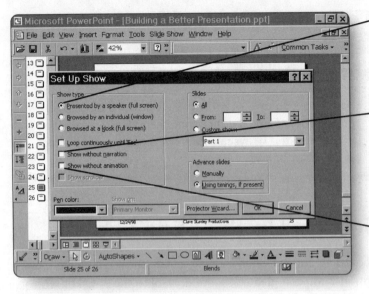

3. Click on the **Presented by a speaker (full screen) option button**. The option will be selected.

4. Click in the **Show without narration check box** if you added narration to the presentation but do not wish to use it. A ✓ will appear in the box.

5. Click in the **Show without animation check box** if you applied slide transitions or animations and do not want to display them in the presentation. A ✓ will appear in the box.

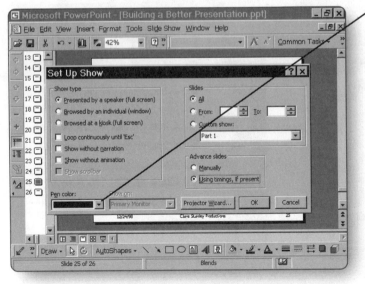

6. If you use the pen to draw on slides during the show and want to change the pen color, **Click** the **down arrow** (▾) next to the Pen color: list box and click on a color. The color will appear in the list box.

NOTE

You don't have to use all of a presentation all the time. Select a group of slides in a presentation to use as a slide show.

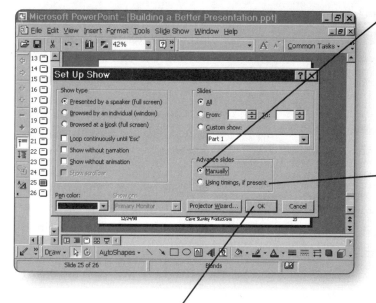

7a. Click on the **Manually option button** if you want the speaker to click on a slide in order to advance to the next slide. The option will be selected.

OR

7b. Click on the **Using timings, if present option button** to have the presentation use the timings that you set to advance through the slides. The option will be selected.

8. Click on **OK**. You can now view this slide show by clicking on the Slide Show button or by pressing the F5 key.

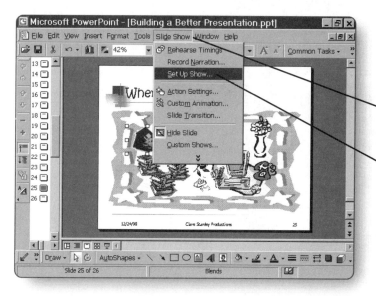

Allowing an Audience to Browse a Presentation

1. Click on **Slide Show**. The Slide Show menu will appear.

2. Click on **Set Up Show**. The Set Up Show dialog box will open.

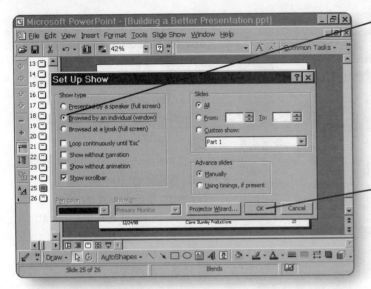

3. Click on the **Browsed by an individual (window) option button**. The option will be selected.

4. Change any **other options** as needed. The options will be selected.

5. Click on **OK**. When you run the slide show, the presentation will appear in the PowerPoint viewer.

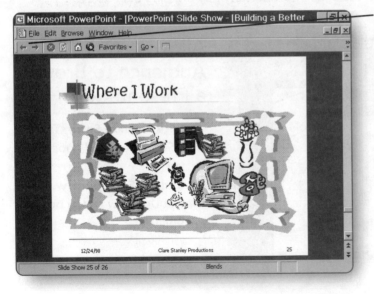

The viewer contains controls for moving back and forth in a presentation, copying slides, printing, and accessing the Internet.

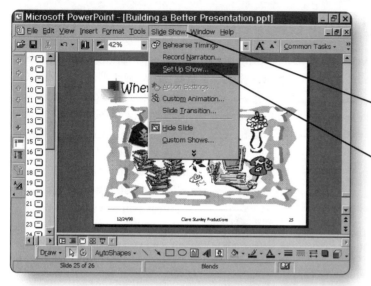

Setting Up a Self-Running Presentation

1. Click on **Slide Show**. The Slide Show menu will appear.

2. Click on **Set Up Show**. The Set Up Show dialog box will open.

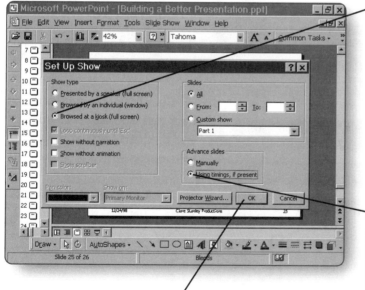

3. Click on the **Browsed at kiosk (full screen) option button**. The option will be selected.

4. Change any **options** as needed. The options will be selected.

TIP

If you run your presentation at a kiosk, you'll want to advance slides using timings.

---

5. Click on **OK**. Your presentation is now ready to run unattended.

Using the Pack and Go Wizard

If you'll be displaying the presentation on a variety of computers, you'll want to consider the Pack and Go wizard. The Pack and Go wizard can make a copy of your presentation along with a viewer, the fonts, and any linked files, to a diskette, CD-ROM, or network drive. No matter which computer you use to display the presentation, it will look as you originally formatted it. You don't even need to worry if the computer you will use has the appropriate programs or viewers to display the presentation. Your presentation is a self-contained traveling show.

Packing a Presentation

1. Click on **File**. The File menu will appear.

2. Click on **Pack and Go**. The Pack and Go wizard will open, and the Start page of the wizard will appear.

3. Click on **Next**. The Pick files to pack page of the wizard will appear.

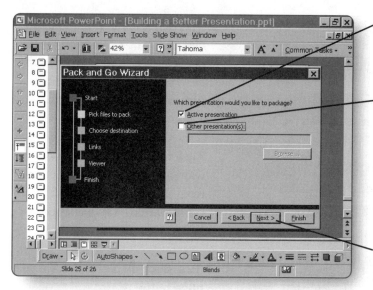

4. Make sure that there is a ✓ in the **Active presentation check box**.

5. If you want to pack other presentations along with the open presentation, **Click** in the **Other presentation(s): check box** and type the path and filename of the other presentations.

6. Click on **Next**. The Choose destination page of the wizard will appear.

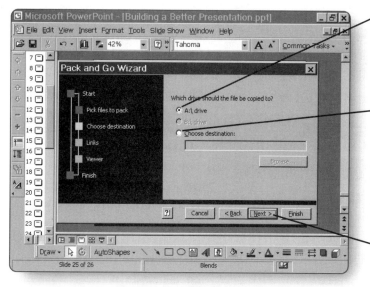

7. Click on the **A:\ drive option button** to save the presentation to a floppy disk. The option will be selected.

8. To save the presentation to another location, **Click** on the **Choose destination: option button** and type the directory path where you want to store the packed presentation.

9. Click on **Next**. The Links page of the wizard will display.

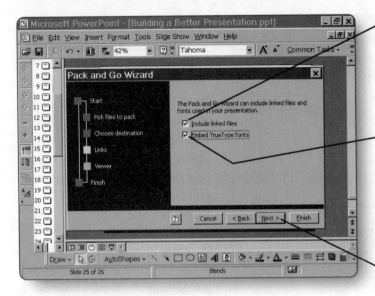

10. Click in the **Include linked files check box** to add to the packed presentation any files that are linked to the presentation. A ✓ will appear in the box.

11. Click in the **Embed True Type fonts check box** if you want any fonts that you applied to text to be packed with the presentation. A ✓ will appear in the box.

12. Click on **Next**. The Viewer page of the wizard will appear.

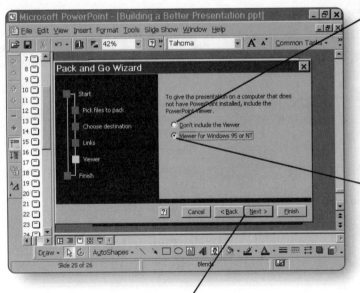

13. Click on the **Don't include the Viewer option button** if the person who will be unpacking and looking at the presentation has PowerPoint and does not need a separate viewer to see the presentation. The option will be selected.

14. Click on the **Viewer for Windows 95 or NT option button** if the person will need a means for viewing the presentation. The option will be selected.

15. Click on **Next**. The Finish page of the wizard will appear.

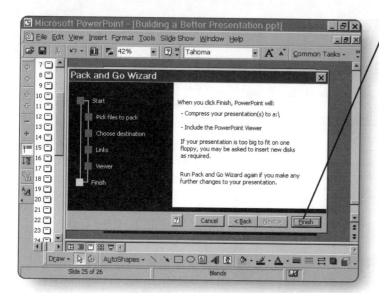

16. Click on **Finish**. The Pack and Go Status dialog box will open, and your presentation will be packed away to the destination you specified. When the process is complete, a confirmation dialog box will appear.

NOTE

If you pack your presentation onto floppy disks, you may need more than one disk.

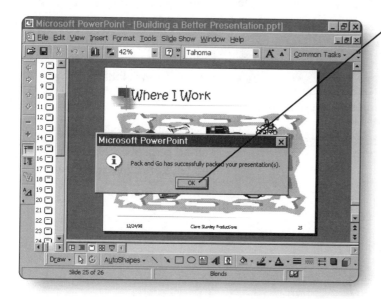

17. Click on **OK**. You're now ready to pass that presentation along to others for their viewing pleasure.

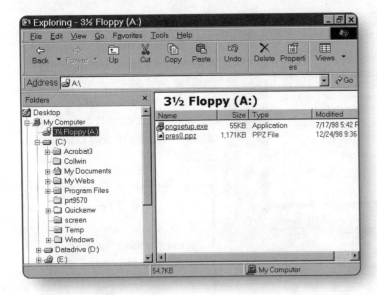

Unpacking a Presentation

1a. **Insert** the **disk or CD** onto which you packed the presentation in the computer where you want to unpack the presentation. The disk or CD will be in the drive.

OR

1b. **Connect** to the **network** where the packed presentation is stored. A connection to the network will be made.

2. Open Windows Explorer. Windows Explorer will appear.

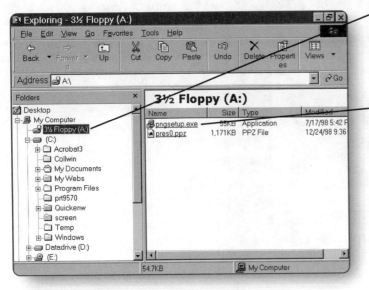

3. Navigate to the **drive and folder** where the packed presentation is located. The drive and folder will be selected.

4. Double-click on the file named **pngsetup.exe**. The Pack and Go Setup dialog box will open.

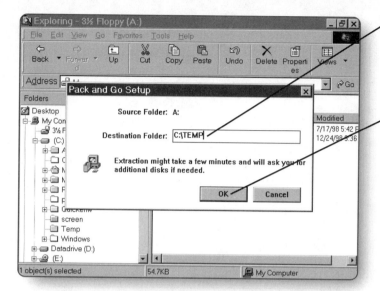

5. **Type** the **drive and path** where you want to store the presentation in the Destination Folder: text box.

6. **Click** on **OK**. The presentation will unpack to the specified directory. When the process is finished, a confirmation dialog box will open.

7. **Click** on **Yes**. The presentation will open.

TIP

You can run the slide show at a later time. Just open the folder where you unpacked the presentation. Right-click on the presentation (it's the one with the .ppt extension) and click on Show.

18

Preparing Your Presentation for the Web

One way to share your presentation with a large number of people who may be scattered over a large area is to publish it on the World Wide Web. Before you publish your presentation, you may want to add a few Web elements, such as hyperlinks. If your audience is familiar with browsing the Internet, these additions will make it easier for them to navigate through the presentation. In this chapter, you'll learn how to:

- Make a GIF image from a slide
- Create hyperlinks and other navigation controls
- Get your presentation ready for the Web
- Publish your Web presentation

Turning a Slide into a GIF Image

A popular file format used on the Internet for graphics is GIF (or Graphics Interchange Format). GIF images work well on Web pages; all browsers can display GIF files. Their small file size makes them a good choice for e-mail attachments. If recipients use an e-mail program that displays HTML format, they can view the GIF file from their mail program.

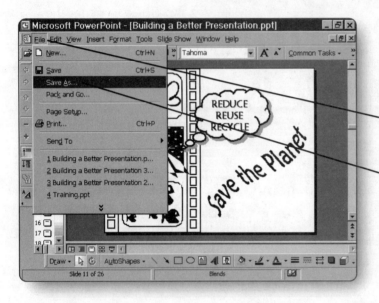

1. **Open** the **slide** that you want to save as a GIF image. The slide will appear in the Normal or Slide view.

2. **Click** on **File**. The File menu will appear.

3. **Click** on **Save As**. The Save As dialog box will open.

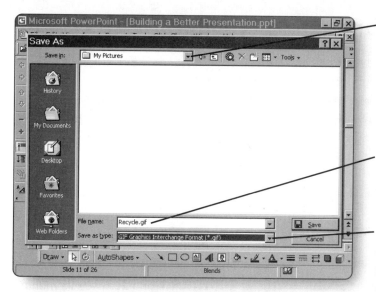

4. **Click** on the **down arrow** (▾) next to the Save in: list box, and click on the folder in which you want to store the GIF file. The folder will appear in the Save in: list box.

5. **Click** in the **File name: text box** and type a name for the GIF file.

6. **Click** on the **down arrow** (▾) next to the Save as type: list box and click on GIF Graphics Interchange Format. The option will appear in the list box.

7. **Click** on **Save**. A confirmation dialog box will open.

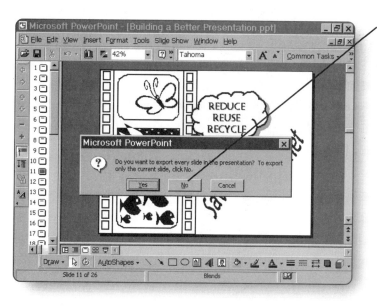

8. **Click** on **No**. Only the selected slide will be saved in the GIF format.

Designing Navigation Controls

Navigation controls help your audience move around inside your presentation and link to places outside your presentation. These controls can take the form of buttons that move your audience between slides. They can also be text or image hyperlinks that move the audience from slide to slide, or to someplace else on the Web.

Using Action Buttons to Navigate a Presentation

PowerPoint includes a number of navigation controls (called Action buttons) that make moving around a presentation easy. These buttons allow you to go to the first page of the presentation with a single click or move to the next or previous slide in the presentation. You can add navigation controls either to each individual slide or to the Slide Master. Action buttons placed on the Slide Master will appear on each slide.

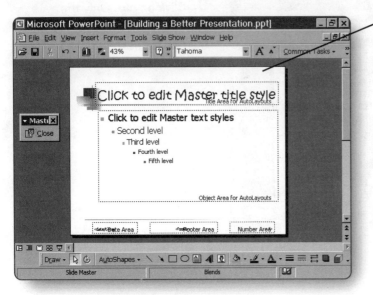

1. **Open** the **slide** on which you want to place the Action buttons. The slide will appear in the Slide view.

NOTE

For help with the Slide Master, see Chapter 8, "Customizing Your Presentation."

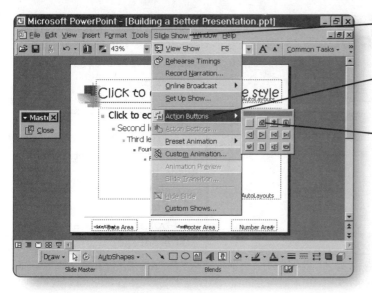

2. Click on **Slide Show**. The Slide Show menu will appear.

3. Click on **Action Buttons**. A submenu will appear.

4. Click on the **button** that you want to insert into the slide. The mouse pointer will turn into a crosshair.

NOTE

The most commonly used navigation buttons are the Home, Back, and Forward buttons.

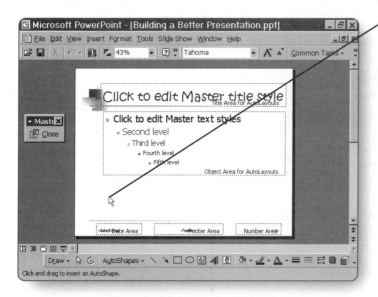

5. Click on the **slide** where you want to place the navigation button. The button will appear in a predefined size, and the Action Settings dialog box will open.

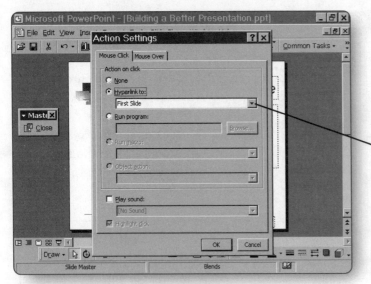

6. Click on **OK** to accept the default links. The button will be used as a hyperlink to the specified page.

TIP

If you want to change the slide that the button links to, click the down arrow next to the Hyperlink to: list box and select a different slide.

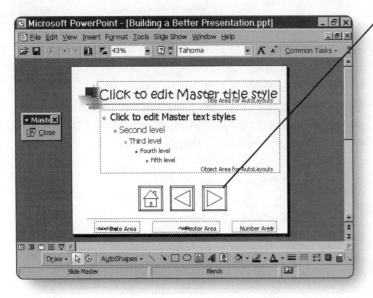

7. Add additional **Action buttons** to the slide as needed. The Action buttons will appear on the slide in the selected position.

NOTE

You can move, resize, and reshape Action buttons in much the same way as other images and shapes you place on a slide. See Chapter 9, "Adding Graphics to a Presentation" for help positioning and resizing images.

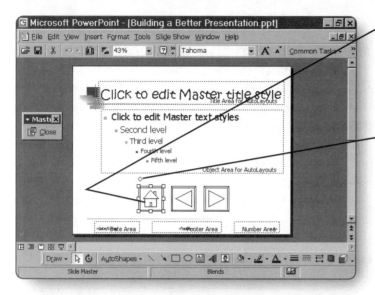

1. Click on the **button** to change the look of an Action button. The button will be selected, and a diamond will appear.

2. Click and drag the **diamond** to change the beveled-edge effect of the button.

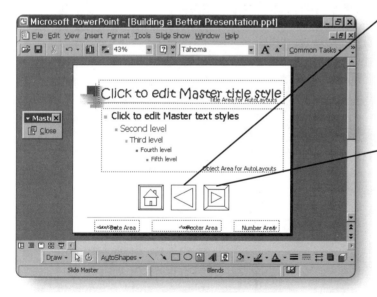

3a. Drag the **mouse pointer** to the left. The beveled edge will turn into a single line appearing around the button.

OR

3b. Drag the **mouse pointer** to the right. The beveled edge will become larger.

Creating a Hyperlink to Another Slide in the Presentation

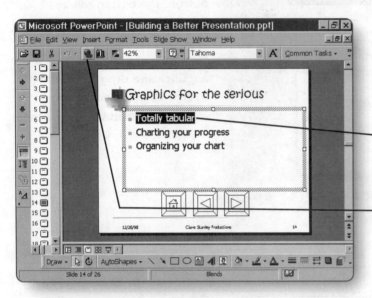

1. **Open** the **slide** onto which you want to place a hyperlink that links to another slide within the presentation. The slide will appear in Normal or Slide view.

2. **Select** the **text** that you want to use as the hyperlink. The text will be selected.

3. **Click** on the **Insert Hyperlink button**. The Insert Hyperlink dialog box will open.

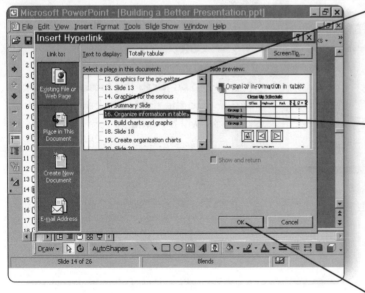

4. **Click** on the **Place in This Document button** found in the Link to: list. A list of slides found in the presentation will appear in the center of the dialog box.

5. **Click** on the **slide** in the Select a place in this document: list box that you want to appear when a visitor clicks on the hyperlink. The slide will be selected, and a preview of the slide will appear in the Slide preview: box.

6. **Click** on **OK**. The hyperlink will be created.

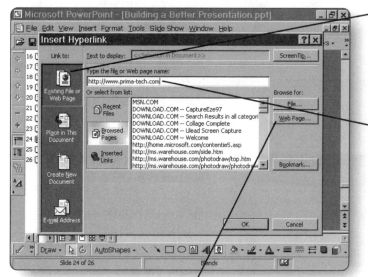

Creating Hyperlinks to Web Sites

1. Open the **slide** into which you want to place the hyperlink. The slide will appear in Normal or Slide view.

2. Select the **text or image** that will be used as the hyperlink. The text will be selected.

3. Click on the **Insert Hyperlink button**. The Insert Hyperlink dialog box will open.

4. Click on the **Existing File or Web page button** in the Link to: list. The dialog box will change to allow you to enter a Web page URL address.

5. Click in the **Type the file or Web page name: text box** and type the URL address of the Web page to which you want to create the hyperlink.

6. Click on **OK**. The hyperlink will be created.

TIP

If you don't know the URL address, and if it's a page you visited recently using your Web browser, click on the Browsed Pages button and select from the list. You can also click on the Web Page button and connect to the Internet.

Creating an E-mail Hyperlink

To give your audience an easy way to contact you, place an e-mail hyperlink on one of the slides. When people click on the e-mail hyperlink, a new message window will open from their default e-mail program. Your e-mail address (or any other address you specify) will appear in the To: field. They just need to type a message and send it to you.

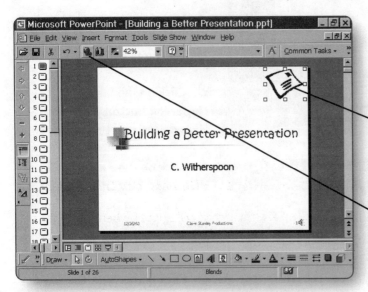

1. Open the **page** where you want to place the e-mail hyperlink. The page will appear in Slide or Normal view.

2. Select the **text or image** that you want to use as the e-mail hyperlink. The item will be selected.

3. Click on the **Insert Hyperlink button**. The Insert Hyperlink dialog box will open.

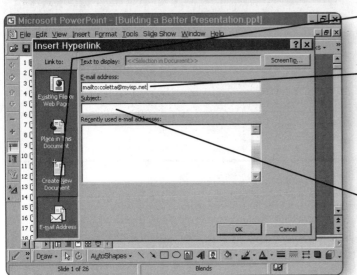

4. Click on the **E-mail Address button** in the Link to: list.

5. Click in the **E-mail address: text box** and type the e-mail address to which you want to create the link.

NOTE

If you want e-mail sent from this link to contain a specific message header, type it in the Subject: text box.

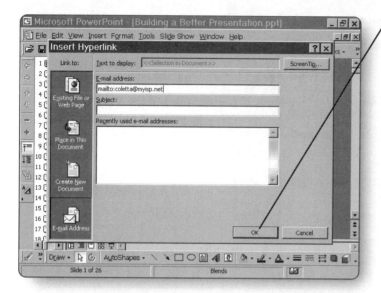

6. Click on **OK**. The e-mail hyperlink will be created.

Adding Special Effects to Hyperlinks

You can add special effects that will appear when the mouse pointer is held over a hyperlink. You can turn a hyperlink into a different color and have a sound play.

1. Right-click on the **hyperlink** to which you want to add the effect. A shortcut menu will appear.

2. Click on **Action Settings**. The Action Settings dialog box will open.

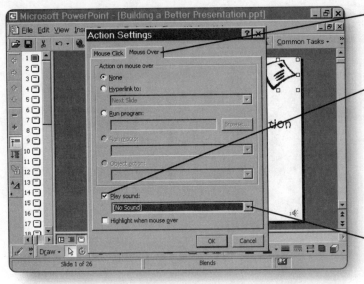

3. **Click** on the **Mouse Over tab**. The Mouse Over tab will move to the front.

4. **Click** in the **Play sound: check box** if you want a sound to play when the mouse pointer is held over the hyperlink. A ✓ will appear in the box, and you will be able to select from a list of sounds.

5. **Click** on the **down arrow** (▼) next to the Play sound: list box. A list of sounds will appear.

6. **Click** on a **sound**. The sound will appear in the list box.

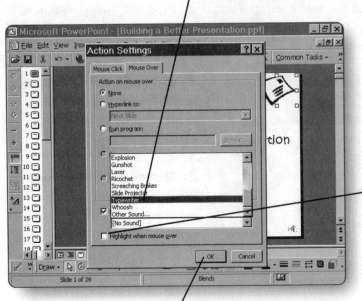

NOTE

If you have a sound stored on your computer that you would like to use, click on Other Sound in the Play sound: list box.

7. **Click** in the **Highlight when mouse over check box** if you want the hyperlink to change colors when the mouse pointer is held over it. A ✓ will appear in the box.

8. **Click** on **OK**. The effects will be applied to the hyperlink.

Using the Notes and Outline Panes in a Web Presentation

When you publish a presentation to the Web, the text and images you placed in the Outline and Notes panes will automatically appear as part of the Web presentation. You can use this information to help your audience navigate through your site and find other useful information.

Hiding the Notes and Outlines Panes

If you don't want to use the Notes and Outline panes, you can turn them off. The notes and outline won't appear when your audience views the presentation in a Web browser.

1. Click on **Tools**. The Tools menu will appear.

2. Click on **Options**. The Options dialog box will open.

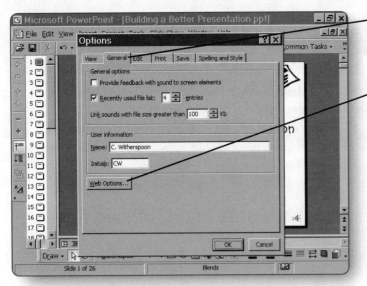

3. Click on the **General tab**. The General tab will move to the front.

4. Click on **Web Options**. The Web Options dialog box will open.

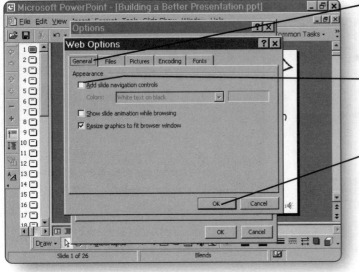

5. Click on the **General tab**. The General tab will move to the front.

6. Click in the **Add slide navigation controls check box**. The check box will be cleared.

7. Click on **OK**. The Options dialog box will appear.

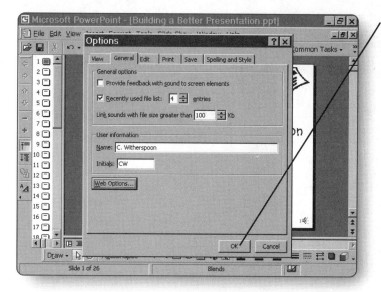

8. Click on **OK**. The notes and outline will not appear in the Web presentation.

Changing Background and Text Colors

If you do want to use the notes and outline in your Web presentation, you have the option of changing the colors of the text and background.

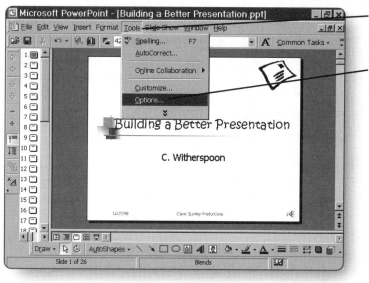

1. Click on **Tools**. The Tools menu will appear.

2. Click on **Options**. The Options dialog box will open.

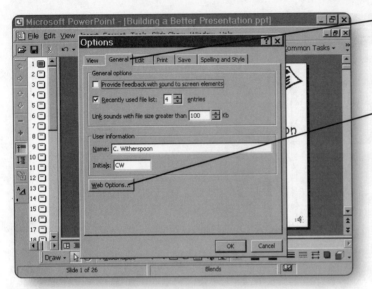

3. Click on the **General tab** if it is not already displayed. The General tab will move to the front.

4. Click on **Web Options**. The Web Options dialog box will open.

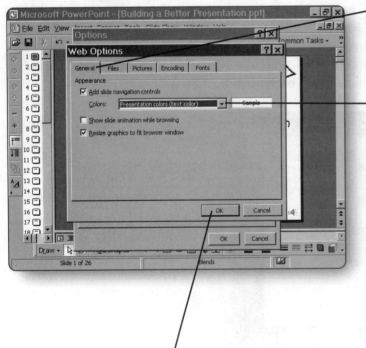

5. Click on the **General tab** if it is not already displayed. The General tab will move to the front.

6. Click on the **down arrow** (🔽) next to the Colors: list box and select a color scheme from the list. You'll see a preview of the selection to the right of the list box.

NOTE

If the Colors: list box is not available to you, place a ✓ in the Add slide navigation controls check box.

7. Click on **OK**. The Options dialog box will reappear.

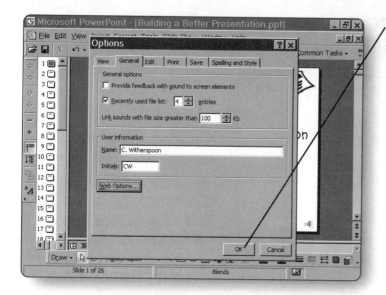

8. Click on **OK**. The colors selected for the text and background will be used when displayed in a Web browser.

Previewing the Presentation Before You Publish

Before you publish your presentation to the World Wide Web where everyone can see it, you'll want to see what it looks like when viewed from a Web browser.

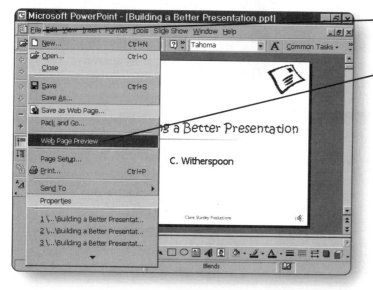

1. Click on **File**. The File menu will appear.

2. Click on **Web Page Preview**. The presentation will open in your default Web browser. If you're using Internet Explorer 5, an additional set of navigation controls will appear along the bottom of the window.

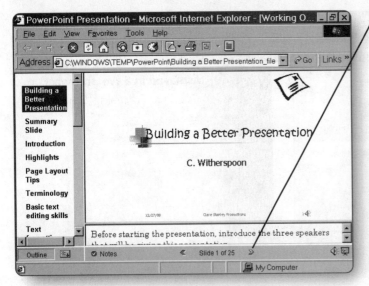

3. Navigate through the **presentation**. Check for navigation ease, spelling errors, and areas that could be improved.

4. Click on the **Close** (☒) **or Minimize** (▬) **button** to return to the presentation. The browser window will disappear from the screen.

Publishing the Presentation

When you're satisfied with how your presentation will work on the Web, it's time to publish it. Before you can publish your Web presentation, you'll need an account with an Internet Service Provider (ISP). Your ISP will give you the instructions you need to copy files to your Web space on their server.

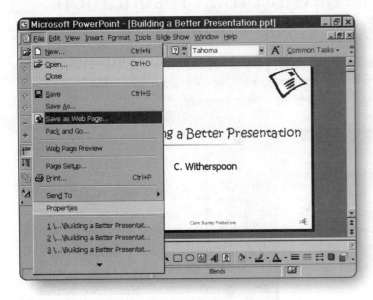

> ## NOTE
> You'll need to connect to your Internet Service Provider or other network before you can publish your Web presentation.

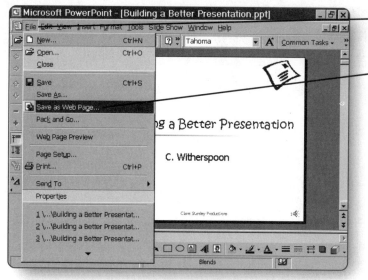

1. Click on **File**. The File menu will appear.

2. Click on **Save as Web Page**. The Save As dialog box will open.

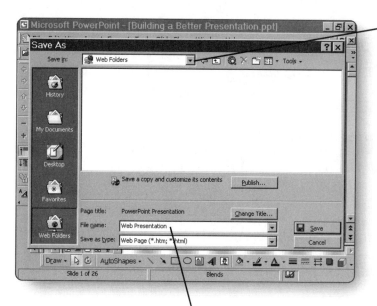

3. Click on the **down arrow** (▼) next to the Save in: list box, and click on the folder to which you want to publish the Web presentation. The folder will appear in the list box.

NOTE

If you haven't done so, you'll need to set up access to your ISP using the Add/Modify FTP Locations command in the Save in: list box.

4. Click in the **File name: text box** and type a different name for the Web presentation, if you want to distinguish your Web presentation from the original presentation.

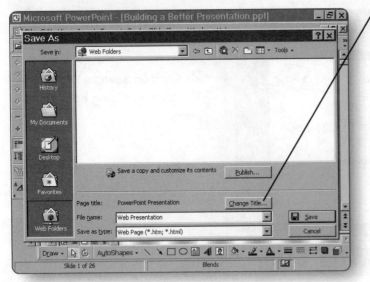

5. **Click** on the **Change Title button**. The Set Page Title dialog box will open.

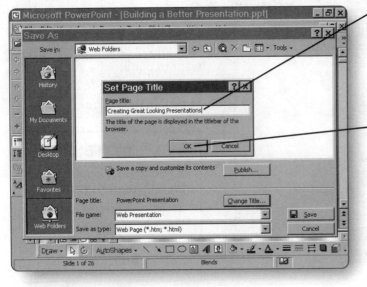

6. **Click** in the **Page title: text box** and type a title for the presentation. This title will appear in the title bar of the Web browser.

7. **Click** on **OK**. The Save As dialog box will reappear.

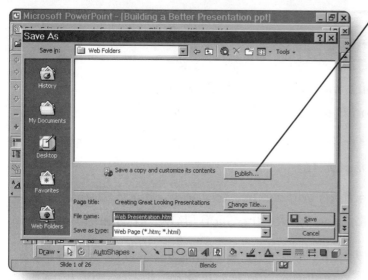

8. Click on **Publish**. The Publish as Web Page dialog box will open.

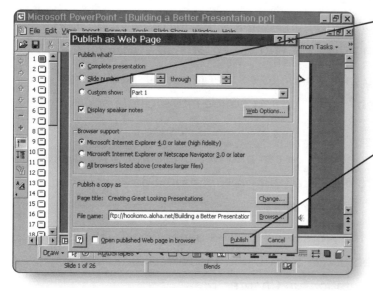

9. To only publish a part of the presentation, **Click** on either the **Slide number** or **Custom show option buttons** and select the slides you want to publish. The slides will be selected.

10. Click on **Publish**. Your presentation will be published to the location you specified.

Part V Review Questions

1. How do you customize the way handouts appear when printed? See "Using Notes and Handouts" in Chapter 16

2. Why would you want to hide slides in a presentation? See "Using Hidden Slides" in Chapter 16

3. What are the two methods you can use to apply timings to your presentation? See "Rehearsing for the Slide Show" in Chapter 16

4. How do you make sure a presentation looks as good in grayscale as it does in color? See "Working in Shades of Gray" in Chapter 17

5. What are the three options from which you can choose to run a slide show? See "Setting Up the Slide Show" in Chapter 17

6. How do you save a presentation so that you can display it on any computer? See "Using the Pack and Go Wizard" in Chapter 17

7. What format can you save a slide as so that it can be used more efficiently on the Web? See "Turning a Slide into a GIF Image" in Chapter 18

8. Name the different controls you can add to a presentation to make it easier for visitors to navigate your presentation. See "Designing Navigation Controls" in Chapter 18

9. Is it possible to hide the Notes and Outline panes when viewing the presentation as a Web page? See "Using the Notes and Outline Panes in a Web Presentation" in Chapter 18

10. How can you be sure your presentation will display on the Web in just the way you want? See "Previewing the Presentation Before You Publish" in Chapter 18

PART VI

Appendixes

A

Office 2000 Installation

Installing Office 2000 is typically very quick and easy. In this appendix, you'll learn how to:

- Install Office 2000 on your computer
- Choose which Office components you want to install
- Detect and repair problems
- Reinstall Office
- Add and remove components
- Uninstall Office 2000 completely
- Install content from other Office CDs

Installing the Software

The installation program for the Office 2000 programs is automatic. In most cases, you can simply follow the instructions onscreen.

> ## NOTE
>
> When you insert the Office 2000 CD for the first time, you may see a message that the installer has been updated, prompting you to restart your system. Do so, and when you return to Windows after restarting, remove the CD and reinsert it so that the Setup program starts up automatically again.

1. **Insert** the **Office 2000 CD-ROM** into your computer's CD-ROM drive. The Windows Installer will start and the Customer Information dialog box will open.

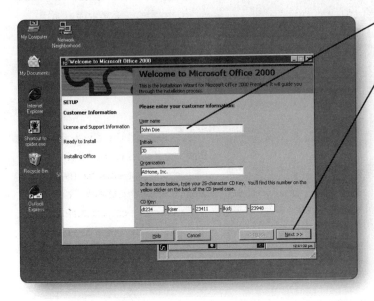

2. **Type** all of the **information** requested.

3. **Click** on **Next**. The End User License Agreement will appear.

> ## NOTE
>
> You'll find the CD Key number on a sticker on the back of the Office CD jewel case.

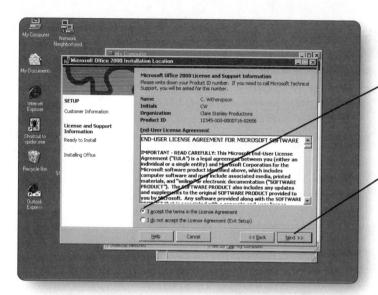

4. Read the **License Agreement**.

5. Click on the **I accept the terms in the License Agreement option button**. The option will be selected.

6. Click on **Next**. The Ready To Install dialog box will open.

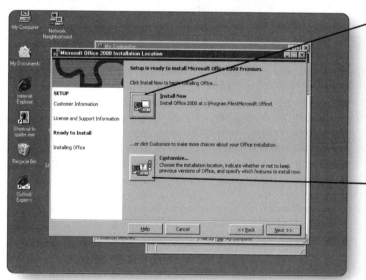

7a. Click on the **Install Now button.** Use this option to install Office on your computer with the default settings. This is the recommended installation for most users.

OR

7b. Click on the **Customize button**, if you want to choose which components to install or where to install them. The Installation Location dialog box will open. Then see the next section, "Choosing Components," for guidance.

8. Wait while the **Office software** installs on your computer. When the setup has completed, the Installer Information box will open.

9. Click on **Yes**. The Setup Wizard will restart your computer. After your computer has restarted, Windows will update your system settings and then finish the Office installation and configuration process.

Choosing Components

If you selected option 7b in the previous section, you have the choice of installing many different programs and components.

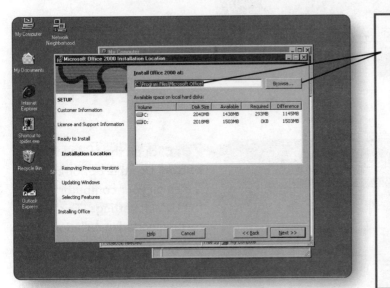

NOTE

For a custom installation, you have the option of placing Office in a different location on your computer. It is recommended that you use the default installation location. If you want to install Office in a different directory, type the directory path in the text box or click on the Browse button to select a directory.

1. Click on **Next**. The Selecting Features dialog box will open.

2. Click on a **plus sign (+)** to expand a list of features. The features listed under the category will appear.

3. Click on the **down arrow (▼)** to the right of the hard drive icon. A menu of available installation options for the feature will appear.

4. Click on the **button** next to the individual option, and choose a setting for that option:

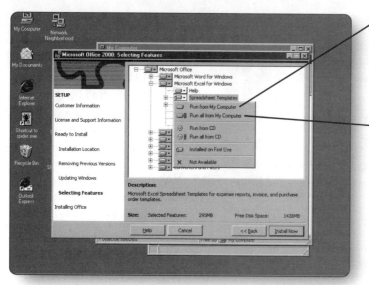

- **Run from My Computer**. The component will be fully installed, so that you will not need the Office CD in the CD-ROM drive to use it.

- **Run all from My Computer**. The selected component and all the components subordinate to it will be fully installed.

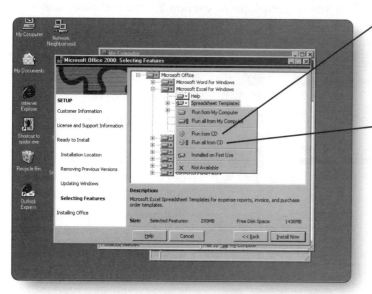

- **Run from CD**. The component will be installed, but you will need to have the Office CD in the CD-ROM drive to use it.

- **Run all from CD**. The selected component and all the components subordinate to it will need to have the Office CD in the CD-ROM drive to use it.

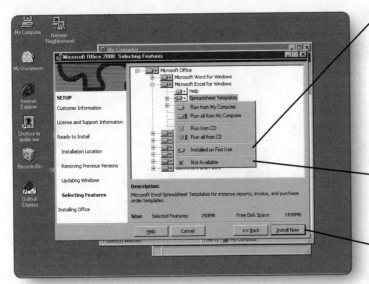

• **Installed on First Use**. The first time you try to activate the component, you will be prompted to insert the Office CD to fully install it. This is good for components that you are not sure whether you will need or not.

• **Not Available**. The component will not be installed at all.

5. Click on **Install Now**. The Installing dialog box will open.

In a Custom installation, you'll be asked whether you want to update Internet Explorer to version 5.0. Your choices are:

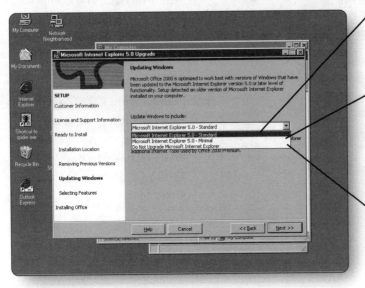

• **Microsoft Internet Explorer 5.0—Standard**. This is the default, and the right choice for most people.

• **Microsoft Internet Explorer 5.0—Minimal**. This is the right choice if you are running out of hard disk space but still would like to use Internet Explorer 5.0.

• **Do Not Upgrade Microsoft Internet Explorer**. Use this if you don't want Internet Explorer (for example, if you always use another browser such as Netscape Navigator, or if you have been directed by your system administrator not to install Internet Explorer 5).

Working with Maintenance Mode

Maintenance Mode is a feature of the Setup program. Whenever you run the Setup program again, after the initial installation, Maintenance Mode starts automatically. It enables you to add or remove features, repair your Office installation (for example, if files have become corrupted), and remove Office completely. There are several ways to rerun the Setup program (and thus enter Maintenance Mode):

- Reinsert the Office 2000 CD. The Setup program may start automatically.

- If the Setup program does not start automatically, double-click on the CD icon in the My Computer window.

- If double-clicking on the CD icon doesn't work, right-click on the CD icon and click on Open from the shortcut menu. Then double-click on the Setup.exe file in the list of files that appears.

- From the Control Panel in Windows, click on the Add/Remove Programs button. Then on the Install/Uninstall tab, click on Microsoft Office 2000 in the list, and finally, click on the Add/Remove button.

After entering Maintenance Mode, choose the button for the activity you want. Each option is briefly described in the following sections.

Repairing or Reinstalling Office

If an Office program is behaving strangely, or refuses to work, chances are good that a needed file has become corrupted. But which file? You have no way of knowing, so you can't fix the problem yourself.

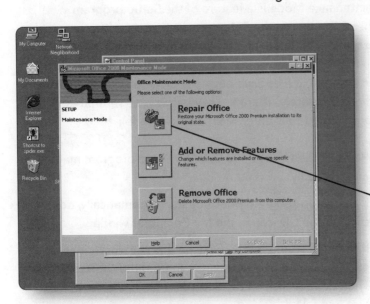

If this happens, you can either repair Office or completely reinstall it. Both options are accessed from the Repair Office button in Maintenance Mode.

1. **Click** on the **Repair Office button** in Maintenance Mode.

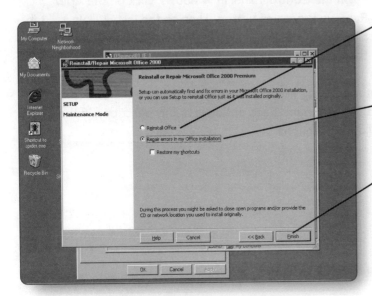

2a. **Click** on **Reinstall Office** to repeat the last installation.

OR

2b. **Click on Repair errors in my Office installation** to simply fix what's already in place.

3. **Click** on **Finish**. The process will start.

> **TIP**
>
> You can also repair individual Office programs by opening the Help menu in each program and clicking on Detect and Repair. This works well if you are sure that one certain program is causing the problem, and it's quicker than asking the Setup program to check all of the installed programs.

Adding and Removing Components

Adding and removing components works just like selecting the components initially.

1. Click on the **Add or Remove Features button** in Maintenance Mode. The Update Features window will appear. This window works exactly the same as the window you saw in the "Choosing Components" section earlier in this appendix.

> **NOTE**
>
> Some features will attempt to automatically install themselves as you are working. If you have set a feature to be installed on first use, attempt to access that feature. You will be prompted to insert your Office 2000 CD, and the feature will be installed without further prompting.

Removing Office from Your PC

In the unlikely event that you should need to remove Office from your PC completely, click on Remove Office from the Maintenance Mode screen. Then follow the prompts to remove it from your system.

After removing Office, you will probably have a few remnants left behind that the Uninstall routine didn't catch. For example, there will probably still be a Microsoft Office folder in your Program Files folder or wherever you installed the program. You can delete that folder yourself.

CAUTION

If you plan to reinstall Office later, and you have created any custom templates, toolbars, or other items, you may want to leave the Microsoft Office folder alone, so that those items will be available to you after you reinstall.

Installing Content from Other Office CDs

Depending on the version of Office you bought, you may have more than one CD in your package. CD 1 contains all the basic Office components, such as Word, Outlook, PowerPoint, Excel, Access, and Internet Explorer. It may be the only CD you need to use.

The other CDs contain extra applications that come with the specific version of Office you purchased. They may include Publisher, FrontPage, a language pack, or a programmer and developer resource kit. Each of these discs has its own separate installation program.

The additional CDs should start their Setup programs automatically when you insert the disk in your drive. If not, browse the CD's content in My Computer or Windows Explorer and double-click on the Setup.exe file that you find on it.

B

Using Keyboard Shortcuts

You may have noticed the keyboard shortcuts listed on the right side of several of the PowerPoint menus. You can use these shortcuts to execute commands without using the mouse to activate menus. These shortcuts can help speed your productivity, and help decrease wrist strain caused by excessive mouse usage. Windows applications all share the same keyboard combinations to execute common commands. Once you get accustomed to using some of these keyboard shortcuts in PowerPoint, try them out on some of the other Microsoft Office programs. In this appendix, you'll learn how to:

- Get up to speed with frequently used keyboard shortcuts in the Help system
- Use keyboard combinations to edit text
- Perform often-used presentation commands

Getting Help

It is possible to maneuver your way through the Office Assistant for help and navigate the Help screens without the aid of a mouse. Keep these shortcut guides close at hand and practice using those keyboard shortcuts. You'll find that with a little time, you'll be using the keyboard as naturally as you once used the mouse.

Asking the Office Assistant for Help

To execute this command	Do this
Use the What's This? Button	Press the Shift and F1 keys simultaneously (Shift+F1)
Ask the Assistant a question (if turned on) or display the Help contents (if Assistant is off)	Press the F1 key
Open a help topic from the Assistant's list	Press Alt+[number] (Alt+1 opens the first topic listed, Alt+2 opens the second)
View more of the Assistant's list	Press Alt+Down Arrow
Go back to the previous list	Press Alt+Up Arrow
Close the list of help topics	Press Esc

Moving Around the Help System

The following table shows you a few of the more common keyboard shortcuts that you may want to use when working with the Help files.

To execute this command	Do this
Display the Contents tab	Press the Alt and C keys simultaneously (Alt+C)
Move between the navigation pane and the topic pane (when the Contents tab is displayed)	Press F6
Move between books and topics in the navigation pane	Press the Up Arrow to move up the list, Press the Down Arrow to move down the list until the desired book is selected
Open a selected book or Help topic	Press Enter
Display the Answer Wizard tab	Press Alt+A
Display the Index Tab	Press Alt+I

Working with Text

The easiest keyboard shortcuts to learn are those that manipulate text. Try your hand at selecting, editing, and formatting text using some of the commonly used text combinations.

Selecting Text

Before you can edit and format the text in your presentation, you'll need to select it. This table shows you how to use keyboard combinations to select text. Before you start, you'll need to move the cursor to the beginning of the text that you want to select.

To execute this command	Do this
Highlight the character to the right of the cursor	Press Shift+Right Arrow
Highlight the character to the left	Press Shift+Left Arrow
Highlight an entire word	Press Ctrl+Shift+Right Arrow
Highlight an entire line	Press Shift+End
Highlight a paragraph	Press Ctrl+Shift+Down Arrow
Select an entire page	Press Ctrl+A

Editing Text

Once you have selected the text to which you want to make the editing changes, apply one of the combinations in the following table.

To execute this command	Do this
Delete the character to the left of the cursor	Press Backspace
Delete the character to the right	Press Delete
Delete the word to the left of the cursor	Press Ctrl+Backspace
Delete the word to the right	Press Ctrl+Delete
Delete selected text	Press Ctrl+X
Make a copy of selected text	Press Ctrl+C
Paste the copied text	Press Ctrl+V
Spell check a presentation	Press the F7 key
Find text on a slide	Press Ctrl+F
Replace text on a slide	Press Ctrl+H
Undo an action	Press Ctrl+Z
Redo an action	Press Ctrl+Y

Formatting Text

To make your text look good, you may want to change the font, font style, or one of the many standardized paragraph styles.

To execute this command	Do this
Change the font	Press Ctrl+Shift+F
Change the size of the font	Press Ctrl+Shift+P
Make selected text bold	Press Ctrl+B
Make selected text italic	Press Ctrl+I
Center a paragraph on a slide	Press Ctrl+E
Left align a paragraph	Press Ctrl+L
Right align a paragraph	Press Ctrl+R
Left indent a paragraph	Press Ctrl+M
Right indent a paragraph	Press Ctrl+Shift+M
Apply a style	Press Ctrl+Shift+S

Finding Your Way around a Presentation

Here are a few simple keyboard shortcuts you can use while you're working with your presentation. There's lots more shortcut keys that you can use; this appendix has only shown you a sampling. You can find more shortcut keys by typing "Shortcut Keys" in the Office Assistant or by looking for the "Shortcut Keys" topic in the Contents tab of the Help system.

Working with Your Presentation

To execute this command	Do this
Create a new presentation	Press Ctrl+N
Open a presentation	Press Ctrl+O
Close a presentation	Press Ctrl+W
Save your presentation	Press Ctrl+S
Print a presentation	Ctrl+P
Run a slideshow	Press the F5 key

Organizing the Outline

To execute this command	Do this
Move a selected outline item up in the outline list	Press Alt+Shift+Up Arrow
Move a selected outline item down	Press Alt+Shift+Down Arrow
Promote a selected item in the outline	Press Alt+Shift+Left Arrow
Demote a selected item	Press Alt+Shift+Right Arrow

Running a Slide Show

To execute this command	Do this
Move to the next slide in the presentation	Press the Spacebar
Go to the previous slide	Press Backspace
Display a specific slide	Type the slide number and press Enter
End the slide show	Press Esc

Glossary

3-D. Having or appearing to have three dimensions: width, height, and depth.

A

Accessibility. The ease of use and access to the program is enhanced to aid those with limited vision or impaired movement.

Agenda slide. A slide that lists items for the agenda or headings for main sections of your presentation.

Animation. The addition of special effects such as movement or sound to objects in your presentation.

Annotate. To draw or write on a slide during a presentation using the annotation pen.

Answer wizard. The Answer wizard lets you formulate your question in your own words, and then automatically directs you to the proper place within Help for your answer.

AutoShape. A ready-made shape for you to use in your presentations. The AutoShapes menu can be found on the Drawing toolbar.

B

Bitmap. A graphic file with its graphic information stored pixel by pixel. Bitmap images cannot be directly converted into PowerPoint images.

Bullet. A character, number, or graphic object used to delineate special sections of the text.

C

Callouts. These are text additions to the slide that point to specific items and give information about them. In PowerPoint, these are drawing objects that may be sized, rotated, and otherwise manipulated along with the information contained within them.

Caption. An alternative description of a picture, chart, or other graphic that may be used in a presentation to indicate the content of the picture, chart, and so on.

Chart. A graphic representation of a data array, such as a pie-shaped graphic sliced to show spending or budget contributions.

Clip Gallery. This contains a large number of graphic objects and pictures that you can use to enhance and illustrate your slides.

Clip art. This is the name applied to various graphics that are freely available for you to use in presentations.

Collapse. When working in Outline view, clicking on the (-) at the beginning of a major heading will hide the subheadings shown indented below the main heading. This can be used to show an Outline view that has only major headings.

Color scheme. A set of eight colors that you can use in combination within your presentation to give a uniform appearance.

Comments. Notes added to the slides by you, or perhaps others, that are not automatically shown with the slides in the presentation because they are separate from the slides and may be turned on or off.

Connector lines. Three types of lines that you may use to connect objects: straight, angled, and curved. These remain attached to the object when it is moved and may be reshaped by handles on the connector lines to make rearranging objects easier.

Crop. Trimming the horizontal and vertical edges of a picture using the cropping tool on the Picture toolbar.

D

Drag and drop. Moving or otherwise manipulating an object by clicking on the left mouse button and "dragging" the mouse pointer until the object is placed where desired.

Drawing object. A text box, WordArt drawing, AutoShape, or other clip art object that you can insert into a picture.

Duplicate. You can make more than one copy of a slide for the same presentation or for use in other presentations by selecting the object to duplicate and then clicking on Duplicate on the Edit menu.

E

Embedded objects. Information inserted into a file from another file (source file) that becomes part of the file into which it is inserted (destination file) after it becomes embedded. Double-clicking on the embedded object launches the original application in which the object was created.

Emboss. A shadow effect available on the drawing toolbar that you may apply to drawing objects to give them 3-D effects.

Engrave. Effect on the drawing toolbar that gives texture effects to drawing objects.

Expand. When working in the Outline view, clicking on the (+) sign beside a major heading in an outline will display the subheadings cascading down in outline format.

F

FastTips. Microsoft has established an automated (and toll free) service to provide you with some quick answers for lots of common technical questions. It's open 24 hours a day, seven days a week. Call 1-800-936-4100 from any touch-tone telephone in the United States. Outside the United States, you'll have to get information from your local Microsoft subsidiary.

Fill. You can fill drawing objects with solid or shaded colors, textures, or even pictures.

Flip. You can rotate an object 90 degrees in either direction, and you can flip them horizontally or vertically.

Font. A family of type characters all of the same design, such as Garamond or Times New Roman.

Footer. The text at the bottom of the page that reflects the page number, the document name, or other similar information and that prints on the bottom of every page.

Format. The organized way in which objects and text are placed on a page or slide.

Freeform object. An object created by selecting a freeform shape from the Autoshapes menu and then dragging and reshaping it with the handles.

G

Gradient. A way of adding a pattern to an object to make it appear shaded.

Graph. A visual representation of an array of data organized to show trends.

Grayscale. A method that converts color images into black and white. Different amounts of black and white are combined to produce shades of gray that more closely represent the different shades of color in the image.

Grid. A space with evenly spaced lines (often invisible) in which objects may be dragged and then inserted exactly by having their boundaries snap to a grid line.

Gridline. A line upon a grid on which drawing objects may be exactly placed by using the snap function.

Group. To assemble drawing objects together and bind them so that they can all be manipulated together and still maintain their relative positions regarding each other.

Guide. Guides are available to help you align objects and text on your slide

H

Handle. A diamond-shaped handle is used to change the shape of most AutoShapes; there are also handles on the connecting lines to allow you to move drawing objects.

Header. A text box or graphic that is inserted on the top of each page in a document with information such as the company name, date, document title, or page number.

Hue. You can change the color of the shadow fills by clicking on Shadow on the Drawing toolbar and then clicking on Shadow settings. On the Shadow Settings toolbar, click on the arrow next to Shadow Color.

Hyperlink. A link from a place in your document to another document or another place inside your document.

I

Import. To bring text or graphics into PowerPoint from other programs for inclusion as a PowerPoint object in a presentation or stored in the PowerPoint clip art gallery.

K

Kiosk. A standalone computer that plays a presentation on a continuous basis. A kiosk is usually unattended or used as a part of a display, and the presentation is set up to automatically move from slide to slide.

L

Line art. Graphics that are redrawn on the screen from a set of vectors contained in a file as opposed to a pixel-by-pixel graphic map such as a bitmap.

Linked objects. Objects (information) in a file that remain connected to, and receive updates from, the original application in which they were created.

M

Macro. A small script used to simplify repetitive tasks and reduce keyboard strokes.

Multimedia. Elements such as animation, music, and video that you can add to your presentation.

N

Normal View. In Normal view, three panes are visible: the Outline pane, Slide pane, and Notes pane. The ability to focus on all aspects of the presentation simultaneously is helpful. Dragging the pane borders can change the size of the different panes.

Notes Master. There are masters for both the Notes and Handouts. The master can contain the header and footer information or any picture or icon that you want to appear on all the Notes pages or handouts.

O

Office Assistant. A handy little artificial-intelligence-enhanced assistant that can help you sort through the Help files for the specific information you request and that spontaneously offers help with tasks.

Organization chart. PowerPoint has a program that builds organization charts, offering tools and templates for you to create, edit, and modify the charts.

Outline view. A view of a document showing section headings and detailed subheadings in outline form. Text may be moved and the overall order of elements changed by dragging and dropping the outline heads in another spot in the document.

Overhead. A slide shown with an overhead projector on a screen.

P

Placeholder. A small, dotted-line box that marks the position of text or objects on a slide. You can add text by typing it into the placeholder.

Presentation. An organized collection of text and graphics displayed to an audience to orient, teach, advertise, market, and so on.

Presentation Broadcasting. You can broadcast presentations over the Web and make them accessible to viewers in remote locations.

Preview. You may preview all your Web pages and video and animation effects before using them in a presentation.

R

Regroup. You may use the Drawing toolbar to reassemble objects that previously were grouped. Select Draw and then Regroup.

Rotate. To turn an object on its axis, such as rotating a picture or a graphic on a slide.

S

Scan. Pictures can be imported into PowerPoint from a scanner or a digital camera if the hardware is TWAIN-compatible.

Shadow. You can apply shadows to drawing objects by selecting Shadow on the Drawing toolbar.

Slide Master. PowerPoint comes with a Slide Master slide. The Slide Master controls text characteristics, background color, and special effects, such as shadowing and bullet style. It also contains placeholders for text and layout attributes such as headers and footers.

Slide Show. An ordered presentation of slides, often accompanied by narration or animation and other special effects.

Slide Sorter view. In Slide Sorter view, the whole presentation is shown in miniature. You can add slide transitions and preview them in this view.

Slide view. By clicking on the controls in the bottom-left corner of the PowerPoint window, you can select from several views: Normal, Slide Show, Slide Sorter, and Slide. In Slide view, you see the slides in full size one at a time.

Spell check. You may spell check your documents in PowerPoint as you do in other Office applications. You can have PowerPoint check as you type or have the spell check done all at one time.

Style Checker. PowerPoint automatically checks your presentation for consistency and style. The Office Assistant must be turned on to have this feature available.

Summary Slide. By clicking Summary Slide on the Slide Sorter toolbar, you can create a slide that contains all the agenda items for the presentation.

T

Table. Tables are handy ways of including data and other objects into your presentation. You can format a table of your own or you can import tables from other programs, such as Microsoft Word.

Text Box tool. You can enter text easily with the Text Box tool on the Drawing toolbar.

Transparent. You can set transparent areas in objects such as pictures. You can make the background of the picture transparent and just show certain objects in the picture, without the background.

U

Undo. A handy function accessible by the button on the Standard toolbar shaped like a left-curving arrow. Should you need to do so, you may undo any mouse or keyboard action and its result by clicking on the Undo button.

Ungroup. You can remove objects grouped in a drawing object by clicking on the Ungroup selection found in the Draw menu selection on the Drawing toolbar.

V

Voice narration. You may add voice narration to your presentation in PowerPoint. If you do so, the narration can be archived and shown later or used as a Web presentation.

W

Watermark. You may create your own watermark by inserting any graphic that you want from the clip art gallery or AutoShapes (from the Drawing toolbar) or even a picture.

Z

Zoom. To move the viewer's perspective closer or farther away by either enlarging a detail (Zoom in) or by displaying the complete object (Zoom out).

Index

W

Z

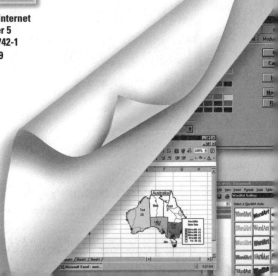